CUMULATIVE INDEX

HANDBOOK OF POLITICAL SCIENCE

CUMULATIVE INDEX

FRED I. GREENSTEIN Princeton University
NELSON W. POLSBY University of California, Berkeley

 ADDISON-WESLEY PUBLISHING COMPANY

Reading, Massachusetts
Menlo Park, California · London · Amsterdam · Don Mills, Ontario · Sydney

ISBN 0-201-02609-0
ABCDEFGHIJ-HA-798765

CUMULATIVE INDEX

Aaron, Henry J., **6:** 200

Abbott, Freeland, **3:** 80

Abbott, Grace, **6:** 220

Abboushi, W. F., **3:** 365

Abdel-Malek, Anouar, **3:** 369

Abel, Elie, **6:** 415; **8:** 345

Abel, Theodore, **1:** 217

Abeles, Ronald P., **7:** 235

Abelson, Philip, **6:** 91

Abelson, Robert, **2:** 15, 140; **7:** 146, 188, 189, 191, 194, 196, 197, 198, 203, 223; **8:** 191

Abendroth, Wolfgang, **3:** 320

Aberbach, Joel D., **2:** 110; **4:** 103, 159; **6:** 349

Abernathy, James R., **7:** 297

ABM (Anti-Ballistic Missile) System, **8:** 258, 298, 305–306, 307

Abraha, Gedamu, **3:** 254

Abraham, Henry, **5:** 334, 343, 346, 361

Abram, Michael E., **5:** 291

Abrams, Charles, **6:** 270, 313

Abrams, Mark, **7:** 298

Abramson, Paul R., **2:** 101, 102, 105, 106, 107, 108, 111, 112, 115, 116, 120, 131, 132, 138; **4:** 245

Absolute ethic, **5:** 20

Absolutism
  baroque, **5:** 59
  sanctioned, **5:** 60
  strategic, **1:** 351

Absolutist monarchies, **3:** 582

Abstraction process, human, **5:** 13–14

Abu-Laban, Baha, **2:** 202

Accelerators, revolutionary, **3:** 491

Achaean League, **5:** 94

Acheson, Dean G., **6:** 404, 407; **8:** 343, 422

Achinstein, Peter, **1:** 216, 218

Ackerman, Nathan W., **2:** 73

Ackley, Gardner, **6:** 77

Ackoff, Russell, **2:** 320, 336; **8:** 344

Act-descriptions, **1:** 371

Action, irrationalist emphasis on, **3:** 235

Action vs. movement, **1:** 161, 164

Activism, right- and left-wing, **3:** 525

Activists, **4:** 39–40, 42, 60–61

Adam, Heribert, **3:** 73, 327

Adamany, David, **4:** 254

Adams, Richard N., **3:** 26

Adams, Robert F., **6:** 312, 342

Adams, Walter, **6:** 86; **7:** 309

Adcock, F. E., **3:** 116

Adelman, Irma, **3:** 13, 62, 171

Adelson, Joseph, **2:** 106, 111, 112, 133, 136, 193

Ad hoc hypotheses
  analysis of, **8:** 112–191
  testing, **8:** 90–91, 92, 97, 100

Adler, Norman, **2:** 94

Administration, comparative, **5:** 373
  of developing nations, **5:** 373, 374
  of the Soviet Union, **5:** 382, 385
  of Western Europe, **5:** 373, 375, 389

Administrative law, **5:** 346–347, 351

Administrative man, **2:** 327

Administrative Reforms Commission, **5:** 150
Administrative totalitarianism, **3:** 340
Adorno, Theodor W., **2:** 25, 47, 65, 66; **3:** 363, 613; **5:** 241
Adrian, Charles R., **4:** 232
"Adventure capitalism," **3:** 596
Adversary proceedings, **5:** 329, 332, 340, 346, 347, 352
Advice, as influence in bureaucracy, **5:** 375–380
Advisory Commission on Intergovernmental Relations, **5:** 149, 151
Advisory committees, **5:** 404–405
Affect
    definition of, **7:** 275
    political, **7:** 275–278
Africa, federalism of, **5:** 97–98, 124–125, 126–127
African political parties, typologies of, **3:** 325–326, 369
Agathon, **1:** 239
Agger, Robert E., **6:** 16
Aggregative analyses, **2:** 31, 60–68
    "building up," **2:** 66–67
    linkage, **2:** 66
    literature on aggregation, **2:** 60–65
    "nonadditivity," **2:** 67
    psychological needs and the international conflict, **2:** 62
    relating frequencies, **2:** 67
    "working back," **2:** 67–68
Aggression
    animal, studies of, **3:** 487
    frustrations producing, **3:** 487
    instinctive drive to, **3:** 487
    model of, **8:** 153–155
Ahmavaara, Y., **7:** 154
Ahmed, Bashiruddin, **4:** 22, 58
Aiken, Michael, **2:** 357; **6:** 311, 336, 338, 339, 341, 343, 344; **7:** 64
"Airborne alert," **8:** 289
Aiyar, S. P., **5:** 150
Ake, Claude, **8:** 374
Alberdi, Juan Bautista, **5:** 112
Alberoni, Francesco, **3:** 485
Albrow, Martin, **5:** 390, 429
Alcock, N., **8:** 190
Alderman, R. K., **5:** 231
Aldrich, Howard, **5:** 407
Alegal opposition, **3:** 272
Alexander, DeAlva Stanwood, **5:** 307
Alexander, Paul, **5:** 139, 140

Alexander v. *Holmes County Board of Education,* **6:** 292
Alford, Robert A., **4:** 3, 160, 244; **6:** 311, 325, 327, 328, 331, 336, 338, 339, 341, 343, 344, 362
Alger, Chadwick, **7:** 225, 241, 246
Aliber, Robert Z., **6:** 77
Alienation, **1:** 380
Alignment behavior, model of, **8:** 155–163
Alinsky, Saul, **6:** 169
Alker, Hayward R., Jr., **2:** 337; **3:** 3, 9, 40; **6:** 16, 400; **7:** 64, 140, 141, 143, 146, 147, 149, 154, 156, 157, 159, 168, 169, 184, 201, 202, 203, 204, 227; **8:** 193, 221
Alker, Henry A., **2:** 17, 45
Allegiance, **5:** 38, 48, 51, 52, 56, 70–71
Allen, C. K., **5:** 322, 328
Allen, Howard W., **7:** 47
Allen, Richard V., **3:** 360
Allen, William Sheridan, **3:** 248, 363
Alliance politics, **8:** 302, 331
Alliances, **5:** 101; **8:** 93, 206, 208, 212, 215, 221
Allison, Graham T., **2:** 4, 320, 322, 325, 326, 344, 349, 359; **5:** 375, 381, 384; **6:** 17, 382, 387, 389, 390, 393, 395, 398, 405, 409, 415, 418, 421; **8:** 231, 324, 345
Allport, Floyd Henry, **7:** 280
Allport, Gordon, **2:** 32, 34; **7:** 96
Allport, Gordon Willard, **6:** 249
Almanacs, **7:** 16
Almond, Gabriel, **1:** 134, 141, 170, 194, 309, 310; **2:** 156, 160, 308; **3:** 2, 3, 16, 17, 27, 32, 34, 35, 36, 78, 91, 96, 97, 171, 180, 274, 352, 357; **4:** 3, 22, 32, 60, 160, 177, 178, 179, 180, 199, 221, 233, 236; **5:** 177; **6:** 381, 413; **7:** 99, 105, 110, 121, 275, 279
Alston, William P., **1:** 295, 314
Alt, James E., **6:** 339, 362
Altbach, Philip G., **2:** 68
"Alternative world orders," **8:** 316
Althoff, Phillip, **2:** 180, 196, 197
Althusius, Johannes, **5:** 160
Altmeyer, Arthur, **6:** 119, 220
Altshuler, Alan, **6:** 349
Ameillon, B., **3:** 369
American Assembly, **5:** 156; **8:** 300
American Association for Public Opinion Research, **7:** 327
American Constitutional Convention, **3:** 116
American Institute of Public Opinion, **7:** 324
American Political Science Association, **1:** 34, 35, 42, 54; **4:** 237

American Psychiatric Association, **2:** 45
American Public Welfare Association, **6:** 119, 121, 212
American Youth Commission, **7:** 309
"Amoral familism," **1:** 173
Amphoux, Jean, **5:** 206
Analysis of variance, **7:** 215, 244
Analytic neofunctionalism, **8:** 378
Analytic theory, **8:** 12
Anarchists, **8:** 247
Anarchy, **1:** 388
   and hierarchy, **8:** 47
   international, **8:** 35, 68
Andersen, Kristi, **4:** 68
Anderson, Charles W., **3:** 365, 367; **5:** 267
Anderson, Frank Maloy, **7:** 4
Anderson, Martin, **6:** 446
Anderson, Norman H., **2:** 133, 140
Anderson, Patrick, **5:** 223, 376
Anderson, Ronald E., **2:** 134; **4:** 90, 100, 102, 159; **7:** 286
Anderson, William, **1:** 4; **5:** 148, 156; **6:** 113, 305
Andrade, E. N. de C., **8:** 4
Andrain, Charles, **2:** 354
Andreski, Stanislav, **3:** 367, 538
Andrews, Charles M., **5:** 46
Andrews, William G., **5:** 228
Angell, Norman, **8:** 79
Angell, Robert C., **6:** 361, 363
Anglo-American law, **5:** 328
Angyal, Andras, **8:** 68, 78
Annals of the American Academy of Political and Social Science, **8:** 326
Anomie, **2:** 75
Anscombe, G. E. M., **1:** 166
Anthony, Earl, **6:** 297
Anthropomorphism, **1:** 179, 182; **5:** 10–12, 13
Anticonstitutional movements, **5:** 85
Antidemocratic mass parties, **3:** 248
Antidiscrimination policy, **6:** 246, 290–291
Antifederalists, **5:** 152–153
Anti-Semitism, **3:** 316, 611
Anton, Thomas J., **6:** 329
Apartheid, **3:** 327, 328; **6:** 275; **7:** 281
Apathy, **3:** 570–571
Apel, Karl-Otto, **1:** 217
Apollo missions, **6:** 85
Apollo-Soyuz Test Project, **8:** 273
Appellate courts, **5:** 350–356, 362
   uses of, **5:** 357–362
Appellate opinion, **5:** 330

Appleby, Paul, **5:** 133
Appraisal
   alternatives, **6:** 14–15
   arenas, **6:** 9
   base values, **6:** 9–10
   criteria for, **6:** 13–14
   effects, **6:** 10
   external relations, **6:** 4
   functions and structures, **6:** 4
   goals of, **6:** 10–14
   internal relations, **6:** 4
   model, **6:** 4
   outcomes, **6:** 10
   participants, **6:** 8–9
   perspectives, **6:** 9
   process of, **6:** 8–10
   projections, **6:** 14–15
   scientific task, **6:** 4–5
   strategies, **6:** 10
   trends, **6:** 14–15
Appraisals, **1:** 315–316, 317
Appropriations Committee, **5:** 287
Apter, David, **2:** 354; **3:** 3, 12, 13, 19, 20, 31, 32, 55, 294, 322, 357, 364, 370; **7:** 82, 99
Aquarone, Alberto, **3:** 199, 202, 210, 219, 270, 308, 310, 360, 361, 362, 367, 368, 371
Arab-Israeli war, **8:** 72–73
Aranson, Peter H., **3:** 468
Arbitrary administration, **5:** 77
Arbitration, **3:** 455–461; **5:** 324, 326, 327
Archive movement, **8:** 95, 96
Archive on Political Elites in Eastern Europe, **7:** 50
Archives, **7:** 27–34, 45–67
Ardant, Gabriel, **3:** 527, 528
Area studies, **3:** 1, 2
Areal division of powers, **5:** 141–143
Arenas, vs. transformative legislatures, **5:** 277–296
Arendt, Hannah, **1:** 212, 272; **3:** 188, 193, 212, 217, 221, 223, 225, 241, 512, 513; **6:** 260
Argyris, Chris, **2:** 12; **6:** 392, 403
Aristotle, **1:** 9, 162, 206, 230, 233–234, 237, 240, 244, 245, 248, 249, 252, 253, 259, 260, 263, 323, 326; **5:** 24, 26, 39, 40, 42; **8:** 3, 4
Arkes, Hadley, **6:** 408
Armacost, Michael H., **6:** 88, 412; **8:** 323
Armaments, **8:** 175, 176
Arms control and disarmament, **8:** 299–302, 305–313, 317–321, 332–339
Arms Control and Disarmament Agency, **8:** 300, 317

Arms control treaties, **6:** 93
Arms-length bargaining, **5:** 136
Arms race, pre-World War I, **8:** 263, 268
  implications of, **8:** 178–188
  models of, **8:** 174–191
Armstrong, J. Scott, **7:** 153, 154
Armstrong, John A., **3:** 336; **4:** 232
Armstrong, W. E., **3:** 437, 446
Arne, S., **5:** 206
Arnoff, E. Leonard, **8:** 344
Aron, Raymond, **3:** 187, 370; **8:** 51, 54, 69, 203, 230, 264, 284, 343
Aronson, Elliot, **7:** 249, 250
Arrested totalitarianism, **3:** 336
Arrow, Kenneth, **1:** 341; **2:** 343, 358; **3:** 414, 416, 417, 419, 420, 423, 424, 425, 426, 427, 429, 431, 437, 445, 446, 450, 461; **7:** 374, 375, 376, 397
Arrow's (Im)possibility Theorem, **7:** 375
Art, Robert J., **5:** 375; **6:** 390, 405, 409, 410, 422; **8:** 323, 344
Articles of Confederation, **5:** 94, 95, 109
Aryan race, **6:** 243–244, 252
Asch, S. E., **2:** 20
Ash Council, **5:** 405, 406
Ashby, C. M., **7:** 33
Ashby, R. W., **1:** 292
Ashby, W. Ross, **2:** 320; **8:** 6, 46, 70, 78
Ashenfelter, Orley, **3:** 470
Asher, Herbert B., **6:** 406
Ashford, Douglas E., **3:** 365
Ashmore, R. D., **2:** 118
"Asiatic mode of production," **3:** 251
Aspaturian, Vernon, **5:** 115, 122; **6:** 412
Assassinated leaders, **2:** 103–105
Associational structures, **3:** 505
Assured Destruction, **8:** 298, 305, 319
Astin, Alexander W., **2:** 70
Athanasiou, Robert, **7:** 306
Atkin, Charles R., **7:** 250
Atomic Energy Commission, **8:** 277, 279
Atomic testing, **8:** 301
Attachment to political system, **2:** 96–117
  adulthood sense of legitimacy of political authority, **2:** 99
  benevolent leader, **2:** 100
  children's "exemplars," **2:** 99–100
  content of, **2:** 96–97
  critiques, **2:** 99–105
  fallible leader, **2:** 100–102
  malevolent leader, **2:** 100–102
  persistence of political system, **2:** 99, 114

preliminary point of view, **2:** 97
  psychodynamic needs, **2:** 98
Attainable combinations, line of, **8:** 156, 157, 158, 159
"Attentive" publics, **5:** 391, 392
Attitude formation, **7:** 242
Attitude measurement
  acquiescence response set, **7:** 292, 294
  bias, **7:** 297
  controversies in, **7:** 289–305
  filter questions, **7:** 304
  index of political cynicism, **7:** 277
  index of political efficacy, **7:** 277, 292, 296
  latent structure analysis, **7:** 318
  levels of conceptualization, **7:** 286, 287
  memory error, **7:** 297
  multiple indicators, **7:** 295
  omission error, **7:** 297
  randomized response, **7:** 297–298
  scaling theory, **7:** 318
  self-anchoring striving scale, **7:** 281
  semantic differential scales, **7:** 276
  social desirability response set, **7:** 297
  split ballots, **7:** 295
  telescoping error, **7:** 297
  validity of, **7:** 290, 304, 306
  voter turnout, **7:** 297
Attitudes, **7:** 274–289, 296–303
  and behavior, **2:** 137
  vs. belief, **7:** 275
  context of, **7:** 280
  definition of, **7:** 274–275
  direction of, **7:** 278
  on foreign policy, **7:** 279
  formation, **4:** 82
  instability, **4:** 84
  intensity of, **7:** 278–279, 285
  level of information, **7:** 279
  and "non-attitudes," **7:** 303–305
  political, **7:** 278–281, 314
  racial, **7:** 280, 289, 300, 303, 309, 326
  toward risk, **2:** 338
  salience, **4:** 88
  stability, **4:** 88, 104, 111; **7:** 285, 303–304
  structure, **4:** 83–89, 99, 101, 104, 105, 107, 109; **7:** 279
  time perspective, **7:** 281
  in wartime Germany, **7:** 313
  in wartime Japan, **7:** 314
Attneave, Fred, **8:** 193
Attorney general of the United States, **5:** 210
Auerbach, H., **3:** 368

Auerbach, Lewis E., **6:** 83, 91
Aumann, Robert J., **3:** 416, 461; **7:** 389, 391, 394, 395, 399
Austin, John, **1:** 307, 309; **5:** 44, 45, 51
Australia, federalism of, **5:** 120–121, 135, 150, 155
Australian Federal Convention, **5:** 112
Austria, federalism of, **5:** 121–122
Authoritarian regimes, **3:** 264–350
  anarchic, **3:** 347
  bureaucratic-military, **3:** 285–306
  and class structure, **3:** 289
  consolidation of, **3:** 299
  consultative, **3:** 344–345
  co-optation of fascism into, **3:** 291
  co-optation of leaders, **3:** 266
  and crisis, **3:** 313–314
  definition of, **3:** 179–180, 264–274
  economic development in, **3:** 294
  fascist-mobilizational, **3:** 321
  historical context, **3:** 292
  ideology of, **3:** 267–269
  incorporation of population in, **3:** 290
  instability of, **3:** 354
  internal evolution of, **3:** 283
  international linkages of, **3:** 300
  legality, perversion of, **3:** 287
  liberalization of, **3:** 273
  limited pluralism of, **3:** 265, 277–278
  mobilizational, **3:** 279, 313–326
  organic statism, **3:** 281, 306–313
  participation, limited, in, **3:** 278
  posttotalitarian, **3:** 326–350
  quasi-pluralistic, **3:** 345
  single party in, **3:** 291
  and social structure, **3:** 295
  the state in, **3:** 308
  subtypes, **3:** 180
  terror in, **3:** 223–224
  threats for, **3:** 290
  transition to and from other regime types, **3:** 281
  typologies of, **3:** 274–350
  unexpected change of, **3:** 355
  utopian element, absence of, **3:** 271, 273–274
Authority, **1:** 192, 287, 303, 304
  loss of, **3:** 490
  traditional legitimate, **3:** 252, 253–259, 323
Authority structure, **2:** 161
"Automated battlefield," **8:** 265, 334
"Automaticity," **8:** 383
Averini, Shlomo, **1:** 15, 229

Avocational politicians, **2:** 157, 161–162
Avril, Pierre, **5:** 189, 195
Awa, E. O., **5:** 124
Axelrod, Robert, **4:** 147; **7:** 146, 180, 183, 184, 185, 189, 236, 283, 287, 385, 396
Axiom of choice, **1:** 197
Axiom of transitivity, **1:** 197
Axioms, **7:** 374, 395
Ayearst, Morley, **5:** 126
Ayres, Richard E., **4:** 22
Azar, Edward E., **6:** 387
Azpiazu, Joaquín, **3:** 307
Azrael, Jeremy R., **3:** 240, 241, 246, 334, 342

Baade, Hans W., **5:** 207, 429
Baar, Carl, **5:** 184, 186
Baar, Ellen, **5:** 184, 186
Baas, Larry R., **7:** 177, 178, 179, 203
Babcock, Richard F., **6:** 291
Bacchus, William I., **6:** 404
Bach, G. L., **6:** 76
Bachelder, Glen, **5:** 161
Bachman, Jerald G., **2:** 129
Bachrach, Peter, **1:** 307; **2:** 289, 352; **3:** 358; **4:** 5; **5:** 384; **6:** 172
Bacon, Francis, **5:** 25, 54, 56, 59, 60, 61, 64, 87
Badger, Wade W., **3:** 454, 455
Baer, Michael A., **2:** 194; **4:** 205, 206; **5:** 223
Bagehot, Walter, **5:** 300
Bahl, Roy W., **6:** 311, 325, 330, 356
Baier, Helmut, **3:** 359
Baier, Kurt, **1:** 318
Bailey, Stephen K., **4:** 217; **5:** 215, 234, 308; **6:** 75; **7:** 14
Bain, Richard C., **5:** 183, 192, 193
Baker, Kendall L., **2:** 100, 112, 115, 116
Baker, Todd A., **7:** 240
Bakunin, Mikhail, **1:** 12
Balance of payments, **6:** 32, 49
Balance of power, **8:** 204, 208–215, 221, 261, 263
Balance-of-power theory, **8:** 2, 5, 33–43, 69, 179
  and competition, **8:** 42
  expectations of, **8:** 42
  meanings of, **8:** 36
  and the motivation of states, **8:** 36–37
  propositions about, **8:** 35–36
  quality of, **8:** 42, 43
  and the security of states, **8:** 36
  and socialization, a38: 42
  testing of, **8:** 42

as theory about environmental constraints, **8:** 41
and uncertainty, **8:** 39
and war, **8:** 36
"Balances of terror," **8:** 204, 208, 209, 213, 221, 288
Balassa, Bela, **8:** 369
Balbus, Isaac D., **2:** 253, 257, 297, 307
Baldwin, Hanson W., **8:** 343
Ballard, John A., **5:** 267, 268
Baltes, Paul B., **2:** 139
"Ban the bomb" groups, **8:** 299
Bandura, Albert, **2:** 42
Banfield, Edward C., **1:** 171, 172–173, 174, 181, 219; **3:** 17, 28, 32; **4:** 250; **6:** 270, 271, 340, 348, 349, 355, 356, 467; **7:** 267
Banks, Arthur, **1:** 312; **3:** 62, 352; **7:** 64, 83; **8:** 131, 135, 141
Banton, Michael P., **6:** 243, 256
Banzhaf, John, **7:** 396
Baran, Paul A., **6:** 252; **8:** 17, 29, 77, 228
Baratz, Morton, **2:** 289, 352; **4:** 4; **5:** 146, 384; **6:** 172
Barber, Benjamin, **3:** 241, 243
Barber, James Alden, **2:** 131
Barber, James David, **2:** 1, 3, 40, 53, 54, 55, 56, 57, 61, 69, 75, 95, 172, 200, 203, 204, 215, 216, 224, 225; **5:** 183, 217, 240, 241, 242; **6:** 394, 395; **7:** 219, 225
Barber, Richard J., **5:** 410
Barbic, Ana, **4:** 13, 16
Bardolph, Richard, **6:** 289, 293
Bargaining, **3:** 455–461, 590; **5:** 329
Bargaining set, **7:** 395–396
Bargaining theory, **8:** 396
Barghoorn, Frederick C., **3:** 31, 126, 216, 218, 221, 232, 336
Barker, Ernest, **5:** 32, 306
Barksdale, Hiram C., **7:** 326, 327
Barlow, David H., **2:** 44
Barnard, Chester I., **2:** 289, 351; **5:** 303; **6:** 403
Barnes, Harry E., **1:** 46
Barnes, Louis B., **7:** 240, 244
Barnes, Samuel H., **2:** 112; **4:** 159, 256
Barnes, Samuel J., **7:** 288
Barnet, Richard, **6:** 391, 414, 416; **8:** 348
Barnett, A. Doak, **3:** 366
Barnett, Clifford R., **3:** 366
Barnett, Malcolm Joel, **5:** 235, 236
Barnett, Richard, **2:** 324
Bärnthaler, Irmgard, **3:** 311
Barringer, Richard E., **8:** 316

Barry, Brian, **1:** 131, 214, 215, 220, 221, 284, 391; **2:** 297, 321, 348; **3:** 413, 415, 453, 466; **5:** 429
Barss, Reitzel & Associates, Inc., **6:** 180
Bartell, Ted, **7:** 235
Barth, Ernest, **2:** 202
Barton, Allen H., **2:** 94; **3:** 239, 346; **4:** 158
Barton, Weldon V., **5:** 151
Bartos, Otomar J., **3:** 470
Barzun, Jacques, **6:** 244
Bast, William, **5:** 134
Bates, F. L., **2:** 355
Bauer, Raymond A., **2:** 245, 332; **3:** 203, 232; **4:** 162, 207; **5:** 287; **6:** 16, 206, 307, 406, 413, 417
Baum, Richard, **3:** 366
Baumgartner, T., **7:** 188
Baumol, William J., **3:** 453; **6:** 211
Bavelas, A., **2:** 231
Bawden, D. Lee, **6:** 468
Baxter, Craig, **3:** 80
Baxter, James P., III, **6:** 84, 95
Baxter, William, **6:** 445
Bay, Christian, **1:** 325; **2:** 75
Bayer, Alan E., **2:** 70
Bayesian analysis, **2:** 346; **7:** 148
Beal, Richard Smith, **7:** 241
Beall, Lynette, **2:** 111, 112
Beard, Charles, **5:** 118; **6:** 360, 361; **7:** 269
Beavin, Janet B., **8:** 78
Bechhoefer, Bernhard G., **8:** 278, 345
Beck, Carl, **3:** 239, 336
Beck, Paul A., **4:** 162
Becker, Gary S., **6:** 14, 16
Becker, H. S., **7:** 104, 105, 125
Becker, Theodore, **5:** 321, 334, 357; **6:** 467
Bedau, Hugo A., **1:** 287
Beer, Samuel H., **1:** 176–177, 181, 219, 390; **2:** 308; **4:** 181, 195, 200, 208, 215, 221, 256; **5:** 36
Behavioral revolution in political science, **3:** 2
Behavioralism, **1:** 58–62; **6:** 439, 440, 459
postbehavioralism, **6:** 439
Behavioralists, **1:** 258
Behaviorism, **1:** 292–293, 294, 295, 297, 299
Behrman, Lucy, **3:** 364
Beinze, Shirley J., **6:** 15
Beitzinger, Alfons J., **7:** 38
Belaunde, Victor Andres, **5:** 111, 119
Belgium, foreign domination in, **3:** 155, 156
Belief systems, **7:** 285–288

Beliefs, **7:** 274, 296–303
  vs. attitude, **7:** 275
  context of, **7:** 280
  political, **7:** 278–281
Belknap, George, **7:** 218
Bell, Daniel, **3:** 95, 363; **6:** 80, 81, 94, 96, 100; **7:** 272
Bell, Winifred, **6:** 118
Benda, Julien, **1:** 255
Bender, Irving E., **2:** 129
Benditt, Theodore M., **5:** 429
Bendix, Reinhard, **2:** 18; **3:** 3, 364; **4:** 3, 31; **7:** 272, 273
Benedict, Ruth F., **2:** 60, 61
Benefit-cost analysis, **7:** 147, 148
Benjamin, Lawrence, **2:** 7
Benjamin, Roger W., **3:** 14, 240
Benn, S. I., **1:** 284, 289, 308
Bennett, Jonathan, **1:** 351
Bennett, William H., **5:** 100, 160
Benney, Mark, **7:** 302
Bennis, Warren, **2:** 352, 357, 358
Bensen, Paul R., Jr., **7:** 240
Benson, George C. S., **5:** 148
Benson, Lee, **4:** 160; **7:** 47
Benson, Oliver, **7:** 223
Bentham, Jeremy, **1:** 12, 14, 220, 326, 360
Bentler, P. M., **2:** 48
Bentley, Arthur, **2:** 73, 244, 245, 246, 248, 249–250, 252, 253, 254, 255, 256–257, 258–259, 260–261, 262, 263, 264, 265, 266, 275, 297, 308; **4:** 173, 174, 175, 208, 223
  epistemological position of, **2:** 246, 250–251, 252, 255–257, 294
  ethical view of American politics, **2:** 260–261
  on government institutions, **2:** 258–259
  group-activity-interest equation, **2:** 253–254
  on group interests, **2:** 257
  on potential activity, **2:** 262
  on regimes, **2:** 259
  on socialism, **2:** 255, 256
  on "spooks," **2:** 255, 257
  on stability-disruption-protest model, **2:** 260–262
  vision of political process, **2:** 253–262
Benton, William, **7:** 6
Benveniste, Guy, **5:** 374, 413
Bequiraj, Mehmet, **3:** 151
Berdyaev, Nicholas, **3:** 363

Berea College v. *Kentucky,* **6:** 272
Berelson, Bernard, **1:** 293; **4:** 3, 7, 159; **7:** 161, 302, 328, 329, 332, 335
Berger, Peter L., **1:** 216
Berghahn, Volker K., **3:** 238
Berghorn, Forrest J., **2:** 188
Bergmann, Barbara R., **6:** 283
Bergmann, Gustav, **7:** 227
Bergson, Abram, **2:** 328, 329
Bergson, Henri, **1:** 233, 261
Berkeley, Humphry, **5:** 232
Berkowitz, L., **2:** 231
Berle, Adolph A., **5:** 304
Berlin, Isaiah, **1:** 292, 389, 392, 398
Berlin crises of 1958–1959 and 1961, **8:** 294
Berman, Daniel M., **5:** 234
Berman, Harold J., **3:** 218, 220; **5:** 330, 365
Bernaut, Elsa, **3:** 221, 225
Berning, Cornelia, **3:** 360
Berns, Walter, **2:** 75
Bernstein, Irving, **4:** 212
Bernstein, Marver H., **5:** 387, 398, 401, 414
Bernstein, Richard J., **1:** 220
Berrington, H. B., **2:** 203, 204
Berrington, Hugh, **5:** 241
Berry, Brian J. L., **6:** 327
Bertalanffy, Ludwig von, **8:** 63, 78, 79
Berton, Peter, **3:** 366
Best, James J., **7:** 278
Bethe, Hans A., **6:** 93
Bettelheim, Bruno, **3:** 363, 619
Beyme, Klaus von, **2:** 163, 171, 182, 190, 196, 203, 204, 207, 208, 226, 227, 229, 231; **5:** 303
Bhansali, R. J., **3:** 443
Bhatt, Anil, **4:** 22, 58
Biasing factors, **7:** 243
Bibby, John F., **5:** 308; **6:** 222
Bicameralism, **5:** 34
Bickel, Alexander M., **7:** 28
Bicker, William E., **2:** 135; **4:** 159; **6:** 343
Biderman, Albert, **6:** 16, 467
Bienen, Henry, **3:** 39, 322, 324, 325, 485, 486, 512
Bigongiari, Dino, **1:** 264
Bill, James A., **5:** 304
Billon-Grand, Françoise, **2:** 99, 100, 112, 113, 115, 116, 120
Bilorusky, John A., **2:** 70
Binary relation, **3:** 416
  ordering, **3:** 416
Binder, Leonard, **3:** 3, 14, 81, 91, 255, 365, 369

Binkley, Robert F., **5:** 97
Binkley, Wilfred E., **4:** 231; **5:** 205, 234
Biometrics, **7:** 143
Biopolitics, **2:** 30
Bios theōretikos, **1:** 240, 245, 259
Bipolarity, **8:** 204, 213, 214, 215, 220, 222, 223, 225, 268
Birch, A. H., **5:** 106, 113, 114, 116, 117, 124, 125, 127, 129, 148
Bisco, Ralph, **7:** 45, 55
Bishop, Donald G., **5:** 222
Bishop, R. L., **3:** 459
Bishop, William W., Jr., **8:** 420
Bitner, Harry, **7:** 12, 27
Black, Cyril E., **3:** 3, 14, 335, 363, 370
Black, Duncan, **1:** 341; **3:** 420, 427, 428, 429, 439; **7:** 369, 370, 373
Black, Gordon S., **2:** 166, 171, 173
Black, Joseph, **6:** 382
Black officeholders in the United States, **6:** 295–296
Black Panthers, **6:** 257, 273–274, 297
Black political socialization, **2:** 106–111
Black Power, **6:** 295
Black Power Conference, **6:** 281
Blackmer, Donald L. M., **3:** 249, 338
Blake, Ralph M., **7:** 214, 216
Blalock, Ann, **2:** 337, 345
Blalock, Hubert M., Jr., **1:** 216; **2:** 27, 337, 345; **6:** 361, 467; **7:** 143, 146, 156, 220, 245
Blank, Blanche D., **2:** 164, 180, 197
Blank, Stephen, **5:** 403
Blankenship, L. Vaughn, **6:** 94, 100
Blau, Julian H., **3:** 424
Blau, Peter M., **1:** 386; **2:** 356; **7:** 273
Blaug, M., **6:** 77
Blechman, Barry, **8:** 347
Blinder, Alan S., **6:** 76
Blissett, Marlan, **6:** 83
Bliven, Naomi, **7:** 17
Bloch, Charles, **3:** 220
Bloch, Marc, **3:** 55
Block, Jack, **2:** 27, 48
Block, Jeanne H., **2:** 27, 69, 70
Block, William, **4:** 180, 215
Blondel, Jean, **3:** 357; **5:** 189, 275
Bloom, Benjamin S., **2:** 127, 129, 130
Bloomberg, Warner, Jr., **6:** 222
Bloomfield, Lincoln P., **8:** 321, 339, 340, 386
Blue Ribbon Defense Panel, **8:** 323
Bluhm, William T., **5:** 122
Blum, Richard H., **6:** 93

Blumberg, Abraham S., **5:** 329
Blumenthal, Henry, **6:** 247, 267
Blumler, J. G., **2:** 112, 113, 116
Blydenburgh, John C., **6:** 386; **7:** 235
Boaden, Noel, **6:** 325, 326, 327, 336, 338, 339, 342, 344, 349, 356, 362
Board, Joseph B., Jr., **5:** 293
Boardman, Robert, **5:** 212
Bobrow, Davis B., **8:** 323
Bochel, J. M., **2:** 197
Bochenski, J. M., **8:** 7
Bochner, Stephen, **7:** 249
Bodde, Derk, **5:** 328
Bodenheimer, Susanne, **3:** 97
Bodin, **1:** 12, 13
Boguslaw, Robert, **6:** 97
Bohannan, Paul J., **5:** 325
Bollens, John C., **6:** 312, 356
Bolsheviks, **8:** 40
Bombwall, K. R., **5:** 123
Bonapartism, **3:** 314
Bonding rules, **7:** 196–198
Bonham, G. Matthew, **7:** 189
Bonilla, Frank, **6:** 17
Bonjean, Charles M., **2:** 75; **7:** 306
Bonnor, Jean, **5:** 183, 202
Boocock, Sarane S., **7:** 241
Books, John W., **2:** 131
Booms, Bernard H., **4:** 64
Boorman, Scott, **8:** 315
Booth, Charles, **7:** 265, 268
Borch, Karl, **2:** 336
"Borda method," **3:** 420
Borkenau, Franz, **3:** 250, 298, 313, 315, 369
Bottomore, T. B., **7:** 273
Boucher, W. I., **6:** 95; **8:** 323
Boulding, Kenneth E., **3:** 489; **6:** 395; **8:** 76, 209, 346
Bourdeaux, Michael, **3:** 359
Bourne, Peter G., **2:** 64, 65
Bourricaud, François, **3:** 253
Bouxsein, Sandra, **7:** 235
Bowen, Don R., **6:** 327
Bowen, Ralph H., **3:** 306
Bowen, William G., **4:** 22
Bower, Joseph, **2:** 321, 322, 357, 361
Bowie, R. R., **5:** 145
Bowles, Samuel, **6:** 16
Bowman, Lewis, **2:** 181, 190, 197, 201
Boyd, Richard W., **4:** 68, 128, 133, 135; **7:** 277, 279, 282, 286
Boyle, Edward, **5:** 219

Boyle, Lawrence, **6:** 340, 362
Boynton, G. R., **2:** 115, 116, 180, 181, 184, 189, 190, 197, 201, 223, 225, 233
Bracher, Karl Dietrich, **3:** 220, 225, 248, 336, 359, 362, 363, 368; **6:** 244, 260
Bradburn, Norman M., **7:** 297, 298, 299
Bradshaw, Kenneth, **5:** 235
Brady, David, **5:** 289
Brady, Richard A., **7:** 179
Brady, Robert, **4:** 187
"Brain drain," **3:** 602
Braithwaite, R. B., **3:** 457
Brams, Steven, **7:** 384, 397
Bramson, Leon, **2:** 63
Brand, J. A., **6:** 340
Brand, Katherine E., **7:** 35, 36
Brandenburg, Hans-Christian, **3:** 209, 358
Brandt, Richard, **1:** 217, 321
Brannon, Robert, **7:** 299
Braudel, Fernand, **3:** 530
Braungart, Richard G., **4:** 197
Braunthal, Gerard, **5:** 198, 238
Braybrooke, David, **1:** 306, 308; **2:** 322, 332; **5:** 384; **6:** 421; **8:** 433
Brazer, Harvey, **6:** 130, 307, 311, 321, 322
Brazil, federalism of, **5:** 119, 155
Brazilian Congress, **5:** 267–268
Break, George F., **5:** 149
"Breakthrough coup," **3:** 57
Brecher, Michael, **6:** 382, 383, 384, 390, 395, 419
Brecht, Arnold, **5:** 105, 121; **7:** 212, 213
Breckinridge, Sophonisba, **6:** 320
Breger, Louis, **2:** 11
Breines, Paul, **1:** 274, 275
Bremer, Stuart, **8:** 13, 144, 148
Bremner, Robert H., **7:** 268
Brennan, Donald G., **8:** 300
Brenner, Hildegard, **3:** 358
Breslauer, George W., **3:** 208, 217, 219, 223, 225, 226, 228
Breton, Albert, **5:** 142, 143, 158
Breton, Raymond, **3:** 619
Bretton, Henry L., **3:** 322, 325, 370
Brewer, Garry D., **3:** 96; **6:** 15, 17; **8:** 343, 347
Brewer, Thomas L., **6:** 398, 400, 421
Bribery, **3:** 593
Bridgman, P. W., **7:** 334
Brierly, John E. C., **5:** 339
Brierly, J. L., **8:** 432
Briggs, Ellis O., **6:** 404
Bright, John, **5:** 94

Brinton, Crane, **3:** 521, 532, 539
Britain
    decisiveness of elections in, **3:** 164–165
    organized violence in, **3:** 137
British Association for the Advancement of Science, **7:** 61, 65
British colonies, federalism of, **5:** 96, 120
Brito, Dagobert L., **8:** 191
Brodbeck, May, **1:** 216, 217, 286, 299, 330
Broder, David, **5:** 421
Brodie, Bernard, **8:** 278, 283, 284, 315, 318, 340, 342, 343
Brodie, Fawn M., **2:** 40
Brody, Andras, **7:** 146
Brody, Richard A., **1:** 186; **3:** 224; **4:** 26, 60, 68, 106, 126, 160; **6:** 387; **7:** 188, 215, 222, 225, 227, 241, 246; **8:** 96, 123, 124, 127, 128, 193
Broetsky, Michael, **6:** 98
Bromley, David, **2:** 123, 190, 191, 192
Brooke, John, **5:** 307
Brookings Institution, **6:** 464; **8:** 348
Broszat, Martin, **3:** 215, 220, 225, 368
Browder, Robert, **6:** 413, 417
Brown, A. H., **5:** 222, 227, 231, 232
Brown, B. C., **7:** 82
Brown, Dee Alexander, **6:** 248, 259
Brown, George Rothwell, **5:** 307
Brown, J. F., **3:** 337
Brown, James R., **2:** 112, 113, 116
Brown, Josephine, **6:** 220
Brown, L. Carl, **6:** 252
Brown, Lester R., **6:** 99; **8:** 372
Brown, Michael Barratt, **8:** 30, 76, 77
Brown, Norman O., **1:** 250, 274; **2:** 31
Brown, Robert, **1:** 313
Brown, Robert E., **5:** 118
Brown, Roger, **2:** 49
Brown, Seyom, **8:** 342
Brown, Steven R., **2:** 44; **4:** 86, 158; **7:** 157, 177, 178, 179, 203, 244, 248
Brown, Stuart Gerry, **5:** 226
Brown, Thad A., **2:** 110, 140; **4:** 147, 162
Brown v. *The Board of Education,* **6:** 292
Browne, Eric C., **5:** 198
Browne, William P., **4:** 198, 199, 200, 204
Browning, Rufus P., **2:** 67, 75, 172, 189, 214, 215; **5:** 242
Brownlow, Louis, **5:** 223
Brownlow Committee, **5:** 405, 416
Brownstein, Charles N., **7:** 188, 235, 242, 249
Bruce-Briggs, Barry, **7:** 419
Bruck, H. W., **6:** 389, 421; **8:** 89, 94, 231

Bruner, Jerome S., **2:** 9, 13, 26, 34, 35, 51; **4:** 84; **7:** 278, 287
Brunner, Ronald D., **3:** 96; **6:** 15, 17
Bruno, Frank J., **6:** 220
Brunswik, Egon, **7:** 222, 248
Bryce, James, **2:** 205; **4:** 237; **6:** 335
Bryce, Lord, **5:** 184, 187, 188
Brymer, Richard G., **5:** 423
Brzezinski, Zbigniew, **3:** 95, 187, 188, 221, 225, 229, 336, 359, 361, 370; **6:** 80; **7:** 279
Buchan, Alastair, **8:** 222, 284, 345
Buchanan, Garth, **7:** 240
Buchanan, James M., **1:** 205, 220; **2:** 329; **3:** 424, 438, 444, 445, 453, 454, 470; **5:** 148; **7:** 86
Buchanan, William, **2:** 190, 191; **4:** 162; **5:** 303; **6:** 16
Bucher, Rue, **2:** 322, 323, 353
Buchheim, Hans, **3:** 187, 202, 210, 215, 216, 220, 225, 317, 359, 361, 363
Buck, Phillip W., **2:** 162; **5:** 183, 202
Buckley, Walter, **7:** 182; **8:** 78
Budget Message, **6:** 39
Bukharin, Nikolai, **8:** 79
Bull, Hedley, **8:** 75, 300
Bullitt, William C., **2:** 38
Bullock, Alan, **3:** 362
Bullock, Charles S., III, **2:** 94, 107
Bulpitt, J. G., **6:** 362
Bundesministerium für Gesamtdeutsche Fragen, **3:** 362
Bundesrat, **5:** 140
Bundestag of Germany, **5:** 293
Büntig, Aldo J., **3:** 78
Burchard, John, **6:** 362
Burckhardt, Jacob, **8:** 34
Bureau of Applied Social Research, **7:** 50
Bureau of the Budget, **5:** 377, 416
Bureau of the Census, **6:** 182, 284; **7:** 6, 33, 63, 67, 270, 271, 308
Bureau of Labor Statistics, **7:** 62
Bureaucracy, **5:** 373–429
  corporate, **5:** 399
  and the courts, **5:** 419–420
  expertise in, **5:** 374–380
  implementation in, **5:** 382–385
  nongovernmental, **5:** 399–411, 427
  organizational capabilities, **5:** 380–385, 405
  and the press, **5:** 421–422
  private vs. public, **5:** 407–411
  public, **5:** 399–411
  and its publics, **5:** 390–399

and rationality, **5:** 388–390
representative, **5:** 423–424
responsibility of, **5:** 411–428
size of, **5:** 425
and society, **5:** 412–413
and the United States Congress, **5:** 418–419
and the United States president, **5:** 417–418
Bureaucratic empire, **3:** 55–56
Bureaucratic expertise, **5:** 374–390
  as source of influence, **5:** 403–405
Bureaucratic-military authoritarian regimes, **3:** 285–306
  policies of, **3:** 299–300
  political institutionalization of, **3:** 300
  socioeconomic conditions for, **3:** 287–288
Bureaucratic politics, actors in, **6:** 393, 408–409
Bureaucratic responsibility, **5:** 411–428
  in China, **5:** 412
  control, forms of, **5:** 415–427
  ombudsman, **5:** 420–421
  trends of, **5:** 427–428
  in underdeveloped countries, **5:** 412–413
Bureaucratic routines, **5:** 381, 382–383
Bureaucratic theory, **8:** 16
Burger, Ewald, **7:** 382, 397, 398
Burgess, Philip M., **6:** 387; **8:** 99, 101
Burke, Edmund, **1:** 247, 371; **5:** 63, 87
Burke, Kenneth, **2:** 38
Burke, Peter J., **7:** 272, 335
Burks, Jesse D., **6:** 361, 363
Burks, R. V., **3:** 84, 362
Burnham, Walter Dean, **4:** 2, 138, 144, 145, 147, 148, 160, 161, 247, 269; **5:** 289; **7:** 67
Burns, Arthur, **8:** 204
Burns, Haywood, **6:** 253, 273
Burns, James M., **4:** 237, 255; **5:** 232; **7:** 37
Burns, Tom, **2:** 322, 357; **7:** 182, 188
Burrowes, Robert, **3:** 241; **8:** 130, 134, 136
Burt, Al, **3:** 261
Burwen, Leroy S., **2:** 23
Busch, Peter, **7:** 397; **8:** 193
Bush, Richard C., Jr., **3:** 359
Bush, Vannevar, **6:** 84
Business cycle, **5:** 146; **6:** 51–54
Busing, **6:** 257
Busshoff, Heinrich, **3:** 311
Butler, D. E., **5:** 219
Butler, David, **2:** 124, 127, 129; **4:** 27, 110, 160, 234, 245; **5:** 225; **7:** 282, 283, 302, 303, 304
Butler, Rohan, **3:** 363
Butt, Ronald, **5:** 236

Buttinger, Joseph, **3:** 98
Button, Christine Bennett, **2:** 138
Buzzard, Anthony, **8:** 284
Bwy, Douglas P., **3:** 9

Cabinet, British, **5:** 175, 194, 200–201, 211, 214, 216, 218
Cabinet, Canadian, **5:** 201–202
Cabinet officers, American, **5:** 198, 200, 202
Cabinet responsibility, collective, **5:** 215
Cabinet Secretariat, British, **5:** 224
Caciquismo, **3:** 263–264
Caesarism, **3:** 187, 315
Cahalan, Don, **7:** 297
Cahn, Anne H., **6:** 94, 95
Cahoon, Lawrence, **7:** 179
Cain, Glen, **6:** 467
Calhoun, John C., **1:** 391
Calkins, Susannah E., **5:** 150; **6:** 77
Callard, Keith, **5:** 123
Calvert, Peter, **3:** 522
Calvin, John, **1:** 230, 234
Calvinism, **5:** 52
Camau, Michel, **3:** 369
Cameron, David R., **2:** 120
Cameron, James R., **5:** 30
Campaign activity, **4:** 10, 13, 18, 35, 50–52
Campbell, Alan K., **6:** 330, 363
Campbell, Angus, **2:** 9, 49, 67, 102, 103, 124, 125, 127, 134, 137, 184, 332; **4:** 27, 85, 90, 98, 99, 100, 112, 133, 148, 159, 160, 162, 234, 248; **6:** 246; **7:** 57, 59, 60, 214, 218, 277, 286, 287, 312
Campbell, Colin D., **3:** 428
Campbell, Donald T., **2:** 6, 11, 23, 134; **6:** 442, 453, 454, 455, 467; **7:** 59, 146, 204, 217, 219, 221, 222, 229, 231, 232, 237, 238, 240, 243, 244, 246, 253, 295, 322
Campbell, John Franklin, **6:** 404, 408
Campbell, Norman, **1:** 216
Camps, Miriam, **5:** 230
Canada, federalism of, **5:** 112, 120, 135–136, 150–151, 154–155
Candidate image, **2:** 332
Candidate selection, **4:** 257–260
  leadership recruitment, **4:** 257
Cannell, Charles F., **7:** 312
Canonical analysis, **8:** 130, 137
Cantor, Norman F., **2:** 21
Cantori, Louis J., **8:** 215
Cantril, Albert H., **7:** 282
Cantril, Hadley, **2:** 216; **7:** 281, 282, 290, 325
Capitalism, **1:** 247

and imperialism, **8:** 20, 21, 25, 31
and war, **8:** 20
Capitalism, financial and industrial, **3:** 306, 316
and fascism, **3:** 321
Capitalist economic system, disillusionment with, **3:** 311
Caplan, Nathan, **2:** 110
Cappelletti, Mauro, **5:** 339
Caraley, Demetrios, **6:** 84
Care, Norman S., **1:** 293
Career structures, political, **5:** 199
Carey, George W., **1:** 114, 276; **6:** 439
Carey, William D., **5:** 224; **6:** 96
Carling, Ann, **3:** 460
Carlsmith, J. Merrill, **2:** 137; **7:** 249, 250
Carlson, Rae, **2:** 32
Carmichael, Stokely, **6:** 295
Carmines, Edward G., **6:** 223
Carney, Fredrick S., **5:** 160
Caro, Francis G., **6:** 307, 349
Carr, E. H., **3:** 618; **8:** 199, 263
Carr, Leslie G., **2:** 75
Carr, Raymond, **3:** 363
Carroll, Holbert, **5:** 308; **6:** 401
Carroll, J. D., **7:** 157, 175, 178, 179, 188
Carroll-Chang Individual Differences Scaling (INDSCAL), **7:** 175–178
Carsten, Francis L., **3:** 303, 315
Carter, Byrum E., **5:** 183, 193, 200, 219, 222, 226, 227, 229
Carter, Gwendolen M., **3:** 322, 325; **6:** 276
Cartwright, Dorwin, **7:** 311
Cartwright, John R., **3:** 369
Carzo, Rocco, **2:** 319, 320
Case-method teaching, **7:** 105
Case study, **7:** 79–132
  and clinical study, **7:** 81
  and comparative study, **7:** 81–86, 116
  defined, **7:** 84
  options on utility of, **7:** 92–96
  species of, **7:** 94
  and testing theories, **7:** 113
  types and uses of, **7:** 96–123
Caspary, William R., **6:** 413; **7:** 279; **8:** 101, 191
Casper, Jonathan D., **5:** 340
Cassinelli, C. W., **1:** 289, 330; **4:** 233
Cassirer, Ernst, **8:** 34
Castes, **3:** 25, 68, 326; **6:** 245, 246, 252
Casuistry, **1:** 378
Cater, Douglass, **5:** 391, 421; **6:** 413
Catlin, George E. G., **1:** 8, 46, 49
Cattell, David B., **6:** 335

Cattell, Raymond B., **7:** 153, 154, 156, 230, 231, 245, 247, 251
Caudillismo, **3:** 263–264
Causal approach, **2:** 336
Causal inference, **7:** 144, 153, 157, 245
Causal models, **7:** 140, 152, 164, 201
Causal relations, **7:** 195–196
Causal structure, **1:** 135, 136
Causal theories, **7:** 214
Causation, **1:** 300–301, 305; **7:** 141–142
Caywood, Craig P., **7:** 240
Central American Common Market, **8:** 385, 389
Central Intelligence Agency, **5:** 212; **6:** 406; **8:** 277
   "black operations," **8:** 329
   and Congress, **8:** 330
Centralization, **2:** 356
   and substantive rationality, **2:** 357
Centralized bureaucratic empires, **3:** 12
Centralized government, **5:** 99, 100–102, 109, 139, 147, 158
   degrees of, **5:** 101
Cerny, Karl H., **5:** 145
Certainty and decision making, **2:** 328, 336, 337, 347
Ceteris paribus assumptions, **7:** 140, 182, 184
Chabasinski, T., **2:** 118
Chadwick, Richard W., **7:** 228; **8:** 368
Chaffee, Steven H., **7:** 250
Chalmers, Douglas A., **4:** 268
Chamberlain, Lawrence H., **5:** 234, 307
Chamberlayne, Donald W., **6:** 223
Chambers, Clarke A., **6:** 220
Chambers, William N., **4:** 231, 246
Chambliss, William J., **7:** 272
Chammah, Albert, **2:** 343; **3:** 466; **7:** 182
Chancellor of the exchequer, **5:** 212, 213
Chanda, Asok, **5:** 150
Chandler, Alfred D., **5:** 289; **6:** 83
Chang, J. J., **7:** 157, 175, 178, 179
Chapman, Brian, **3:** 217
Chapman, Dwight, **7:** 312
Charisma, **3:** 207, 229, 323, 339, 362
   routinization of, **3:** 339
   transformation of, **3:** 339
Charity Organization Societies, **6:** 120, 161, 164
Charles, Bernard, **3:** 369
Charles, Joseph, **4:** 231
Charlot, Jean, **5:** 189, 195, 237
Chatterji, Manus, **8:** 191
Chaudhury, G. W., **5:** 123

Chauvinism, **2:** 97
Chauvinistic nationalism, **3:** 290
Chayes, Abram, **8:** 422
Checks and balances, system of, **5:** 6, 34, 35, 41
Cheever, Daniel S., **6:** 402
Chein, Isador, **2:** 118, 134
Chemical and biological warfare (CBW), **8:** 269, 336
Chen, S. H., **3:** 358
Cherington, Paul, **6:** 88; **7:** 324
Cherryholmes, Cleo H., **4:** 162
Chester, D. N., **5:** 232
Chevalier, Louis, **3:** 500
Chi square, **8:** 131
Chigier, M., **5:** 342
Child-welfare services, **6:** 116, 122, 126, 145, 147
Childe, V. Gordon, **1:** 5
Chiliastic systems, **3:** 274
China, political acculturation in, **3:** 20–21
Chinese law, **5:** 328
Chinese Revolution, **3:** 490
Chittick, William O., **6:** 413
Chiu, Chang-wei, **5:** 307
Choice function, **3:** 418, 423
Choice set, **3:** 418, 431
Chomsky, Noam, **1:** 274; **2:** 6
Chorley, Katherine, **3:** 538
Choucri, Nazli, **8:** 115, 131, 132, 139, 140
Christensen, Cheryl, **6:** 400
Christensen, Reo M., **1:** 398
Christianity, **1:** 232, 240, 241, 245
   conflict with Nazism, **3:** 317
   medieval, **1:** 242
Christie, Richard, **2:** 47, 48, 49, 50, 51, 52, 124
Christoffel, Tom, **6:** 280, 281
Chubb, Basil, **5:** 310
Churchman, C. West, **2:** 346, 348; **8:** 344
Cities, United States, collapse of public order in, **6:** 306–307
Citizen noninvolvement in government, **5:** 265
Citizens Association of New York, **7:** 269, 270
Citizens' Conference on State Legislatures, **5:** 297
Citizenship, **3:** 183, 602–605, 607–608
   dual, **5:** 38, 57
   national, **5:** 38
   state, **5:** 38
Citrin, Jack, **2:** 12, 51, 52, 117, 134, 137, 138, 140, 141
City size, **6:** 319, 320
Civic consciousness, national, **5:** 36
Civil Aeronautics Board, **5:** 407

Civil disobedience, **5:** 69–70, 71
  baronial tradition of, **5:** 7, 47–48
  colonial, **5:** 7
  constitutionalization of, **5:** 7
  institutionalization, **5:** 6
Civil law, **5:** 322, 329, 355
Civil liberties, **2:** 134
Civil Rights Acts, **6:** 276, 288, 291, 292–293, 449
Civil rights movement, **2:** 290–295
Civil violence, **3:** 8, 10
Civil war, **3:** 523
Civilizations, **1:** 232, 235, 242, 246, 247, 250
Clapp, Charles L., **5:** 291
Clark, Jane Perry, **5:** 148, 153
Clark, Keith C., **5:** 208, 223; **6:** 402; **8:** 323
Clark, Kenneth B., **2:** 118; **6:** 169, 176
Clark, Leon Pierce, **2:** 39
Clark, M. K., **2:** 118
Clark, Peter B., **2:** 163, 289; **4:** 184
Clark, Terry N., **6:** 321, 323, 327, 329, 336, 338; **7:** 324
Clarke, Harold D., **2:** 196
Clarke, James A., **6:** 343, 345
Clarke, James W., **2:** 104, 164, 193
Class analysis, **2:** 249, 286, 290, 304
Class cleavage, **4:** 244
Class, divisions and alliances, **3:** 496
Classical administrative theory, **2:** 350
Classical political philosophy, **2:** 249
Classification, **1:** 309–310
Claude, Inis L., Jr., **6:** 419; **8:** 203, 204, 206, 363
Clausen, Aage R., **7:** 297
Clausen, P.E., **4:** 60
Clausewitz, Karl von, **3:** 301
Cleavages, **3:** 125
Clement of Alexandria, **1:** 241
Clientele agencies, **5:** 396–399
Clientelistic politics, **3:** 288
Cliffe, Lionel, **3:** 326
Clinical vs. experimental studies, **7:** 84
Clogg, Richard, **3:** 286
Clotfelter, James, **6:** 409
Cloward, Richard A., **5:** 426; **6:** 148, 173, 212, 221, 279
Clubb, Jerome M., **7:** 45, 47, 54, 325
Clubok, Alfred B., **2:** 188
Cnudde, Charles F., **1:** 313; **3:** 5, 65; **4:** 2, 32, 33; **6:** 223
Coalition governments, **5:** 189, 198
  between members and challengers, **3:** 531–532
  class, **3:** 496

continuity of, **3:** 578–582
  formation of, **3:** 521; **7:** 241, 389, 390, 392
  French revolutionary of 1789–94, **3:** 540
  member-nonmember, **3:** 511
  structure of, **3:** 574–578
Coalition theory, **8:** 155
Cobb, Richard, **3:** 499, 538
Cobb, Roger W., **7:** 285, 296; **8:** 99
Cobb, Stephen, **6:** 87
Cobban, Alfred, **3:** 542
Cobbs, Price M., **6:** 295
Cochran, W. G., **7:** 312
Cocks, Paul, **3:** 188, 229, 340, 343
Codding, George A., **5:** 113
Coddington, Alan, **3:** 457, 459, 460, 469; **7:** 395
Code of Federal Regulations, **7:** 24
Code of Justinian, **5:** 325
Coercion, **1:** 299; **5:** 263
Coercive diplomacy, **8:** 389
Coercive power, **8:** 382
Coercive resources, **3:** 503
Cohen, Bernard, **4:** 183; **5:** 375; **6:** 273, 381, 389, 393, 397, 399, 400, 402, 405, 413, 418, 421; **7:** 334; **8:** 323
Cohen, Jacob, **5:** 146; **6:** 467, 468
Cohen, Jerome, **5:** 324, 331, 364
Cohen, Lenard, **3:** 286
Cohen, Michael D., **2:** 349
Cohen, Morris L., **7:** 12, 13, 27
Cohen, Morris R., **7:** 211, 221
Cohen, Robert S., **1:** 219; **2:** 107, 108, 115
Cohen, Ronald, **3:** 364
Cohen, Stephen D., **8:** 386, 388
Cohen, Wilbur J., **6:** 125, 130, 151
Cohn, Norman, **3:** 82, 221, 225
Cohn-Bendit, Daniel, **2:** 165
Cohn-Bendit, Gabriel, **2:** 165
Cohort analysis, **2:** 132
Colby, Kenneth M., **7:** 190, 196, 202
Cold War, **3:** 241; **8:** 200, 210, 213, 216, 217, 225, 229, 268
Cole, G. D. H., **4:** 34
Cole, George F., **2:** 307
Cole, Jonathan R., **6:** 83
Cole, Michael, **2:** 26
Cole, Stephen, **6:** 83
Cole, Taylor, **5:** 124
Coleman, James C., **6:** 363
Coleman, James S., **3:** 2, 91, 171, 180, 322, 357, 444, 445, 468, 470, 574, 616, 617, 618; **4:** 7, 177, 178, 182, 233, 236; **5:** 124; **6:** 294, 447, 449, 463; **7:** 99, 121, 397
Coles, Robert, **2:** 139; **6:** 253

Collective action, **3:** 464–467, 506–509
  competitive, **3:** 506–507
  proactive, **3:** 507, 518
  reactive, **3:** 507, 518
Collective goods, **7:** 355–358
Collective leadership, **3:** 208
Collective resistance, **3:** 510
Collective security, **8:** 253, 254
Collective violence, **3:** 514–517
  accomplished by agents of the state, **3:** 495
  likelihood of, **3:** 546
Collectivities, **1:** 298–299
Collier, David, **3:** 14; **8:** 371
Collingwood, R. G., **1:** 180
Collins, Barry E., **2:** 137, 354
Collins, John N., **8:** 130, 137
Collins, Lora S., **6:** 223
Collins, Orvis F., **5:** 183
Colonial rule, **3:** 256, 322, 327, 582
Colonialism, **3:** 58, 327
Columbia University School of Political Science, **1:** 27
Comas, Juan, **6:** 249
Commercialization of agriculture, **3:** 12, 14
Commission of the European Community, **8:** 385
Commission on Freedom of the Press, **6:** 11
Commission on Intergovernmental Relations, **5:** 148
Commitment, enduring, **2:** 121, 128
Committee chairmen, congressional, **5:** 200
Committee on Comparative Politics, **6:** 384
Committee for Economic Development, **6:** 54
Committee on Economic Security, **6:** 116, 117
Committee on Foreign Affairs Personnel, **6:** 403, 408
Committees for the Defense of the Revolution in Cuba, **3:** 225
Common law, **5:** 18, 23, 26, 47, 48, 322–323, 328, 329, 337, 339, 342, 361
Common-law judge, **5:** 21, 22, 23
Common-law jurisdiction, **5:** 50
Common-law king, **5:** 49, 56
Common Market, and security, **8:** 331, 364
Commonwealth, concept of, **5:** 35
Commonwealth Grants Commission, **5:** 150
Communal group, **3:** 45, 46
Communal structures, **3:** 505
Communications Satellite Corporation (COMSAT), **5:** 409
Communism, **1:** 244; **3:** 21, 32, 56, 84
  compared to fascism, **3:** 234–237
  group politics in, **3:** 245

polycentrism of, **3:** 338
"Slavophile" interpretation of, **3:** 244
Communist federalism, **5:** 97
Communist Manifesto, **8:** 20
Communist party, **3:** 203, 215–216; **4:** 232–233
Communist regimes, **3:** 336–337
  comparison of, **3:** 365–366
  foreign policy of, **3:** 359–360
Communist self-government, **3:** 343
Community Action, meaning of, **6:** 175–182
Community Mental Health Services Act of 1964, **6:** 129
Community power, **6:** 306, 307, 319
Comparative analysis in foreign policy, **6:** 384–385, 386–387
  hindrances to, **6:** 385
  types of, **6:** 384–385
Comparative history approach to political development analysis, **3:** 3
Comparative study
  and case study, **7:** 81–86, 116
  defined, **7:** 85
Competitive markets, **6:** 25
Comptroller General, United States, **6:** 221
Comrades courts, **3:** 225
Conant, James B., **8:** 4, 9
Concepts
  categorical, **1:** 309–311
  comparative, **1:** 311–314
  extreme-type, **1:** 311
  quantitative, **1:** 313–314
Conceptual dependency analysis, **7:** 188–198
  atomic relations within, **7:** 191–194
Conceptual development in foreign policy, **6:** 385–388
Conceptual framework, use of, **1:** 140; **6:** 386–387, 388
Conceptualization, **7:** 191
Conciliar Controversy, **5:** 31, 46
Concert of Europe, **5:** 117; **8:** 48, 261
Concordance system, **7:** 7; **8:** 388, 390
Concurrent majorities, **1:** 391
Conde, Francisco Javier, **3:** 361
Condorcet, M. J. A. N. C., **1:** 247, 341
Confederacy, **5:** 71–72, 74
Confederate Congress, **5:** 75
Confederation of British Industries, **5:** 403
Conference on Mutual and Balanced Force Reductions, **8:** 331
Configurative-idiographic study, **7:** 96–99
  assumptions of, **7:** 97
  and clinical study, **7:** 97
  weaknesses of, **7:** 97–98

Confirmed knowledge, **7:** 211
Conflict, **1:** 191; **2:** 321
  management of, **2:** 326
Conflict of interest, **7:** 363–368, 385
Conflict, involvement in, **4:** 8–9
  and voting, **4:** 9
Conflict predispositions, measurement of, **7:** 154, 170
Conflict resolution, **5:** 321–333, 338–340, 342, 343, 344, 345, 352, 354
Conformity, compulsive, **2:** 20, 53, 76
Congress, United States, **5:** 275–276, 284–287, 288–291, 300–301
Congressional committees, **5:** 276
Congressional Directory, **7:** 6
Congressional Record, **7:** 19, 20
Connell, R. W., **2:** 99, 104, 112, 123, 124, 125
Connolly, H., **2:** 118
Connolly, William, **1:** 286, 318; **2:** 297, 309
Connor, Walker, **3:** 89, 97
Conquest, Robert, **3:** 219, 221, 222, 225
Conrad, A. H., **6:** 195
Conrad-Martius, Hedwig, **3:** 363
Conring, Hermann, **7:** 141
Consensus, **1:** 170, 193; **2:** 347, 361
Consensus iuris, **5:** 44, 45
Consensus theory of politics, **7:** 332
Consent, **5:** 322–323, 333, 338
  substitution of law and office for, **5:** 325–328
Consent of the governed, **5:** 264
Consequentialism, **1:** 395
Conservatism, **1:** 247; **3:** 559, 575
Conservative decision maker, **2:** 338
Conservative modernization, **3:** 252
Conservative party, **1:** 177; **5:** 190
Consociational democracies, **3:** 312, 331
Constituency
  and bureaucratic responsibility, **5:** 422
  development of, **5:** 393–396, 398, 400
  as source of power, **5:** 401–403, 407
Constituent government, **5:** 99, 100, 109, 137, 138, 139, 145, 147
  bargaining among, **5:** 150
Constituent meanings, **7:** 190
Constituent units, **5:** 142
Constitution, **1:** 20, 21
  American, **5:** 6–7, 26, 34, 35–36, 37, 38, 41, 45, 50, 66–70, 77–78
  Bacon's, **5:** 60–61
  British, **5:** 27, 47–48, 62
  Canadian, **5:** 112
  English, and *Calvin's Case,* **5:** 54–61
  ideal-typical, **5:** 17

imperial, and *Calvin's Case,* **5:** 61–66
  Whig, **5:** 68, 75
Constitutional choice, **3:** 451–456
Constitutional crisis of 1776, **5:** 50
Constitutional democracy, **5:** 1–2, 4
  liberal, **5:** 6
  theorists of, **5:** 2
Constitutional government, **5:** 41–42
Constitutional history, **5:** 29–30, 57
Constitutional mechanics, baroque, **5:** 76–78
Constitutional monarchy, **5:** 28
Constitutional morality, **5:** 3, 5
Constitutional order, **5:** 4, 17
Constitutional theorists, **5:** 59
Constitutional theory, **5:** 26, 27, 30, 31, 38, 45, 71–72
Constitutional thought, modern, **5:** 35
Constitutional tradition, **5:** 37
Constitutionalism, **5:** 1–87
  American, **5:** 35, 36
  "Americanists," **5:** 36
  ancient, **5:** 3
  "Anglican" theorists of, **5:** 36
  anthropology of, **5:** 7–28
  British, **5:** 6–7, 31, 32
  British contribution to, **5:** 48
  central problem of, **5:** 34–35
  classical background of, **5:** 37–40
  comparative, **5:** 4
  debate over, **5:** 28–37
  and dictatorships, **5:** 4
  German, **5:** 27
  jurisprudential essentials of, **5:** 43–44
  "medieval," **5:** 26, 30–31, 32, 34, 63
  medieval background of, **5:** 44–50
  modern, **5:** 3, 5–6, 33, 34, 35, 75, 81–82, 84
  mystique of, **5:** 1–7
  myth of, **5:** 78–87
  rationalist, **5:** 84, 85–86
  utopian sense of, **5:** 86
  zenith of, **5:** 2
Constitutions of Clarendon, **5:** 28
Constitutions, Cromwellian, **5:** 35, 68
Constitutive meanings, **1:** 168–171, 173, 176, 178, 181, 206, 208, 209; **7:** 197–198
Constitutive norms, **1:** 167, 207
Consultative authoritarianism, **3:** 344–345
Consumer protection, **5:** 391–392
Content analysis, **7:** 146, 148, 152, 157
Contexts of foreign policy, **6:** 397–400
  concurrent, **6:** 400
  historical, **6:** 399–400
  sequential, **6:** 400

Contini, Bruno, **3:** 459, 460
Control, **1:** 300, 301, 305
Controlled nuclear war, **8:** 318–319
Conventions, **1:** 133, 167–168, 178, 208
  American national, **5:** 186, 187
  Canadian, **5:** 190
Converse, Jean M., **7:** 295
Converse, Philip E., **2:** 9, 49, 76, 103, 116, 121,
    122, 125, 127, 128, 130, 131, 134, 137, 140,
    184, 332; **3:** 443, 485, 512; **4:** 27, 60, 68, 84,
    85, 88, 90, 98, 99, 100, 133, 158, 159, 160,
    162, 248; **5:** 225, 242; **7:** 45, 54, 55, 135,
    218, 248, 277, 278, 284, 285, 286, 288, 290,
    303, 304, 305
Conversion variables in foreign policy, **6:**
    420–423
  bureaucratic politics as, **6:** 422
  incrementalism as, **6:** 421–422
  obsolescence as, **6:** 422–423
  rationality as, **6:** 421
Conway, John S., **3:** 359
Conway, M. Margaret, **2:** 166, 197
Conze, Werner, **3:** 248
Cook, Peggy, **2:** 47
Cook, Stuart W., **2:** 131
Cook, Thomas J., **7:** 240, 248
Cooke, Jacob E., **7:** 3, 281
Coombes, David, **5:** 236
Coombs, C. H., **3:** 429; **7:** 159, 167, 306
Coombs, Fred E., **7:** 275, 276
Coon, Carleton S., **6:** 279
Cooper, Joel, **7:** 235
Cooper, Joseph, **5:** 291
Cooper, Richard N., **6:** 416; **8:** 368, 369, 390,
    393, 401
Cooper, W. W., **2:** 334
Cooperative activity, **4:** 11–12
Co-optation, **5:** 266–268; **6:** 277
Cornblit, Oscar, **3:** 75
Cornelius, Wayne, **3:** 36, 37, 486; **6:** 349, 358
Cornford, Francis M., **5:** 12, 15, 16, 17
Corning, Peter, **8:** 341, 347
Cornwell, Elmer E., Jr., **2:** 180–181, 228; **5:**
    225
Corporate bureaucracies, **5:** 373, 403
Corporate management, **5:** 266
Corporate system, **3:** 51
Corporation, modern, **5:** 266
Corporative democracy, **3:** 184, 307
Corwin, Edward S., **5:** 24, 110, 145, 154, 160,
    182, 206, 213, 221, 232; **6:** 401; **7:** 24
Cosio Villegas, Daniel, **3:** 358
cosmopolis, **1:** 245

Cost-benefit analysis, **2:** 328; **8:** 290
  and distribution effects of public policy, **2:**
    328–331
  interpersonal utility comparisons, **2:** 329
  marginal value, **2:** 329
  and optimum distribution of welfare, **2:** 330
  and water resource decisions, **2:** 329
Costello, C. G., **2:** 44; **7:** 84, 85, 95
Cotler, Julio, **3:** 312
Cotter, Cornelius P., **2:** 182
Cotton, John F., **6:** 357
Cottrell, Leonard S., Jr., **7:** 316
Couch, Arthur, **2:** 75
Coulam, Robert F., **8:** 323
Coulborn, Rushton, **3:** 55
Coulter, Philip B., **6:** 305
Council of Economic Advisers, **5:** 377, 379; **6:**
    24, 36, 38, 39, 40, 41, 42, 55, 283, 463
Counterforce, **8:** 257, 258, 298, 305, 310
Counterinsurgency, **8:** 302–303
Counterrevolutionary conservatism, **3:** 306–
    307
Coup d'état, **3:** 523
Court, David, **2:** 112
Court politics, **3:** 362
Courts
  administrative, **5:** 341
  American, **5:** 329, 331, 332, 360
  appellate, **5:** 350–356
  avoidance of, **5:** 334, 341
  Chinese, **5:** 330, 331, 335
  English, **5:** 329, 331, 335, 355, 356, 363, 364
  European, **5:** 329, 337, 341, 346, 355, 363
  feudal, **5:** 334, 335
  imperial, **5:** 334, 336, 363
  Japanese, **5:** 331
  as lawmakers, **5:** 342–349
  logic of, **5:** 349–350
  popular, **5:** 334, 338, 362–365
  prototype of, **5:** 321
  and the regime, **5:** 336–338
  Russian, **5:** 347
  and taxation, **5:** 335, 336
  trial, **5:** 350–356
Coverdale, John F., **3:** 367
Covert operations and foreign policy, **8:** 330
Cowart, Andrew T., **6:** 223
Cox, Donald W., **6:** 90
Cox, Edward, **5:** 402; **6:** 467
Cox, Oliver C., **6:** 249, 252
Cox, Richard, **1:** 275
Cox, Robert W., **8:** 391, 393
Coxon, Anthony P.M., **7:** 176

Crabb, Cecil, **6:** 415
Craig, Albert M., **3:** 20, 97, 365
Craig, Gordon A., **8:** 284
Crain, Robert L., **6:** 338, 341, 342
Crane, Peggy, **6:** 332, 340, 362
Crane, William W., **1:** 38
Cranston, Maurice, **1:** 387
Crassweller, Robert D., **3:** 261
Crecine, John, **2:** 321, 322; **6:** 329; **8:** 323
Creighton, D. G., **5:** 112
Crenson, Matthew A., **5:** 384
Crick, Bernard, **1:** 38, 252; **2:** 253; **4:** 172; **5:** 235, 297
Crime rate as predictor of revolution, **3:** 491
Criminal law, **5:** 329, 339, 340, 356, 359, 364
Crisis government, **3:** 186, 187
Crisp, L. F., **5:** 197
Criteria, aggregation of, **1:** 342–344
  conflicts among, **1:** 349–357
  interpretability of, **1:** 342
Criteria of evaluation, **2:** 324
Crittenden, John, **2:** 132
Croan, Melvin, **3:** 337
Croce, Benedetto, **1:** 258, 260
Cronin, Thomas E., **5:** 207, 224, 232, 377
Crosland, Anthony, **5:** 219
Cross, J. A., **5:** 231
Cross, J. G., **3:** 459, 460, 469
Crossley, Archibald M., **7:** 325
Crossley, Helen M., **7:** 297
Crossman, Richard, **5:** 221, 231, 232
Cross-national hypotheses, **8:** 128–141
Crotty, William T., **2:** 104; **4:** 253
Crow, Ralph E., **3:** 171
Crowe, Eyre, **8:** 206
Crozier, Michael, **2:** 21, 353, 355; **3:** 594; **5:** 413
Crucial-case studies, **7:** 113–131
  advantages of, **7:** 120–121
  characteristics of, **7:** 118
Cruse, Harold, **2:** 313
Crutchfield, Richard, **7:** 312
Cruz, Jose B., Jr., **8:** 191
Cuba
  political culture of, **3:** 31, 84–85
  under Batista, **3:** 262–263
Cuban missile crisis, **2:** 343; **5:** 383; **6:** 85; **8:** 295, 300, 301, 324
Culliton, Barbara J., **6:** 94
Cult of personality, **3:** 195, 206
  rejection of, **3:** 208
Cultural fragment theory, **3:** 22–23
Cultural meanings, **2:** 303–305
Cultural Revolution in China, **3:** 205–206, 347

Culture, **2:** 25–26
  vs. personality, **2:** 25–26, 61
  political, **2:** 25
Cumming v. *County Board of Education,* **6:** 272
"Cumulative knowledge," **1:** 3
Cunliffe, Marcus, **5:** 205, 211
Currie, Elliot P., **5:** 338
Curry, R. L., Jr., **7:** 86
Curtis, John S., **3:** 359
Curtis, Michael, **3:** 241; **5:** 182
Curtis, Richard G., **3:** 454
Cutright, Phillips, **3:** 3, 5, 6, 65, 171; **6:** 200
Cybernetic theory, **2:** 334
Cyclical majorities, **7:** 373
Cyert, Richard M., **2:** 322, 354; **5:** 303; **6:** 403
Czechoslovakia, **3:** 345–346
  political opposition in, **3:** 126, 128
Czudnowski, Moshe M., **2:** 157, 171, 172, 176, 198, 199, 202, 207, 219, 220, 221, 228, 229, 231, 232

Daalder, Hans, **3:** 133, 171, 331; **5:** 206
Dabelko, David D., **7:** 240
Daedalus, **3:** 364
Dahl, Robert A., **1:** 156–160, 285, 287, 290, 291, 301, 304, 306, 311, 312, 313, 363, 390, 394; **2:** 247, 248, 252, 267, 268, 269, 270, 271, 272, 273, 275, 285, 286, 287, 288, 290, 309, 310, 354; **3:** 5, 6, 32, 35, 77, 84, 98, 148, 171, 180, 181, 182, 183, 250, 327, 352, 355, 358, 363, 444, 619; **4:** 4, 27, 34, 70, 149, 222; **5:** 160, 234, 304, 305, 407, 409; **6:** 307, 308, 415, 440; **7:** 99, 109, 121, 184, 266, 267, 280, 284, 329, 332; **8:** 395
  democratic regimes, recent work on, **2:** 267
  democratic theory, recent work on, **2:** 248
  on norms of the American political regime, **2:** 247, 269–272
  on political leadership, **2:** 270
  on political process, **2:** 268–269
  on stability-disruption-protest model, **2:** 270–272
Dahlgren, H. E., **2:** 125; **7:** 301, 302
Dahlstrom, W. Grant, **2:** 45
Dahrendorf, Ralf, **1:** 191, 192, 193; **2:** 310; **3:** 231, 363, 368; **6:** 185
Daland, Robert T., **6:** 313
Dale, Richard, **3:** 327
Dalfiume, Richard M., **7:** 317, 318
Dallin, Alexander, **3:** 208, 217, 219, 223, 225, 226, 228; **6:** 413; **7:** 169
Dallin, David J., **3:** 228

Dallmayr, Fred R., **1:** 276
Damage Limiting policy, **8:** 298, 305, 311
  and psychological effect of Vietnam War, **8:** 305
  reexamination of, recent, **8:** 318
  stability in, **8:** 289
D'Amato, Anthony A., **8:** 419
Danhof, Clarence H., **6:** 81, 87
Daniels, George H., **6:** 82
Daniels, Robert B., **2:** 74
Daniels, Robert Vincent, **3:** 202, 206, 236, 247, 336, 362
Dann, Uriel, **3:** 367, 369
Dante, **1:** 10, 262
D'Arcy, Eric, **1:** 371
Darcy, R., **7:** 240
Darley, John M., **7:** 235
Darrah, William Culp, **6:** 83
Das Gupta, Jyotirindra, **3:** 69, 87
Data
  arrangement of, **8:** 165
  availability, **8:** 95
  banks, **8:** 95
  collection of, **8:** 89, 93, 95, 96, 101
  manufacture of, **8:** 95
  problems, **8:** 94, 95, 96
  sets, **8:** 95
Data analysis, **7:** 146
Data archives, **7:** 45–67. *(See also individual listings.)*
  additional services of, **7:** 47
  data cleaning, **7:** 56
  "data laboratories," **7:** 45
  data sharing, **7:** 60
  development of, **7:** 57–62
  holdings of, **7:** 59
  misuse of data in, **7:** 61
  operation and utilization of, **7:** 51–56
  training programs, **7:** 47
Data sources, **7:** 62–67. *(See also individual listings.)*
  public record, **7:** 54, 56
Data theory, **7:** 159, 167, 182, 202
DATUM, **7:** 51
Daumard, Adeline, **3:** 500
David, Martin H., **6:** 84, 130
David, Paul T., **5:** 183, 192, 193, 197
David, René, **5:** 339, 343
Davidson, Donald, **1:** 217, 297
Davidson, K. H., **7:** 33
Davidson, P. O., **2:** 44; **7:** 84, 85, 95
Davidson, Roger H., **5:** 308; **6:** 222
Davies, A. F., **2:** 34, 37, 38, 46

Davies, Bleddyn, **6:** 327, 336, 339, 344, 356, 357, 362
Davies, James C., **2:** 5, 30, 63, 127, 212, 233; **3:** 8, 488, 526, 528
Davies, Richard O., **7:** 269
Davies, Robert W., **6:** 335
Davis, Allen F., **6:** 220
Davis, Allison, **7:** 309, 310
Davis, David Brion, **6:** 250, 263, 264
Davis, David H., **5:** 427; **6:** 407, 422
Davis, David W., **5:** 148; **6:** 177
Davis, E. Eugene, **5:** 329
Davis, F. James, **5:** 329
Davis, James A., **7:** 290
Davis, James W., **5:** 183, 188, 385, 387; **6:** 467
Davis, John M., **3:** 437
Davis, John P., **7:** 317, 318
Davis, Kenneth C., **5:** 385, 419
Davis, Kingsley, **6:** 310
Davis, Lance E., **6:** 83
Davis, Morton, **7:** 384, 398
Davis, Otto, **3:** 442, 449; **4:** 113, 125, 160; **6:** 329, 330; **7:** 377, 384
Davis, Rufus, **5:** 106, 131
Davis, Vincent, **6:** 88; **8:** 322
Davison, W. Phillips, **6:** 412
Dawes, Robyn, **7:** 159
Dawson, John P., **5:** 327, 335, 363
Dawson, R. MacGregor, **5:** 202
Dawson, Raymond H., **6:** 412
Dawson, Richard E., **2:** 94, 127; **3:** 65; **4:** 243; **5:** 157; **6:** 223
Dawson, W. F., **5:** 310
Dawson, William H., **6:** 345
Deakin, Alfred, **5:** 112
Deakin, F. W., **3:** 359
Deane, Phyllis, **7:** 54
Debate, **5:** 281
Debreu, Gerard, **7:** 397
Decentralization and uncertainty, **2:** 356
Decision-making, **1:** 203; **6:** 389
  distinction between context and issue, **6:** 398–399
Decision-making hypotheses, **8:** 113–128
Decision-making models, **6:** 390
Decision process, **6:** 1, 2, 4
Decision rules, **3:** 417–418
  binary, **3:** 420
  domain of, **3:** 417, 419, 429
  multi-stage, **3:** 433–437
  Pareto-inclusive, **3:** 420
  range of, **3:** 417, 419
  simple, **3:** 452–453

Decision theory, **2:** 320, 341
  certainty, **2:** 335
  and compromise, **2:** 326, 349
  risk, **2:** 320, 335
  transitivity of choice, **2:** 326
  uncertainty, **2:** 320, 335–347
  viewed as process, **2:** 326
Deckard, Barbara, **5:** 291
Declaration of Independence, **1:** 21
Decline-of-community model, **4:** 33–38
de Coulanges, Foustel, **3:** 170; **5:** 87
Dédoublement fonctionnel, **8:** 417
De facto republic, **5:** 68
De Felice, Renzo, **3:** 248, 315, 336, 361, 369, 370
Defense affairs, **8:** 251
Deference voting, **5:** 271–272
Definitional measurement, **7:** 146
Definitions, **1:** 290–291
  explicative, **1:** 290–291, 308
  persuasive, **1:** 323–327
  reportative, **1:** 291, 308
  stipulative, **1:** 290
de Glanvill, Ranulf, **5:** 26
Degler, Carl N., **3:** 70; **6:** 242, 265, 266, 268, 278, 286
de Grazia, Alfred, **5:** 232
de Grazia, Sebastian, **1:** 274
de Jouvenel, Bertrand, **1:** 212, 273
de Kadt, Emanuel, **3:** 78
Dekmejian, R. Hrair, **3:** 367, 369
Delafons, John, **6:** 349
Delaney, Paul, **6:** 277
Delian League, **5:** 94
Deliberation, process of, **5:** 42, 260, 273
Delphi technique, **7:** 426–427
Delzell, Charles F., **3:** 315
Demagoguery, **5:** 41
DeMeyer, Frank, **3:** 428
De Miguel, Amando, **3:** 288, 367
Deming, William Edwards, **7:** 308
Demobilization, **3:** 504
Democracy, **1:** 306–307, 313, 386, 390–394; **5:** 40, 41
  as maximin consent, **1:** 390
  parliamentary, **3:** 496
Democratic centralism, **3:** 184, 206, 362
Democratic character, **2:** 36
Democratic government, **3:** 92
  breakdown of, **3:** 249, 333
  definition of, **3:** 182–183
  diversity of, **3:** 181

elitist theory of, **3:** 358
  establishment by foreign intervention, **3:** 186
  and nondemocratic polities, **3:** 182–185
  stability of in economically developed countries, **3:** 182
Democratic participation, **4:** 2, 4
Democratic performance, measures of, **3:** 353
Democratic pluralism, **3:** 307
Democratic political institutions, **3:** 59, 60, 62
Democratic revolutions, **5:** 5
Democratic theory, **7:** 266–267, 300, 330, 331
  and randomization, **7:** 322
Democratization, dimensions of, **3:** 119–120
Demography, historical, **3:** 499
Demonstration, political, **3:** 515
Dempster, M., **6:** 329, 330
Denison, Edward F., **6:** 76, 99
Deniston, O. Lynn, **6:** 440
Denitch, Bogdan, **3:** 239, 346
Denney, Reuel, **2:** 46
Denney, William Michael, **4:** 143
Dennis, Jack, **2:** 94, 95, 96, 97, 98, 99, 100, 102, 106, 112, 113, 114, 116, 120, 124, 125, 127, 132, 134, 140; **7:** 61, 278, 302
Dennison, Edward F., **6:** 135
Dennison, Eleanor E., **6:** 401
Denny, Brewster C., **6:** 100
Dentler, Robert A., **1:** 132
d'Entrévès, Alexander Passerin, **1:** 264, 277, 321
Denzin, Norman K., **2:** 8
Department of Agriculture, **5:** 394, 423
Department of Commerce, **3:** 171
Department of Defense, **5:** 212, 375, 376, 378, 391, 395–396, 408; **6:** 44, 406; **8:** 277, 280, 292
  belief systems in, **6:** 408
Department of Defense Science Board, **6:** 90
Department of Education and Science, **6:** 86
Department of Health, Education, and Welfare, **6:** 44, 73, 141, 144, 207–208, 457, 462; **7:** 63
Department of Housing and Urban Development, **6:** 457
Department of Housing and Urban Development, Office of International Affairs, **6:** 313
Department of Justice, **5:** 400; **7:** 284
Department of Labor, **5:** 394, 396, 407
Department of State, **5:** 212, 375, 394; **6:** 403–404, 420

belief systems in, **6:** 408
Department of Transportation, **5:** 399
Depoliticization, **3:** 269, 351; **8:** 397
Depository libraries, **7:** 19–20
Depré, Roger, **6:** 339, 344
Deprivation
  collective violence and, **3:** 493, 494
  measures of, **3:** 494, 495
de Rivera, Joseph H., **2:** 63; **6:** 394; **7:** 228; **8:** 316
Derthick, Martha, **5:** 111, 148; **6:** 114, 221, 342
de Santillana, Giorgio, **6:** 93
de Solla Price, Derek, **6:** 100
Despotism, **5:** 40, 68
  monarchial, **5:** 69
De-Stalinization, **3:** 240, 336
Destler, I. M., **5:** 379; **6:** 92, 406, 409; **8:** 323
De Swaan, Abram, **7:** 396
Detente, **8:** 208
Deterrence, **8:** 256, 257, 279, 282, 288
  credibility in, **8:** 289
  and ending the arms race, **8:** 300, 306
  and "Massive Retaliation" policy, **8:** 287
  minimum deterrence, **8:** 299–300
Deterrent, vulnerability of, **8:** 288–289, 300
de Tocqueville, Alexis, **1:** 14; **2:** 204, 207, 290; **3:** 139, 144, 176; **6:** 83, 215, 244; **7:** 406, 407
Deutsch, Karl W., **1:** 140, 141, 277, 297, 305; **3:** 2, 3, 27, 32, 68, 72, 97, 503, 571, 603; **4:** 33; **5:** 114, 115; **6:** 308, 390, 467; **7:** 45, 54, 64; **8:** 110, 146, 212, 215, 223, 364, 365, 366, 375, 378, 379, 380, 381
Deutsche Arbeitsfront (DAF), **3:** 201
Deutscher, Irwin, **7:** 296
Developmental analyses, **2:** 42
Developmental interpretations, **2:** 43
Devine, Edward T., **6:** 220
Devletoglou, Nicos E., **3:** 470
Devons, Ely, **6:** 87
DeVos, George A., **7:** 289
Dewey, John, **2:** 73, 276; **5:** 32, 45, 407
Dexter, Lewis Anthony, **1:** 231; **2:** 245, 332; **4:** 162, 205, 207; **5:** 287; **6:** 407, 413, 417
Diamant, Alfred, **3:** 311; **5:** 373
Diamond, Martin, **5:** 160
Diamond, Sigmund, **7:** 270
Díaz Elís, **3:** 359
Dickerman, Charles Robert, **8:** 399
Dickinson, Edwin DeWitt, **8:** 428
Dickman, Kern, **7:** 154
Dicks, Henry V., **2:** 61, 65; **3:** 221, 225
Dickson, Paul, **6:** 464

Dickson, W. J., **2:** 351
Dickson, William, **6:** 457
Dictatorship, **3:** 185–187; **5:** 58, 263
  constitutional, **3:** 185
  definition of, **3:** 187
  historical origins of, **3:** 185
  military, **3:** 582
  of the proletariat, **3:** 234
  royal, **3:** 186, 276, 288
  sovereign, **3:** 186
Diederich, Bernard, **3:** 261
Diesing, Paul, **2:** 332; **8:** 78
Dietze, Gottfried, **5:** 160
Diffuse system support, **2:** 112, 114, 115, 134
  measures of, **2:** 115
Diffusion patterns, **8:** 371
Dikshit, R. D., **5:** 121
Dilemma of collective action, **7:** 182
Dillehay, Ronald C., **2:** 47
Dilthey, W., **7:** 122
Diminishing marginal utility, **1:** 387
Dinerman, Helen, **7:** 297, 312
Di Palma, Giuseppe, **2:** 20, 51, 53; **7:** 289
Diplomacy, **5:** 50
Dirección General de Estadística, **3:** 71
Dirección Nacional de Estadística, **3:** 71
Directive correlation, **7:** 168
Di Renzo, Gordon J., **2:** 54, 216, 217, 359
Disch, Robert, **6:** 254, 280
Disciplined-configurative study, **7:** 99–104
  chain of inquiry in, **7:** 100
  utility of, **7:** 103–104
Discounting function, **3:** 460
Discretion, administrative, **5:** 385–388, 402, 410–411, 420
Discrimination, **6:** 63–64
Disenfranchisement, **3:** 309
Dispositional concepts, **1:** 301
Dispositional practices, **1:** 294
Dispute settlement, **5:** 338
Distribution of power, **3:** 47
Distributive authority, **5:** 58
Dittmer, Lowell, **5:** 412
Division of functions of government, **5:** 101, 109–111
  horizontal, **5:** 105
  vertical, **5:** 104
Division of Program Surveys, Department of Agriculture, **7:** 311
Djilas, Milovan, **5:** 412
Dobson, Richard B., **3:** 232
Dodds, Eric R., **5:** 15

Dodge, Richard W., **7:** 234, 248
Doenhoff, Marion, **8:** 255
Dogan, Mattei, **2:** 159, 183, 204, 208, 232; **5:** 183, 199, 201, 202, 203; **6:** 16
Doig, Jameson E., **5:** 183, 202, 203
Dolbeare, Kenneth M., **2:** 116; **5:** 385, 387; **6:** 467
Dolkart, Ronald, **3:** 263
"Dollar diplomacy," **6:** 416
Dollard, John, **2:** 34; **7:** 298, 309, 310
Domestic sources of foreign policy, **6:** 410–420
  economic variables, **6:** 416–418
  political variables, **6:** 414–416
  societal variables, **6:** 412–414
  types of, **6:** 411
Dominance, **1:** 365–368
Dominance theory, **7:** 161, 198
Dominated strategy, **7:** 381, 387
Domínguez, Jorge I., **3:** 25, 78, 84, 190, 366
Dominion theory, **5:** 57
  and federalism, **5:** 70–73
Donald, David, **2:** 40, 104
Donley, Richard E., **2:** 75
Donnellan, Keith S., **1:** 296
Donnison, D. V., **6:** 313
Donovan, John C., **6:** 222, 391, 408
Doob, Leonard, **3:** 29
Dorfer, Ingemar, **6:** 98
Dorfman, Robert, **6:** 16
Döring, Hans Joachim, **3:** 219
Dornbusch, Horst D., **6:** 467
Dorsey, John T., Jr., **5:** 183
Dos Santos, Theotonio, **8:** 367
"Double majesty," theory of, **5:** 30, 35, 49, 54, 57, 58, 59, 61, 63–64, 65–70, 74
Dougherty, Richard, **6:** 389
Douglas, Mary, **1:** 216
Douglas, Paul H., **6:** 220
Douglas Subcommittee on Employment, **6:** 54
Dowling, R. E., **2:** 253, 307
Downes, Bryan T., **6:** 305, 341
Downing, Randal, **4:** 181
Downs, Anthony, **1:** 141, 195–197, 198–199, 200, 201; **2:** 321, 325, 326, 327, 333, 358; **3:** 442, 443, 465, 468; **4:** 95, 98, 160; **5:** 401; **6:** 218; **7:** 86, 376, 377, 384
Dowty, Alan, **8:** 79
Drachkovitch, Milorad M., **3:** 236
Draper, Theodore, **3:** 366
Dror, Yehezkel, **6:** 11
Dubester, Henry J., **7:** 67
Dubin, Robert, **2:** 353
Du Bois, William Edward Burghardt, **6:** 271

Ducasse, Curt J., **7:** 214, 216
Duchacek, Ivo O., **5:** 99, 106
Ducoff, Louis J., **7:** 295
Dudman, Richard, **4:** 197
Duff, Ernest A., **5:** 310
Dulles, John Foster, **8:** 284, 286, 287, 290
Dummett, Michael, **3:** 424, 430; **7:** 399
Dumont, René, **3:** 190, 366
Duncan, Otis D., **1:** 386; **2:** 27; **6:** 184; **7:** 146, 273, 291, 295
Duncanson, Dennis J., **3:** 98
Dunlap, Riley, **2:** 69, 70
Dupeux, Georges, **2:** 76, 103, 116; **4:** 248; **5:** 225, 242
Duprat, Gérard, **3:** 369
Dupre, J. Stefan, **6:** 81, 82
Durkheim, Emile, **2:** 2; **3:** 307; **5:** 12; **8:** 78
Duties, **1:** 371
Duverger, Maurice, **1:** 138; **3:** 237, 617; **4:** 237, 241, 249, 250
Dvorin, Eugene P., **5:** 428
Dye, Thomas R., **2:** 182, 248; **3:** 33, 65; **4:** 264; **5:** 157; **6:** 223, 309
Dynamic programming, **2:** 335, 336
Dynamics, **2:** 41–42, 43
Dyos, H. J., **6:** 333
Dyson, James W., **7:** 235, 240, 242, 248, 249

Eagleton, Thomas F., **6:** 409
Earle, Edward Mead, **8:** 341
East, Maurice A., **6:** 385, 387
Eastin, Roy B., **7:** 22
Easton, David, **1:** 1, 70, 114, 118, 141, 276, 285, 293, 298, 304, 318; **2:** 94, 95, 97, 98, 99, 100, 102, 106, 112, 114, 115, 117, 127, 132, 133, 136, 245, 334; **3:** 3; **6:** 389, 440, 441, 467; **7:** 61, 90, 132, 133, 278, 302; **8:** 43, 44, 45
Eaton, Dorman B., **1:** 33
Eckhoff, Torstein, **5:** 334
Eckland, Bruce C., **5:** 425
Eckstein, Harry, **1:** 190, 191; **2:** 76, 308; **3:** 17, 159, 363, 485; **4:** 3, 60, 181, 234, 265; **7:** 82, 91, 103, 105, 111, 120, 127, 135, 158, 188
École Libre des Sciences Politiques, **1:** 33
Ecological range, **3:** 602–605
Econometrics, **7:** 146, 154, 158
Economic crises, and rise of fascism, **3:** 320
Economic development
  in newly independent nations, **3:** 324
  and political institutions, **3:** 59–66
Economic efficiency, **2:** 321, 360; **6:** 33–34
Economic growth, **6:** 25, 27–28
Economic institutions, **2:** 306

Economic man, **2:** 331; **5:** 82
Economic mechanisms, **6:** 36–44
  macroeconomic policy, **6:** 37–41
  microeconomic policies, **6:** 42–44
  monetary policy, **6:** 41–42
Economic Opportunity Act, **6:** 113, 115, 125,
  133, 166, 167, 169, 186
Economic policy, instruments of, **6:** 44–50
  balanced-budget rule, **6:** 45
  government expenditures and taxes, **6:**
    44–47
  intervention, direct, **6:** 49–50
  money and credit, **6:** 47–49
Economic policy, objectives of, **6:** 26–36
  economic efficiency, **6:** 33–34
  economic growth, **6:** 27–28
  full employment, **6:** 29–30
  international, **6:** 31–33
  price stability, **6:** 30–31
Economic policy, procedural improvements in,
  6: 72–75
  budget control, **6:** 74
  incomes policy, **6:** 75
  program evaluation staffs, **6:** 72–73
  social experimentation, **6:** 73–74
Economic Report, **6:** 39
Economic and social structure, relationship to
  political systems, **3:** 182
Economic variables in foreign policy, **6:** 416–
  418
  participation characteristics of, **6:** 417
  structural characteristics of, **6:** 417
  substantive characteristics of, **6:** 417–418
Economists, types of
  conservative, **6:** 25–26
  liberal, **6:** 26
  radical, **6:** 26
Economy, performance of in United States, **6:**
  50–72
  business cycle, **6:** 51–54
  inflation, **6:** 57–59
  "new" economics, **6:** 54–56
  stabilization, **6:** 51
  unemployment, **6:** 57–59
  Vietnam War inflation, **6:** 56–57
Ecumenicism, attempted, **1:** 3
Edelman, Murray, **2:** 312; **5:** 402; **6:** 17, 467
Edgeworth, F. T., **3:** 458
Edinger, Lewis J., **2:** 40, 185, 189; **4:** 181, 214;
  5: 202, 203, 233, 239
Edmonson, Monro S., **7:** 310
"Educated incapacity," **7:** 438
Education, and economics, **6:** 61–63

Education policy, **6:** 449–450
Edwards, Allen L., **2:** 75; **7:** 305
Edwards, Ward, **1:** 371; **2:** 341; **3:** 437
Efficiency, **1:** 343, 362
Egalitarian democracy, **3:** 118
Egalitarianism, **1:** 286, 309, 311, 313
Ego-psychology, **2:** 10
Egremont, Lord (John Wyndham), **5:** 224
Ehrlich, Thomas, **8:** 422
Ehrmann, Henry, **4:** 181; **5:** 309
Eichholtz, Dietrich, **3:** 232
Eidenberg, Eugene, **6:** 467
Einaudi, Luigi, **3:** 78, 302, 367
Einbinder, Harvey, **7:** 7
Eisenhower, Dwight, **2:** 32, 103–105
Eisenstadt, S. N., **2:** 190; **3:** 3, 19, 25, 55, 74,
  251, 330, 364, 530, 569; **5:** 374
Eisinger, Peter K., **6:** 341
El-Assal, Mohamed, **2:** 70
Elazar, Daniel J., **5:** 94, 104, 105, 110, 140, 153,
  192, 193
Elbow, Matthew H., **3:** 306
Elder, Charles D., **7:** 241; **8:** 99
Elder, Glen H., Jr., **2:** 15, 102
Elder, Robert E., **6:** 402, 403
Eldersveld, Samuel J., **2:** 166, 180, 191, 196,
  197; **4:** 186, 252; **7:** 220, 234, 248, 249, 303
Elections, **4:** 76, 157
  in Africa, **3:** 323
  citizen control over, **4:** 2
  decisiveness of, **3:** 164–165
  electoral laws, **3:** 562
  indirect, **3:** 308
  in Mexico, **3:** 358
  multiple-ballot, **3:** 562–564
  in noncompetitive politics, **3:** 362–363
  plurality, **3:** 562–564
  popular, **5:** 262
  proportional representation, **3:** 562–564
  realignments of party strength, **4:** 137–144
  in Tanzania, **3:** 325–326
  timing of in Britain, **5:** 219
Electoral college, **5:** 185
Electoral competition, **3:** 441–444, 468; **7:** 376,
  380, 383, 384
Electoral participation, **3:** 351
Electoral system, **2:** 181
Electorates, types of, **2:** 174
Electronic countermeasures (ECM), **8:** 272,
  333
Electronic warfare, **8:** 272
Elementary and Secondary Education Act of
  1965, **6:** 129, 132

Elesh, David, **6:** 222; **7:** 239, 249
Eliade, Mircea, **5:** 12
Elites, **2:** 159, 161; **7:** 142
　social background data, **2:** 159
　social composition of, **3:** 232
　sociological history of, **2:** 159
Elkin, Stephen L., **2:** 331
Elkins, Stanley, **3:** 24; **6:** 263
Elliott, William Y., **1:** 49, 50; **5:** 32; **6:** 402
Ellsberg, Daniel, **2:** 341; **6:** 400, 415; **7:** 387; **8:** 321, 343
Ellul, Jacques, **1:** 274
Elman, Richard M., **6:** 274
Emancipation, **6:** 256, 259–260
Emancipation Proclamation, **6:** 264
Emerson, Ralph Waldo, **5:** 269, 270
Emerson, Rupert, **3:** 23, 87; **5:** 124
Emery, Fred E., **2:** 320
Emery, James, **2:** 320
Emmanuel, Arghiri, **8:** 77, 367
Emmet, Dorothy, **1:** 217
Empires, **5:** 108
Empiricism, **1:** 291–292, 294, 297
Encel, S., **5:** 183, 197, 200, 201, 202
Encyclopaedia Britannica, **7:** 7
Encyclopedias, **7:** 16–17
Enfranchisement, **6:** 288
Engelmann, Frederick C., **4:** 258, 265
Engels, Friedrich, **3:** 197, 362, 538; **8:** 20
England, white slavery in, **6:** 254–255
Engler, Robert, **2:** 309
Engstrom, Richard L., **2:** 102, 108, 113, 115, 138
Enke, Stephen, **8:** 293, 303, 323
Enlightenment, **1:** 252
Ennis, Philip E., **7:** 284, 302
Ensor, R. C. K., **6:** 345
Enthoven, Alain C., **6:** 81, 406, 422; **8:** 292, 323
Envelope curve, **7:** 421, 424
Environment, **2:** 6, 7, 12, 15, 19, 20, 26–27, 28–29
　historical processes, **2:** 28
　immediate environmental phenomena, **2:** 16, 28, 69
　objective, **2:** 6
　as perceived, **2:** 6, 7
　situational variables, **2:** 7, 18
Environmental constraints upon nations, **8:** 41, 46
Environmental problems, and economics, **6:** 64–66
Epistemology, **7:** 144, 159, 165, 167

Epstein, Abraham, **6:** 220
Epstein, Erwin, **6:** 221
Epstein, Leon, **2:** 182, 184; **4:** 242, 250; **5:** 291, 306; **6:** 418
Equal Employment Opportunity Commission, **6:** 290
Equality, **1:** 287–288, 310, 343, 361–362, 378, 386–387
　before the law, **1:** 386
　political, **1:** 387
　racial, **1:** 387
　sexual, **1:** 386
　social, **1:** 387
Equation, group-activity-interest, **2:** 246, 253–254, 255, 294, 296
Equilibrium, **7:** 361, 377, 378, 381
Equilibrium, in spatial models of electoral competition, **3:** 441–444
　collective, **3:** 464
　individual, **3:** 464
　of order *r,* **3:** 464
Erbe, William, **3:** 35
Erie, Stephen P., **6:** 306, 332
Erikson, Erik H., **2:** 10, 39, 40, 74, 187; **3:** 619
Erskine, Hazel G., **4:** 79
Escalation, **8:** 298, 318, 319, 320, 321
Eschenburg, Theodor, **3:** 248
Esman, Milton J., **3:** 85, 87, 88; **5:** 412
"Essential equivalence," principle of, **8:** 309
Essentialism, **1:** 290
Essien-Udom, E. U., **6:** 296
"Estates" of Parliament, **5:** 58
Esteban, Jorge de, **3:** 308, 367
Ethnic movements, **3:** 570
Ethnicity, **6:** 245
Ethiopia, assimilation in, **3:** 86
Etzioni, Amitai, **1:** 274; **2:** 324, 349; **3:** 503; **5:** 126, 389; **8:** 380, 382
Eulau, Heinz, **1:** 231, 285, 293, 298, 302; **2:** 157, 173, 189, 190, 191, 193, 200, 201, 202, 204, 206, 207, 208, 228; **4:** 162, 243; **5:** 303; **6:** 16, 331, 338, 440
European Coal and Steel Community (ECSC), **8:** 364
European Economic Community, **8:** 218, 364
European Monetary Union, **8:** 387
European Security Conference, **8:** 331
Evans, John W., **6:** 467
Evans-Pritchard, E. E., **3:** 364; **5:** 338
"Event" data, **7:** 247
Events-data analysis, **6:** 387–388
Evers, Tilman Tönnies, **3:** 367

Everson, David H., **2:** 69, 70
Ewbank, A. J., **2:** 112, 113, 116
"Exchange theory," **1:** 195
Executive-legislative relations, **5:** 233–238
Executive Office of the President, **5:** 417
Executive processes, **5:** 207–208
Executive recruitment, **5:** 183–205
    and political parties, **5:** 183–184
    and social structure, **5:** 183
Executives
    academic literature on, **5:** 173–175, 182
    command of staff resources, **5:** 214–215
    conceptions of their own offices, **5:** 215
    definition of, **5:** 175–183
    expectations of others, **5:** 214
    goals of, **5:** 220
    heads of government, **5:** 184–196
    internal dynamics of, **5:** 205–233
    lame-duck, **5:** 194–195
    and legislatures, **5:** 233–238
    political standing, **5:** 216–217
    powers and obligations of, **5:** 213
    professional reputation, **5:** 215–216
    propinquity to particular policy areas, **5:**
        213–214
    psychological approaches to the study of, **5:**
        238–242
    public prestige, **5:** 216
    recruitment of, **5:** 183–205
    skills and other personal qualities, **5:** 217–
        218
    unified and collegial, **5:** 218–219
Existentialism, **5:** 80–81
Exogenous variables, **2:** 345
Expectations, in bargaining theory, **3:** 459
Experiment
    "action," **7:** 229
    and experience, **7:** 216–220
    field, **7:** 220, 235, 244, 249, 250
    "methodological," **7:** 230
    "natural," **7:** 218, 240
    nonlaboratory, **7:** 242
    number of variables in, **7:** 233–236
    "pilot," **7:** 230
    as planned observation, **7:** 217, 219
    sample surveys as, **7:** 218–219
    "training," **7:** 230
Experimental controls, **7:** 220, 236
    analytic, **7:** 236
    correlational, **7:** 214
    design, **7:** 214, 233
    manipulation of variables, **7:** 236–244

randomization, **7:** 243–244
    temporality, **7:** 244–245
Experimental design, **7:** 215, 230
    case study, **7:** 237
    comparison groups, **7:** 237
    and decision making, **7:** 231
    dimensions of, **7:** 230
    logic of, **7:** 231
    partial factorial, **7:** 239
    Solomon Four Group, **7:** 238–239
    treated groups, **7:** 237
Experimental inquiry, **7:** 217
Experimental manipulation, **7:** 217, 218
Experimental method, value of the, **7:** 220–
    221
    strength of, **7:** 222
Experimental realism, **7:** 249–250
Experimental stimuli, **7:** 242
Experimental units of analysis, representa-
    tiveness of, **7:** 251–253
Experimental variables, **7:** 219, 230–231
    criterion, **7:** 243
    dependent, **7:** 234, 249
    extraneous, **7:** 231, 236, 243
    known, **7:** 246
    manipulation of **7:** 234, 236–244
    multilevel, **7:** 234, 235
    number of, **7:** 233–236
    performance, **7:** 241
    relevant, **7:** 236
    representativeness of, **7:** 245–251
    uncontrolled, **7:** 234
    unknown, **7:** 246
    unspecified, **7:** 246
Explanation of action, interpretative, **1:** 161–
    167, 174, 204, 206
    limitations of, **1:** 182–186
Explanation of action, naturalist, **1:** 156–161
Explanation, quasi-causal, **1:** 186–191, 192,
    204, 208
Explanation, scientific, **1:** 135–140
    "covering-law model," **1:** 136–137, 157
    "explanation-sketch," **1:** 157
    "nomological explanation," **1:** 136–137, 185
Exploitation of the state, **8:** 423
Exponential curve, **7:** 420
"Extinct movement regime," **3:** 340
Extraneous variance, **7:** 251–252
Extraterritoriality, **5:** 337
Eyestone, Robert, **6:** 309, 328, 331, 338, 359
Eysenck, Hans J., **2:** 44
Eysenck, Sybil, **2:** 44

Ezrahi, Yaron, **6:** 92

F scale, **2:** 47, 49, 58, 59
Fabricant, Solomon, **6:** 307, 330
Factionalism, **2:** 233; **3:** 341
Factions, **4:** 230; **5:** 3, 4
Fact-value dichotomy, **2:** 359–360
  and empirical method, **2:** 360
  and equality, **2:** 358
  and ethical knowledge, **2:** 360
Factor analysis, **4:** 13, 15; **7:** 144, 153–157, 158, 167, 248; **8:** 96, 111, 130, 131, 132, 133, 134
  Baas-Brown intensive, **7:** 178–180
  confirmatory, **7:** 156
Fagen, Richard, **3:** 31, 224, 225, 363, 366
Fagin, Henry, **6:** 309
Fainsod, Merle, **3:** 363; **4:** 232, 240; **5:** 266
Fair Employment Practices Commission, **6:** 289
Fairbank, John K., **3:** 20, 97
Fairlie, John A., **6:** 333, 345, 360
Fairweather, G. A., **7:** 240
Fairweather, George W., **6:** 17
Falco, Mario J., **1:** 134
Falk, Richard A., **8:** 433
Falk, Stanley L., **5:** 223
Fall, Bernard B., **3:** 89; **8:** 346
Fallacy of reification, **1:** 286, 322
Fallers, Lloyd A., **3:** 364; **5:** 325
Family assistance plan, **6:** 61, 148, 152–153, 457
Family service agencies, **6:** 121
Fanon, Frantz, **3:** 29, 538
Farkas, Susanne, **4:** 188
Farm Credit Association, **6:** 42
Farnsworth, David N., **6:** 401
Farquharson, Robin, **2:** 321, 342; **3:** 424, 430, 461, 462, 463, 464; **7:** 376, 388, 389, 399
Farr, Helen T., **5:** 146
Farrand, Max, **5:** 109
Farrar, Donald E., **2:** 27
Farrell, R. Barry, **3:** 232, 239, 336
Farris, Buford, **5:** 423
Fascism, **3:** 201, 215–216, 233, 314, 315, 316–321, 496, 518, 527; **5:** 33
  anticapitalism of, **3:** 317
  anticlericalism of, **3:** 317
  appeal to veterans, **3:** 318
  and capitalism, **3:** 321
  compared to communism, **3:** 234–237
  defeated nations, **3:** 318
  definition of, **3:** 316
  destruction of labor movement by, **3:** 317

  function of, **3:** 318
  historical role of, **3:** 321
  Italian, **3:** 311, 334
  Marxist interpretation of, **3:** 320–321
  military models of, **3:** 236–237
  populism of, **3:** 317
  rise of, conditions for, **3:** 298
  style of, **3:** 319
  utopia of, **3:** 319
Fascist Italy, **4:** 232
Fava, Sylvia F., **6:** 333, 334
Fay, Brian C., **1:** 131, 212, 219
Faye, Jean Pierre, **3:** 363
Fearing, Franklin, **2:** 39
Federal Communications Commission, **5:** 386, 400, 407
Federal Home Loan Bank Board, **6:** 42
Federal Housing Authority, **6:** 274
Federal National Mortgage Association, **6:** 42
Federal Open Market Committee, **6:** 41
Federal Register, **7:** 24
Federal Reserve Board, **5:** 386; **6:** 38, 42, 47, 52
Federal Reserve System, **6:** 24, 41, 42
Federal theory, **5:** 38
Federal Trade Commission, **5:** 400, 404, 420
Federalism, **3:** 88; **5:** 93–161
  accidents of, **5:** 141–151
  administrative features of, **5:** 141, 143–144
  administrative problems of, **5:** 145–151
  of Africa, **5:** 97–98, 124–125, 126–127
  asymmetrical units, **5:** 142
  of Australia, **5:** 120–121, 135, 150, 155
  of Austria, **5:** 121–122
  beneficiaries of, **5:** 152–156
  bibliographies of early writers on, **5:** 160
  of Brazil, **5:** 119, 155
  in Canada, **5:** 112, 120, 135–136, 150–151, 154–155
  centralized, **5:** 95, 107–113, 131–133, 137, 138, 140, 157, 158
  classifications of, **5:** 131–133
  Communist, **5:** 97
  conditions of, **5:** 113–131
  congruent, **5:** 142
  constitutional problems of, **5:** 145
  cooperative, **5:** 104; **6:** 119, 161
  definitions of, **5:** 98–106
  and democracy, **5:** 156, 158
  development of, **5:** 106–113
  and division of functions, **5:** 101, 109–111
  and dominion theory, **5:** 70–73
  early modern leagues, **5:** 94–95
  economic conditions of, **5:** 130

and empires, **5:** 108
evaluation of, **5:** 151–159
financial problems of, **5:** 145–151
formalistic, **5:** 142
of the former English colonies, **5:** 96
founding of, **5:** 131
German, **5:** 97, 113, 140–141
ideological writings on, **5:** 159–161
ideology of, **5:** 156–158
of India, **5:** 122–123, 150, 155
and individual freedom, **5:** 157–158
of Indonesia, **5:** 98, 126
initial circumstances of, **5:** 152–153
Latin American, **5:** 95–96, 118–119
linguistic problems of, **5:** 151
and local government, **5:** 156–157
and "majoritarianism," **5:** 157, 158, 159
of Malaya, **5:** 124
"marble cake" theory of, **5:** 104
meaning of, **5:** 93–106
measurement of, **5:** 131–141
moral evaluation of, **5:** 158–159
and nationalism, **5:** 152
of the Netherlands, **5:** 95, 100, 117–118
of New Zealand, **5:** 120
operation of, **5:** 131
of Pakistan, **5:** 122–123
partially centralized, **5:** 133–136
peripheralized, **5:** 107, 108, 111
and pluralism, **5:** 156
primitive leagues, **5:** 93–94
and racism, **5:** 154, 155
root meaning of, **5:** 99
and separate elections, **5:** 134
of the Soviet Union, **5:** 102, 122, 151
of Switzerland, **5:** 94, 99, 112, 117
symmetrical units, **5:** 142, 158
of the United States, **5:** 37–40, 95, 104, 118, 154
in welfare, **6:** 117–119, 163–164, 166, 209
of Yugoslavia, **5:** 100, 126
Federalist papers, **1:** 21
Federalists, **5:** 152
Federations, failures among, **5:** 125–126
Feedback, **2:** 334
Feierabend, Ivo, **1:** 190; **3:** 8, 9
Feierabend, R., **1:** 190; **3:** 8, 9
Feigert, Frank B., **2:** 166, 197
Feigl, Herbert, **1:** 142, 218, 219; **7:** 215
Fein, Leonard J., **3:** 330
Feis, Herbert, **6:** 399; **8:** 21
Feit, Edward, **3:** 73, 367
Feith, Herbert, **3:** 248, 367

Feld, Werner, **8:** 385, 391
Feldheim, Pierre, **7:** 284
Feldman, Jacob J., **2:** 104, 115, 116
Feldman, Kenneth A., **2:** 127
Fellmeth, Robert, **5:** 402; **6:** 467
Fenno, R. F., **5:** 197, 198, 200, 208, 215, 217, 223, 229, 231, 287, 417, 419; **8:** 322
Fenton, John H., **6:** 214, 223
Ferejohn, John, **1:** 202–203; **2:** 332, 362
Ferguson, Jack, **4:** 248
Ferguson, Leroy, **2:** 190, 191; **4:** 162; **5:** 303; **6:** 16
Ferkiss, Victor, **1:** 274; **5:** 374
Fermoselle, Rafael, **3:** 71
Fernandes, Florestan, **3:** 71
Fernández-Carvajal, Rodrigo, **3:** 308, 310
Fesler, James W., **6:** 349
Fest, Joachim C., **3:** 368
Festinger, Leon, **2:** 125
Fetscher, Irving, **1:** 235; **3:** 369
Feudal systems, **3:** 55–57, 253
Feyerabend, Paul K., **1:** 147, 148, 218, 219, 220
Field, John O., **2:** 134, 248; **3:** 41; **4:** 90, 100, 102, 159; **7:** 286
Fielder, Frances, **6:** 403
Fiedler, Fred E., **2:** 17
Fiellin, Alan, **2:** 206; **5:** 291
Figgis, J. N., **5:** 30, 31, 32
Fighter aircraft of the United States, **8:** 271–273
Filibuster, **6:** 242
Filmer, Sir Robert, **1:** 264
Finer, Herman, **3:** 367; **5:** 176, 177, 180, 181, 182, 415, 416, 418, 426; **7:** 84
Finer, S. E., **2:** 203, 204; **3:** 60, 128, 186, 275, 357, 367; **4:** 173, 176, 181, 208, 213, 214
Finifter, Ada W., **2:** 134
"Finite deterrence," **8:** 319
Fink, Clinton F., **3:** 485
Finley, Moses I., **5:** 13
Fiorina, Morris, **1:** 202–203; **2:** 332, 362
First-strike capability, **8:** 282, 288, 300
Fiscal policy, **6:** 44, 48–49
Keynesian, **5:** 146
Fiscal-policy analysis, **6:** 447
Fiscal relations, intergovernmental, **6:** 69–72
conditional grants, **6:** 70
revenue sharing plans, **6:** 69–70, 71, 72
unconditional or general purpose grants, **6:** 70–71
Fischer, Carl W., **6:** 93
Fischer, George, **3:** 336
Fischer, Gregory W., **8:** 323

Fishbein, Martin, **7:** 67, 274, 275, 276, 305
Fishburn, Peter C., **3:** 415, 421, 424, 434, 435, 436, 437, 438, 441, 467
Fishel, Jeff, **2:** 163, 224
Fishel, Leslie H., Jr., **6:** 286
Fisher, Glenn W., **6:** 223
Fisher, Jack C., **6:** 335, 349
Fisher, Louis, **5:** 234, 379, 429
Fisher, Margaret W., **3:** 254
Fisher, R. A., **7:** 143, 217
Fishman, Joshua A., **3:** 332
Fiske, Donald W., **2:** 44; **7:** 246, 295
Fitch, Bob, **3:** 370
Fitch, John S., III, **3:** 294, 301, 304, 367
FitzGerald, Frances, **3:** 21, 98
Five Year Plans, **5:** 266
Fixed-point theorem, **7:** 362
Flacks, Richard, **2:** 69, 70, 76, 127, 128, 130, 131
Flanagan, John C., **7:** 321
Flanagan, Robert J., **6:** 77
Flanigan, William H., **3:** 9, 98
Flanz, Gilbert H., **5:** 126
Flash, Edward, Jr., **5:** 208, 220, 223, 377, 379; **6:** 75
Flathman, Richard E., **1:** 274, 284, 293; **2:** 296, 297
Flax, Michael J., **6:** 307
Fleischman, V., **3:** 261
Fleitas, Daniel W., **7:** 242
Fleming, Denna F., **6:** 399; **8:** 229
Fleming, Donald, **5:** 289
Fleron, F. J., Jr., **2:** 100; **3:** 336, 359, 366; **6:** 412, 418
Fletcher, William C., **3:** 359
Flexible Response, and Kennedy administration, **8:** 285, 290, 292, 297
Flint, Jerry M., **6:** 277
Fodor, Jerry A., **2:** 6
Fogelman, Edwin, **3:** 9, 98
Foldes, L., **3:** 459
"Folk" law, **5:** 21
Folkmoot, **5:** 268, 273
Follett, Mary Parker, **5:** 307
Folsom, Ralph E., **7:** 297
Foltz, William J., **3:** 87, 128, 266, 323; **5:** 127
Fon of Dahomey, **3:** 19, 21
Food and Drug Administration, **5:** 391, 400, 403
Food riot, European, **3:** 518, 542
Food stamps, **6:** 138
Foot, Paul, **6:** 256

Foot, Philippa, **1:** 301, 318
Force structure, **8:** 271, 290
Forced choice, **1:** 344–345
Ford Foundation, **5:** 149
Forecasting, methods of, **7:** 420–426
Foreign conflict behavior, **8:** 129, 132, 134, 135, 138, 139, 140
Foreign domination, effects of, **3:** 155–158
Foreign experts, **3:** 590
Foreign intervention, **3:** 364
Foreign policy
  actors, **6:** 391–396
  belief systems, **6:** 407–408, 410
  and the bureaucracy, **6:** 405
  contexts, **6:** 397–400
  conversion variables, **6:** 388, 420–423
  definition of, **6:** 383
  and Department of State, **6:** 403–404
  domestic sources, **6:** 410–420
  economic variables, **6:** 416–418
  external sources, **6:** 418–420
  governmental institutions and, **6:** 401–410
  input variables, **6:** 385–386, 388, 389
  issues, **6:** 397–400
  output variables, **6:** 388, 423
  political variables, **6:** 414–416
  and the presidency, **6:** 404–405
  scientific study of, **6:** 381–382
  societal variables, **6:** 412–414
Foreign-policy actors, **6:** 391–396
  comparative analysis of, **6:** 396
  governmental, **6:** 392
  human beings as, **6:** 392
  mediating role of, **6:** 415–416
  motivations of, **6:** 392
  nongovernmental, **6:** 392, 420
  perceptions of, **6:** 419
  transnational, **6:** 410–411
  treatment of in literature, **6:** 391
  United States Congress as, **6:** 393
Foreign-policy agendas, **8:** 391–392
Foreign-policy behavior, **8:** 94
Foreign policy, comparative, **8:** 128–141
Foreign-policy scholarship, goal of, **6:** 385
Foreign Service, **6:** 403–404
Foreknowledge, **7:** 88–89
Formal languages, **7:** 353
Formal structure and prescriptive theory, **2:** 350
Formal theory, **7:** 351–399
Formalism, **1:** 290
Forrester, Jay W., **6:** 331, 361

Forsey, Eugene, **5:** 135
Forster, John, **2:** 179
Fortes, M., **3:** 364
Foss, Phillip O., **2:** 309; **5:** 393
Fossum, Egil, **3:** 9
Foster, C. D, **2:** 329, 331
Foster, George, **3:** 18
Foster, Henry H., **5:** 329
Founding Fathers, **5:** 7, 38, 41, 75, 77
Fouraker, Lawrence E., **3:** 470
Fourth Republic, **1:** 136
Fowler, Edmund P., **5:** 405; **6:** 307, 323, 336, 338, 339, 341
Fox, Annette Baker, **8:** 75, 345
Fox, William T. R., **8:** 75, 331, 345
Fraenkel, Ernst, **3:** 200, 336; **5:** 33
Fraga Iribarne, Manuel, **3:** 308, 310
Frameworks in research, **8:** 94
France
　since 1500, **3:** 541
　and political acculturation, **3:** 19, 58
　in seventeenth century, **3:** 542
Franch, Thomas M., **5:** 125
Francis, Wayne, **4:** 207; **7:** 306
Franck, Thomas M., **8:** 418
Franco regime, **3:** 292, 367
Franda, Marcus F., **5:** 133, 136
Frank, André Gunder, **3:** 97; **8:** 367
Franke, Winfried, **8:** 79
Frankel, Charles, **6:** 404
Frankel, Joseph, **5:** 126
Frankel, Lester, **7:** 308
Frankena, William K., **1:** 319, 326, 330
Franklin, John Hope, **6:** 247, 248, 256
Franklin, Julian H., **1:** 14
Franklin, Mark N., **5:** 198
Franks, C. E. S., **5:** 280
Frazier, E. Franklin, **3:** 67; **6:** 252; **7:** 309, 310
Frederickson, George M., **6:** 244
Frederickson, H. George, **2:** 360; **5:** 388
Fredland, J. Eric, **6:** 330
Free, Lloyd A., **7:** 281, 282
Freedman, Anne, **4:** 203
Freedman, Jonathan L., **2:** 8, 137
Freedman, Max, **7:** 35
Freedmen's Bureau, **6:** 263
Freedom, **1:** 287, 288–289, 304, 305, 378, 387–390
　of choice, **1:** 288
　feeling free, **1:** 288–289
　free actions, **1:** 289
　under law, **5:** 18

from restraint, **5:** 18
social or political, **1:** 288
of speech, **1:** 288
systemic, **5:** 18–19
from want, **1:** 288
Freedom of Information Act of 1967, **7:** 32
Freeland, Richard M., **6:** 412
Freeman, E. A., **5:** 94, 305
Freeman, Howard E., **6:** 462
Freeman, J. Lieper, **5:** 103, 234, 403
Freemen, **5:** 271
Freidel, Frank, **7:** 37
Freidson, Eliot, **7:** 279
French, J. P. R., **7:** 220
French Revolution, **3:** 493; **7:** 101–103
Frenkel-Brunswik, Else, **2:** 60, 65; **3:** 363
Freud, Anna, **2:** 10
Freud, Sigmund, **2:** 25, 31, 38, 62; **5:** 15
Freund, Paul A., **5:** 145
Fréville, Yves, **6:** 330, 344
Frey, Frederick W., **2:** 159, 202; **3:** 53, 62, 63; **7:** 182, 288
Fried, Edward R., **6:** 198, 223
Fried, Robert C., **5:** 183, 303; **6:** 321, 322, 323, 324, 329, 333, 335, 336, 339, 340, 342, 344, 345, 349, 362
Frieden, Bernard J., **6:** 349
Friedheim, Robert L., **8:** 219
Friedland, William H., **3:** 324
Friedman, Lucy N., **2:** 124
Friedman, M., **7:** 133
Friedman, Milton, **6:** 75, 76, 77
Friedman, Wolfgang, **5:** 341, 342, 348; **8:** 420
Friedmann, John, **6:** 309, 334
Friedrich, Carl J., **1:** 264, 272, 277, 288; **3:** 92, 187, 188, 189; **5:** 2, 49, 103, 131, 145, 156, 160, 177, 415, 416, 426; **7:** 84
Frohlich, Norman, **4:** 193
Frolic, B. Michael, **6:** 313, 335
Frolich, Norman, **2:** 248, 289
Froman, L. A., Jr., **4:** 162; **6:** 305
Fromm, Erich, **2:** 22, 28, 46, 47, 57, 65, 75; **3:** 363; **8:** 340
Frustration-aggression analysis, **3:** 495
Fry, Brian, **4:** 64; **6:** 223, 306, 467, 468
Frye, Alton, **8:** 322
"Full employment budget," **6:** 46–47
Fuller, J. F. C., **8:** 341
Fuller, Lon, **5:** 324
Functional approach to personality and politics, **2:** 11–12, 13
Functional budgeting, **8:** 292

"Functional cabinets," **5:** 211–212, 233
Functional relationships, **7:** 194–195, 199, 215
Functionalism, **1:** 192; **4:** 236
Functions of government, expansion of, **3:** 38, 41, 52–53
Fundamentalism, **3:** 609–615
   cultural traditions, **3:** 614
   as an ideology, **3:** 614–615
   as a mental disease, **3:** 613
   as a movement of desperation, **3:** 613–614
Funkhousen, Mary Lou, **6:** 93
Furet, François, **3:** 500
Furnivall, J. S., **3:** 67
Future, the study of, **7:** 405–438
   perspective, **7:** 411–415
   usefulness of, **7:** 407–411
Future projections, uses of, **7:** 409–410
Futuribles, **7:** 415–417
   predictability of variables of, **7:** 417–419
Futurology
   motivation for, **7:** 408
   policy development and, **7:** 408

Gaddis, John Lewis, **6:** 399
Galatin, Malcolm, **6:** 468
Galbraith, Jay, **2:** 352, 357
Galbraith, John Kenneth, **4:** 192, 222; **5:** 410, 427; **6:** 75, 130, 174, 404; **7:** 313
Galileo, **8:** 3, 10
Galíndez, Jesús de, **3:** 261
Galkin, Alexander, **3:** 321, 369
Gallagher, John, **8:** 26
Gallagher, Matthew P., **8:** 347
Gallaher, Miriam, **5:** 291
Gallatin, Judith, **2:** 106
Galli, Giorgio, **6:** 340
Gallois, Pierre M., **8:** 289
Galloway, George, **5:** 307
Galloway, Jonathan, **5:** 409
Gallup, George, **7:** 279, 290, 304, 324, 325
Gallup Poll, **7:** 279, 282, 290, 291, 298
Galtung, Johan, **8:** 26, 27, 28, 30, 77, 366, 367
Galula, David, **8:** 346
Game theory, **2:** 320, 336, 342, 348; **3:** 443, 460; **7:** 146, 379–397
   and bargaining, **2:** 348, 349; **7:** 182–183
   cooperative games, **7:** 389–397
   maximum, **2:** 335, 342, 347
   minimax regret, **2:** 335, 342, 343, 347
   minimax strategy, **2:** 337, 342
   noncooperative games, **7:** 384–389
   and opportunity loss, **2:** 343
   Prisoner's dilemma, **2:** 343

saddle point, **2:** 337, 342
two-player constant-sum games, **7:** 380–384
uncertain games, **2:** 342
zero-sum, **2:** 337, 342
Gamm, Hans-Jochen, **3:** 237
Gamson, William A., **3:** 517, 525, 531; **7:** 277
Ganda of Uganda, **3:** 19–20
Gans, Herbert, **6:** 221, 349
Garceau, Oliver, **4:** 203, 207
Garcia, F. Chris, **2:** 102, 106, 111, 138
Gardiner, John A., **6:** 342
Gardiner, Robert K. A., **6:** 267
Gardiner, Samuel Rawson, **5:** 4, 30
Gardner, Lloyd C., **6:** 417
Garfinkel, H., **1:** 216; **6:** 290
Garman, M., **3:** 428
"Garrison state," **8:** 324, 325, 326
Gastil, Raymond D., **6:** 307
Gaudet, Hazel, **4:** 159; **7:** 161, 302, 312, 328, 329
Gavin, James M., **8:** 284
Gawthrop, Louis C., **5:** 411
Geertz, Clifford, **1:** 180; **3:** 97, 257, 259
Geiger, George Raymond, **2:** 73
Geiger, Theodor, **3:** 266
Geis, Florence L., **2:** 50, 51
Gellhorn, Walter, **5:** 420
Gellner, Ernest, **1:** 179, 297; **3:** 364, 365
Gemeinschaft, **5:** 4, 30
General Accounting Office, **6:** 98
General Agreement on Tariffs and Trade, **8:** 373, 391
General possibility theorem, **1:** 341; **3:** 419–427
General-purpose forces, **8:** 270, 293
General systems theory, **8:** 2
Generational differences, **2:** 110–111
Genesis, **2:** 42, 43, 60
Genossenschaften, **7:** 378
Genovese, Eugene D., **6:** 255
George, Alexander L., **2:** 1, 9, 40, 41, 56, 63, 67, 74, 211, 325, 357, 358; **5:** 238, 239, 240, 379; **6:** 11, 394, 395, 406, 419; **7:** 28; **8:** 284, 316, 324, 343, 389
George, Juliette L., **2:** 40, 41, 67; **5:** 238, 239; **6:** 394; **7:** 28
Gerlich, Peter, **5:** 282
German federalism, **5:** 97, 113, 121–122, 140–141
Germani, Gino, **3:** 231, 367, 569
Germino, Dante, **1:** 131, 209, 251, 272, 275, 276; **3:** 209, 361, 362
Gerth, H. H., **3:** 67, 81; **5:** 388

Gertzog, Irwin N., **7:** 235
Gesellschaft, **5:** 4, 30
Getting, V. A., **6:** 440
Ghana Armed Forces, **5:** 264
Ghana Official Handbook, **5:** 264
Ghetto riots, American, **2:** 111; **3:** 489, 493; **6:** 268, 277
Giarda, Pietro, **6:** 340
Gibbs, Jack L., Jr., **5:** 334
Gibson, Quinton, **1:** 216, 323
Gierke, Otto Friedrich von, **5:** 29, 30, 32, 35, 46, 160
Gil, Federico, **5:** 310
Gilb, Corinne Lathrop, **5:** 409
Gilbert, Allan, **1:** 264
Gilbert, Charles E., **6:** 211, 221
Gilbert, Felix, **8:** 34, 35
Gilison, Jerome M., **3:** 362
Gillespie, John V., **8:** 190, 191
Gilmore, Robert, **3:** 263, 367; **5:** 417
Gilpin, Robert, **6:** 93, 98
Gimbel, John H., **3:** 186
Gini index, **8:** 103–110
Ginsberg, Morris, **1:** 327
Girard, Louis, **3:** 519
Gitelman, Zvi Y., **3:** 240, 343
Gittell, Marilyn, **5:** 425
Gittings, John, **3:** 190
Glad, Betty, **2:** 40
Glanzer, M., **2:** 231
Glaser, B. G., **7:** 107
Glaser, R., **2:** 232
Glaser, William A., **4:** 148, 159; **7:** 302
Glass, Gene V., **6:** 455, 467
Glass, Hiram Bentley, **6:** 243
Glasstone, Samuel, **8:** 343
Glauber, Robert R., **2:** 27
Glazer, Nathan, **2:** 33, 46
Glenn, Norval D., **2:** 120, 132, 138
Glick, Henry Robert, **2:** 179
Gliksman, Jerzy G., **3:** 225, 227
Glock, Charles Y., **3:** 614; **7:** 218
Glorious Revolution of 1688, **5:** 63, 68
Gluckman, Max, **3:** 364; **5:** 329, 334, 338
GNP deflator, **6:** 31
Goal displacement, **2:** 358
Goal orientations, **2:** 156
Goals, **2:** 324, 349
Gobineau, Joseph Arthur, de, **6:** 243, 244
Godechot, Jacques, **3:** 543
Godfrey, E. Drexel, Jr., **5:** 189
Goel, M. Lal, **3:** 41
Goethals, George W., **2:** 63

Goffman, Erving, **3:** 619; **8:** 315
Goffman, Irwin W., **7:** 272
Goguel, François, **4:** 112, 159
Golay, John F., **5:** 113, 121
Gold, Alice R., **2:** 124
Gold, David, **4:** 243
Goldberg, Arthur, **1:** 131, 146, 298
Goldberger, Arthur S., **7:** 204
Goldenweiser, Alexander, **1:** 46
Goldhamer, Herbert, **2:** 18; **7:** 54
Goldman, Alvin L., **1:** 217, 297
Goldman, Eric, **6:** 395
Goldman, Ralph M., **5:** 183, 192, 193
Goldner, Fred H., **2:** 324
Goldrich, Daniel, **6:** 16
Goldsby, Richard A., **6:** 243
Goldsmith, Raymond, **3:** 171
Goldwin, Robert A., **5:** 156
Golembiewski, Robert T., **2:** 307
Gong Lum v. *Rice,* **6:** 272
González Casanova, Pablo, **3:** 358
Goodhart, C. A. E., **3:** 443
Goodman, Jay S., **2:** 228
Goodman, L. A., **3:** 446
Goodman, Paul, **1:** 274
Goodman, Roe, **7:** 312
Goodman, Walter, **5:** 308
Goodnow, Frank J., **1:** 39, 91; **5:** 386, 405
Goodwin, Leonard, **6:** 221, 222
Gorden, Morton, **6:** 17
Gordon, Bernard K., **6:** 418
Gordon, David M., **6:** 309, 349, 356
Gordon, Harold J., Jr., **3:** 359
Gordon, Margaret, **6:** 192, 199
Gordon, R. A., **2:** 325, 334; **3:** 619
Gordon Walker, Patrick, **5:** 198, 208, 212, 214, 215, 218, 219, 232
Gorer, Geoffrey, **2:** 61, 62
Görgen, Hans-Peter, **3:** 363
Gorham, William, **6:** 207
Gorz, Andre, **3:** 526
Gosnell, Harold F., **1:** 47; **4:** 112, 249; **7:** 217, 218, 220, 235
Gossez, Rémi, **3:** 500
Gough, Harrison, **7:** 289
Gould, John, **5:** 270, 273
Gouldner, Alvin W., **5:** 411; **6:** 331
Government, **1:** 246
Government-business relations, **6:** 86–87
Government expenditures, **6:** 44–47
Government of India, Ministry of Health, **6:** 361
Government Printing Office, **7:** 19

Governmental institutions, as input variables of foreign policy, **6:** 401–410
  interaction characteristics of, **6:** 408–410, 422
  jurisdiction, **6:** 401–402
  performance characteristics of, **6:** 402–407
  substantive characteristics of, **6:** 407–408
Governors, American state, **5:** 191
Graduated-Deterrence theory, **8:** 284–285, 288, 290
  and Eisenhower administration, **8:** 284
Graff, Henry F., **6:** 404
Graham, George J., **1:** 114, 276; **6:** 439
Gramsci, Antonio, **1:** 235, 243, 256, 260
Granada Television, **5:** 235, 236
Grand inquests, **5:** 259
Granick, David, **3:** 591, 618
Grant, Geoffrey, **2:** 118
Grants-in-aid, **5:** 147–151
  specific-purpose, **5:** 147
  unconditional, **5:** 147
  uncontrolled, **5:** 149
Grassmuck, George L., **6:** 414
Graves, W. Brooke, **5:** 148, 151
Gray, A. P., **7:** 302
Gray, Colin S., **8:** 346, 347
Gray, Virginia, **6:** 223
Gray, Wood, **7:** 67
Graybar, Lloyd J., **6:** 361
Great Dialogue, **1:** 8–11
Great Leap Forward in China, **3:** 347
Great Russian Encyclopedia, **7:** 6
Great Society programs. **6:** 85–86
Greeley, Andrew M., **2:** 128, 130
Green, Harold P., **5:** 308; **8:** 281
Green, Mark J., **5:** 407
Green, Thomas Hill, **5:** 31, 32
Greenberg, Bernard G., **7:** 297
Greenberg, Daniel S., **6:** 90
Greenberg, Edward S., **2:** 94, 102, 106, 107, 108, 115, 138, 140
Greenberg, Gary, **5:** 422
Greenberg, George D., **6:** 90
Greenberg, Sanford D., **5:** ₂07, 224, 377
Greene, Dwight L., **2:** 75
Greene, Murray, **8:** 23
Greenstein, Fred, **1:** 131; **2:** 4, 8, 18, 19, 22, 27, 38, 41, 44, 49, 54, 68, 73, 74, 75, 76, 94, 95, 96, 97, 98, 99, 100, 101, 103, 106, 108, 111, 112, 115, 116, 119, 122, 123, 133, 136, 137, 139, 140, 165, 180, 181, 187, 195, 210, 211, 217; **4:** 143, 243, 250; **5:** 223, 225, 229, 238, 239, 242; **6:** 392, 394; **7:** 122, 274, 278, 302

Greenstone, J. David, **2:** 309, 311, 313; **4:** 171, 213, 217; **6:** 338
Greenwood, Gordon, **5:** 135
Greenwood, John, **8:** 349
Greenwood, Ted, **6:** 88
Greer, Scott, **6:** 335
Gregg, Phillip M., **3:** 352
Gregg, Robert W., **8:** 135
Gregor, A. James, **1:** 134, 284, 289, 309, 310; **3:** 235, 277, 315, 316, 357, 369; **8:** 78
Gressman, Eugene, **7:** 27
Grier, William H., **6:** 295
Griffith, John A. G., **6:** 361, 362
Griffiths, Franklyn, **3:** 336, 339; **4:** 204
Grigg, C. W., **2:** 115
Grigg, Charles M., **7:** 300, 301, 330, 331, 332
Gripp, Richard C., **3:** 239
Grodzins, Martin, **3:** 607, 619; **5:** 104, 105, 110, 134, 140, 146, 408; **6:** 467, 468
Groennings, Sven, **7:** 396
Grofman, Bernard, **3:** 8
Groom, A. J. R., **5:** 212
Gross, Bertram M., **1:** 285; **2:** 351; **5:** 308, 429; **6:** 16, 206, 462
Gross, Leo, **7:** 169
Gross national product (GNP), **6:** 27–28
Grossman, Joel, **4:** 181
Groth, Alexander J., **3:** 230, 232, 239; **6:** 463
Grotius, Hugo, **1:** 230
"Ground alert," **8:** 289, 296
Group conflict, **3:** 343–344
Group hatred, social causes of, **3:** 608–609
Group theories tradition, **2:** 244, 248
  alternatives to, **2:** 248–250
  ethical conflicts within, **2:** 284
  and ethical criticism of American group politics, **2:** 274–275
  limitations of, **2:** 248, 250–253
  overview of, **2:** 246–248
  and problem of social/economic groups, **2:** 250–253
Group politics, **7:** 134
Groupism, **3:** 341
Groups
  community, **7:** 302
  primary, **7:** 301–302, 332
  reference group, **7:** 328
  secondary, **7:** 302, 332
  undemocratic government of, **2:** 282
Gruen, Erich S., **5:** 339
Gruenberg, Barry, **6:** 349, 357
Grumm, John G., **1:** 138; **5:** 295; **6:** 307, 452, 467, 468; **7:** 204

Grunberger, Richard, **3:** 368
Grundy, Kenneth W., **8:** 76
Grunwald, Kurt, **3:** 64
Guerrilla war, **8:** 210–211, 212
Guetzkow, Harold, **2:** 232; **6:** 17; **7:** 222, 225, 241, 246, 248; **8:** 96
Gueyt, Rémi, **3:** 337
Guilbaud, G. Th., **3:** 427, 428
Guild socialism, **5:** 31
Gulick, Luther, **2:** 351; **5:** 397
Gunn, J. A., **1:** 383
Gurin, Gerald, **2:** 124; **4:** 159, 160; **7:** 218
Gurr, Ted Robert, **1:** 190, 220; **3:** 8, 485, 486, 488, 490, 493–496, 526, 528, 532; **7:** 103, 119, 135, 146, 204
Gustafson, W. Eric, **6:** 81
Guterman, Stanley S., **2:** 50
Gutteridge, William F., **3:** 367
Guttman, Louis, **7:** 156, 158, 159, 161, 164, 165, 166, 167, 174, 178, 179, 318
Guttman scaling, **7:** 158, 159, 167
Guttsman, W. L., **2:** 159, 188; **5:** 183, 202
Gwartney, James, **6:** 283
Gwyn, W. B., **5:** 176
Gynther, Malcolm, **2:** 26

Haan, Norma, **2:** 27, 69, 70
Haas, Ernst B., **8:** 36, 204, 235, 315, 364, 365, 366, 367, 378, 379, 380, 383, 384, 396, 401
Haas, Michael, **1:** 312; **8:** 5, 130, 131, 135, 136, 141
Habermas, J., **1:** 134, 217, 219; **7:** 190, 201
Haberstroh, Chadwick, **2:** 319
Hacker, Andrew, **1:** 307; **2:** 183, 189; **4:** 209
Haddow, Anna, **1:** 24
Hadwiger, Don F., **4:** 215
Hagan, Charles, **2:** 307; **4:** 174
Hage, Jerald, **2:** 357
Hagen, Everett Einar, **2:** 62; **3:** 171
Haggi, S. A. H., **5:** 150
Hagood, Margaret Jarman, **7:** 295
Hagstrom, Warren O., **3:** 619
Hah, Chong-do, **3:** 97
Hahn, F. H., **7:** 397
Hahn, Harlan, **6:** 309, 339
Haight, David E., **5:** 224, 226
Hakes, Jay E., **5:** 268
Halberstam, David, **5:** 376; **6:** 391, 400, 405, 407, 408; **7:** 4, 314, 315
Hale, Myron Q., **2:** 253
Hall, Calvin S., **2:** 7, 10, 11
Hall, David K., **6:** 419
Hall, Peter, **6:** 313

Halldorson, James R., **4:** 64
Halle, Louis J., **8:** 68, 340, 342
Haller, Archibald O., **7:** 289
Hallman, Howard, **6:** 178
Halm, George N., **3:** 370
Halperin, Maurice, **3:** 366
Halperin, Morton H., **5:** 375, 384; **6:** 92, 393, 398, 405, 409; **8:** 230, 300, 323, 324, 343, 344
Halpern, Manfred, **3:** 365
Hamer, Philip, **7:** 34
Hamilton, Alastair, **3:** 235, 315
Hamilton, Alexander, **5:** 160
Hamilton, Charles V., **6:** 295
Hamilton, Gordon, **6:** 220
Hamiltonians, **5:** 152
Hammond, Paul Y., **5:** 417; **6:** 87; **8:** 277, 280, 281, 303, 323, 342
Hammond, Phillip E., **2:** 116
Hamon, Léo, **3:** 362
Hampden-Turner, Charles, **2:** 75
Hamsun, Knut, **3:** 619
Handler, Joel F., **6:** 161
Handler, Philip, **6:** 93
Hanna, William John, **6:** 350
Hanrieder, Wolfram, **6:** 384, 386, 415
Hansard, **5:** 276, 277
Hansen, A. H., **5:** 146, 147, 235
Hansen, Edward C., **3:** 263
Hansen, Morris, **7:** 308
Hansen, Roger D., **8:** 368, 381, 401
Hanson, Donald W., **5:** 35, 87, 306
Hanson, Norwood Russell, **1:** 147, 216
Hansson, Bengt, **3:** 421
Harary, Frank, **8:** 111
Harasymiw, Bohdan, **3:** 203
Harberer, Joseph, **6:** 93
Hardgrave, Robert L., Jr., **3:** 25
Hardin, Russell, **3:** 467; **7:** 180, 387
Harding, John, **2:** 118, 134
Hare, R. M., **1:** 318, 319, 322, 330
Harf, James E., **6:** 418
Harger, Alan E., **6:** 98
Hargrove, Erwin L., **5:** 217, 227
Harik, Iliya, **3:** 369
Haring, C. H., **3:** 24, 30; **5:** 111, 119
Harmon, Michael M., **5:** 415, 428
Harr, John E., **6:** 384, 403, 409, 414
Harrar, William S., **6:** 468
Harré, Rom, **1:** 216; **7:** 174
Harrington, Charles, **2:** 94
Harrington, James, **1:** 383; **5:** 35, 46, 63
Harrington, Michael, **6:** 130, 174

Harris, Chauncy D., **6:** 335
Harris, Godfrey, **6:** 403
Harris, Joseph P., **5:** 234, 419
Harris, Nigel, **1:** 378
Harris, P. M. G., **3:** 517
Harris, Robert, **6:** 330
Harris Poll, **7:** 290, 291
Harrison, Jane, **5:** 15, 16
Harrison, Martin, **5:** 189, 195
Harsanyi, John C., **2:** 332, 333; **3:** 448, 449, 450, 451, 452, 454, 455, 457, 458, 459, 461, 470; **7:** 184, 395
Hart, H. L. A., **1:** 160, 212, 284, 302, 303, 320, 378
Hartman, Chester, **6:** 274
Hartmann, George W., **7:** 234
Hartwell, Edward M., **6:** 361
Hartz, Louis, **1:** 252; **2:** 245; **3:** 22, 24, 170, 327; **7:** 273
Harvey, David, **6:** 331, 361
Harvey, Edward, **2:** 320, 322
Hasbrouck, Paul DeWitt, **5:** 307
Haskins, George L., **5:** 331, 336
Hastings, Donald W., **2:** 11
Haug, Marie R., **3:** 153, 171
Haupt, Heinz-Gerhard, **2:** 307
Hauser, Philip M., **6:** 16, 334
Havel, John, **2:** 49
Haveman, Robert, **2:** 329
Haviland, H. Field, Jr., **6:** 402
Hawkins, Bret W., **6:** 309, 337
Hawley, Amos H., **6:** 322, 338
Hayek, F. A., **1:** 326; **5:** 2, 25, 26, 63
Hayes, Paul M., **3:** 315
Hays, Samuel P., **7:** 34
Hayward, Max, **3:** 359
Hazelrigg, Lawrence E., **2:** 131
Hazelwood, Leo A., **8:** 130, 137
Head, Kendra B., **7:** 306
Headey, B. W., **5:** 184, 199, 203, 215, 216, 217
Heads of government, **5:** 184–196
   command of staff resources, **5:** 223–224
   conceptions of the office, **5:** 224–225
   expectations of others, **5:** 223
   goals of, **5:** 220
   interest of in foreign affairs, **5:** 222
   job descriptions of, **5:** 220–221
   political standing, **5:** 227
   power to hire and fire, **5:** 229–233
   powers and obligations of, **5:** 221–222
   professional reputations, **5:** 225
   propinquity to particular policy areas, **5:** 222

   public prestige, **5:** 225–226
   selection processes, **5:** 185–189
   skills and other personal qualities, **5:** 227–228
   surrender of power by, **5:** 194
   tenure, **5:** 194–196
Heady, Ferrel, **5:** 373
Health services, **6:** 133
Heard, Alexander, **4:** 254
Heasman, D. J., **5:** 184, 202, 211, 214
Heath, Shirley Brice, **3:** 86
Heclo, Hugh, **5:** 184, 187, 188, 189, 193, 208, 215; **6:** 223
Hector, Cary, **3:** 367
Hedlund, Ronald D., **2:** 115, 116, 184, 233
Hefner, Ted, **2:** 120, 132, 138
Hegel, Georg, **1:** 230, 231, 234, 235, 239, 243, 248, 252, 254, 255, 260, 262, 264; **8:** 425
Hegemonies, **3:** 118, 126–129
   closed, **3:** 120
   inclusive, **3:** 121
   opposition in, **3:** 126–127
Heidenheimer, Arnold J., **3:** 365; **5:** 140; **6:** 335
Heilbroner, Robert, **5:** 410; **6:** 335
Heinberg, John, **7:** 240
Held, Virginia, **5:** 429
Heller, Francis H., **5:** 223
Heller, Walter, **5:** 149; **6:** 75, 77, 283
Hellmann, Donald C., **6:** 415; **8:** 390
Hellmuth, William F., Jr., **6:** 312
Helmer, Olaf, **6:** 15
Hempel, Carl G., **1:** 132, 138, 142, 145, 155, 158, 159–160, 173, 216, 218, 285, 290, 291, 294, 301, 310, 313; **7:** 86, 99
Henderson, Dan Fenno, **5:** 324
Hendrickson, Walter B., **6:** 83
Henle, Peter, **6:** 198
Hennessey, Timothy M., **2:** 54, 112, 113, 115
Hennessy, Bernard, **2:** 182, 214; **4:** 253
Hennig, Eike, **3:** 232
Hennis, Wilhelm, **5:** 297
Henry, Laurin L., **5:** 183, 194, 196, 197, 198
Henry, Louis, **3:** 499
Hensler, Carl P., **2:** 134
Herbert, Alan Patrick, **5:** 306
Herman, E. S., **5:** 427
Herman, V. H., **4:** 240
Herman, Valentine, **5:** 204, 223, 236, 237, 307
Hermann, Charles F., **6:** 381, 383, 384, 387, 397, 398, 420, 423; **7:** 222, 241; **8:** 96, 113, 316
Hermann, Margaret G., **8:** 96

Hermassi, Elbaki, **3:** 255, 369
Hermeneutical or interpretative circle, **1:** 172–173, 208
Hermeneutics, **7:** 140, 189, 190, 201, 203
Hermet, Guy, **3:** 266, 273
Hero, Alfred O., **2:** 110, 115, 116; **6:** 414
Herre, Vorher F., **3:** 368
Herring, E. Pendleton, **1:** 47; **2:** 244; **4:** 222; **5:** 234, 414
Hersh, Seymour, **8:** 341
Hershey, Gary, **5:** 422
Herson, Lawrence J. R., **6:** 305
Herz, John H., **6:** 392; **8:** 199, 201, 211, 283, 315, 340, 363
Herzberg, Donald, **5:** 297
Hess, Robert D., **7:** 61, 278, 302
Hess, Robert L., **3:** 254
Hess, Ronald D., **2:** 94, 97, 98, 100, 106, 115, 119, 122, 129, 136, 140
Hess, Stephen, **2:** 188
Hesse, Mary B., **1:** 216
Hessler, Ellyn, **8:** 79
Heuristic case study, **7:** 104–108, 188
  criticisms of, **7:** 106
  justification for, **7:** 105–106
Hewison, R. J. P., **5:** 224
Hexter, Jack H., **5:** 307
Heyen, Franz Josef, **3:** 363
Hibbs, Douglas A., Jr., **3:** 9, 10
Hickman, Martin B., **8:** 326
Hicks, J. R., **2:** 322
Hicks, U. K., **5:** 130
Hierarchical structure of social organization, **3:** 25, 67–68, 84
Higham, John, **3:** 611
Higher law, the invention of, **5:** 7–28
Hildebrand, Klaus, **3:** 359
Hildreth, Clifford, **3:** 447, 448
Hilferding, Rudolf, **3:** 357
Hill, Andrew, **5:** 297
Hill, Frances, **3:** 83
Hill, Herbert, **6:** 291
Hill, Richard J., **2:** 75; **7:** 306
Hillgruber, Andreas, **3:** 359
Hilsman, Roger, **6:** 393, 403, 404, 408, 409; **8:** 323, 345, 347
Hilton, Gordon, **8:** 127
Himmelweit, Hilde T., **2:** 129, 130
Hinckley, Katherine, **5:** 303
Hinich, Melvin, **3:** 441, 442, 443, 444, 449; **4:** 113, 125, 160; **7:** 179, 377, 384
Hinrichs, Harley H., **3:** 52

Hinsdale, Mary, **5:** 205
Hinsley, F. H., **8:** 201
Hippler, Arthur E., **7:** 289
Hirsch, Herbert, **2:** 100
Hirsch, Werner Z., **6:** 356
Hirschfield, Robert S., **2:** 164, 180, 197; **5:** 221, 224
Hirschman, Albert O., **3:** 43, 186, 502; **5:** 379; **8:** 155, 158, 159, 160, 161, 162, 163
History, **1:** 248–250, 255
  collective, **3:** 499–501
  philosophy of, **1:** 248
Hitch, Charles J., **2:** 359; **6:** 15, 75, 81, 96; **8:** 292, 303, 323, 344
Hitler, Adolf, **3:** 201, 206, 207, 208, 212, 213, 214, 218, 220, 221, 222, 223, 227, 231, 232, 235, 236, 238, 239, 241, 242, 244, 245, 246, 248, 262, 334, 338, 340, 359, 362
Hitlerism, **3:** 319
Hoag, Malcolm W., **8:** 284
Hobbes, Thomas, **1:** 12, 13, 134, 135, 209, 231, 236, 239, 241, 246, 248, 249, 252, 260, 264, 288; **8:** 364
Hobbs, Edward H., **5:** 223
Hobsbawn, E. J., **3:** 82
Hobson, John A., **8:** 17, 18, 19, 20, 21, 22, 29, 31, 66, 67, 76, 228, 230
Hodgkin, Thomas, **3:** 23, 322, 325
Hodgson, David H., **1:** 398
Hodgson, Richard C., **2:** 67
Hoebel, E. Adamson, **5:** 323, 329, 339, 343
Hoepke, Klaus-Peter, **3:** 319, 363, 367
Hofer, Walther, **3:** 368
Hofferbert, Richard, **3:** 65; **4:** 2; **6:** 223, 306, 463, 467; **7:** 61, 65
Hoffman, George W., **3:** 346
Hoffmann, Erik P., **3:** 359; **6:** 418
Hoffmann, Paul J., **2:** 182
Hoffmann, Stanley, **5:** 160; **6:** 412, 413; **8:** 50, 51, 52, 53, 54, 55, 56, 62, 69, 78, 203, 233, 315, 340, 365, 381, 386, 425
Hofstadter, Richard, **4:** 231, 237, 267; **7:** 287
Hofstetter, Richard C., **2:** 104, 164–165, 218
Hoge, Dean R., **2:** 129
Hoggard, Gary D., **6:** 387
Höhne, Heinz, **3:** 205, 225
Holborn, Hajo, **5:** 113
Holbrooke, Richard, **6:** 404
Holcombe, Arthur N., **1:** 47
Holden, Matthew, **5:** 422
Holism, **2:** 158
Holland, Norman H., **2:** 38

Hollander, E. P., **2:** 49
Hollander, Paul, **3:** 350, 357
Hollander, T. Edward, **5:** 425
Holley, Irving, **6:** 88
Hollingsworth, Ellen Jane, **6:** 161
Hollis, Ernest, **6:** 221
Hollister, Robinson G., **6:** 189, 222; **7:** 321
Hollomon, Herbert, **6:** 98
Holmberg, Allan R., **6:** 16
Holsti, Ole R., **1:** 186; **6:** 394, 407, 410; **7:** 157, 179, 248; **8:** 99, 115, 120, 121, 122, 123, 124, 127, 128, 193
Holt, R. R., **7:** 84, 86, 95, 96, 97, 98, 105
Holt, Robert R., **2:** 32
Holt, Robert T., **1:** 220; **6:** 362, 387
Holt, Stephen, **8:** 385
Holtzman, Abraham, **4:** 205, 208; **5:** 234, 379
Homans, George Caspar, **1:** 195, 216
Homo, Léon, **6:** 361
Hondius, Fritz W., **5:** 126
Honoré, A. M., **1:** 160
Hook, Sidney, **1:** 307; **2:** 28, 29
Hooker, Richard, **1:** 241, 255
Hoopes, Townsend, **5:** 212, 376; **6:** 394, 396, 400, 403
Hoos, Ida R., **6:** 97
Hoover Commission, **5:** 405; **6:** 401
Hoover Institution, **8:** 95
Hopkins, Raymond F., **3:** 325
Hopmann, Terrence P., **8:** 99
Horelick, Arnold, **8:** 294, 331, 345
Horkheimer, Max, **2:** 75
Horn, Wolfgang, **3:** 215, 362
Horowitz, Donald L., **3:** 67
Horowitz, Irving L., **3:** 12, 366, 367; **6:** 17; **7:** 147
Horrell, Muriel, **6:** 246, 275, 276
Horvat, Branko, **3:** 346
Horvath, William J., **8:** 45
Horvitz, Daniel G., **7:** 297
Hoskin, Gary, **3:** 78
Hospers, John, **1:** 397
Hotelling, Harold, **3:** 442
Hough, Jerry F., **3:** 203, 205, 213; **6:** 335
House of Burgesses, **5:** 62
House of Commons, British, **5:** 193, 235–236, 279
    select committees in, **5:** 236
House of Commons, Canadian, **5:** 279–280
House Foreign Affairs Committee, **6:** 401
House of Lords, **5:** 191
    members of, **5:** 199

House of Representatives, **2:** 62; **5:** 278
    Committee on Rules, **5:** 284
House Ways and Means Committee, **6:** 40
Housing subsidies, **6:** 133
Houtart, François, **3:** 78
Hovland, Carl I., **7:** 316
Howe, C., **6:** 335
Howe, Marvine, **6:** 262
Hraba, Joseph, **2:** 118
Hrel index, **8:** 103–110
Huberman, Leo, **3:** 366
Hudson, Michael C., **3:** 3, 68, 97, 171, 358; **7:** 64
Hughes, Barry B., **8:** 368
Hughes, Christopher, **5:** 113
Huitt, Ralph K., **5:** 275, 286, 303
Huizinga, Johan, **1:** 384
Human nature, **2:** 31
Human relations movement, **2:** 351
Humanism, **1:** 242, 250, 261
    anthropocentric, **1:** 238, 241, 243, 246, 249, 261
    metastatic, **1:** 238, 243, 247, 250, 261
    theocentric, **1:** 238, 241, 243, 245, 246, 249–250, 261
Hume, David, **1:** 134, 288; **5:** 8, 9; **8:** 38
Humean ethics, **5:** 9
Hunt, E. H., **5:** 112
Hunter, Floyd, **6:** 172
Huntington, Samuel P., **1:** 347; **3:** 3, 4, 6, 7, 8, 9, 12, 14, 32, 46, 47, 48, 50, 51, 53, 54, 55, 57, 66, 92, 95, 96, 97, 98, 180, 186, 239, 255, 274, 297, 301, 303, 367, 370; **5:** 234, 290, 378, 381, 395, 399, 401; **6:** 406, 408, 416; **7:** 279; **8:** 227, 280, 303, 323, 324, 326, 342, 346, 348, 391
Hurewitz, J. C., **3:** 365, 367, 369
Hurewitz, L., **7:** 119
Hurwitz, Leon, **3:** 7
Hurwitz, Leonid, **2:** 323
Hurwitz, William, **7:** 308
Hutchison, Thomas W., **5:** 338
Huxley, T. H., **6:** 360
Huxtable, Ada Louise, **7:** 31
Hyman, Herbert H., **2:** 25, 94, 123, 127, 131, 136, 187; **4:** 143, 198; **6:** 11, 16, 17; **7:** 45, 46, 266, 275, 278, 288, 297, 298, 300, 302, 312, 313, 324, 325, 328, 335
Hyman, Sidney, **5:** 192
Hymans, Saul H., **6:** 330
Hymer, Stephen, **8:** 77
Hymes, Dell, **7:** 288
Hyneman, Charles S., **1:** 307; **2:** 204; **7:** 214

Hypothesis testing, **7:** 158

Ibo of Nigeria, **3:** 20
ICBM (Intercontinental Ballistic Missile), **8:** 269, 270, 294, 309
Id-centered psychoanalysts, **2:** 10
Idealization of president, **2:** 97–99, 112–113
  assassinated leaders, **2:** 103–105
  benevolent leader, **2:** 100
  Eisenhower, Dwight D., **2:** 103–105
  fallible leader, **2:** 100–102
  Kennedy, John F., **2:** 103–105
  malevolent leader, **2:** 100–102
Ideal-types, **1:** 176
Identitive power, **8:** 382
Identity, and the normative system, **3:** 601–602
Ideology, **2:** 324, 333; **4:** 83–89, 91, 102, 107, 110; **7:** 285–288, 410; **8:** 202, 203, 209, 210, 212, 225
  autonomy and heteronomy of, **3:** 197
  business, **5:** 405
  compromise of, **3:** 565–568
  corporativist, **3:** 306–307
  differences between fascism and communism, **3:** 234–237
  ideologues, **4:** 85
  impact of, **3:** 597–598
  and totalitarianism, **3:** 196–198
  vs. mentality, **3:** 266–267
Iglesias Selgas, Carlos, **3:** 367
Iklé, Fred C., **6:** 395; **7:** 387; **8:** 315, 317, 318
Ilchman, Warren F., **5:** 413; **6:** 16
Illinois Institute of Technology, **6:** 86
Immigration policies of United States and Great Britain, **6:** 256
Immobilism, **3:** 132
Impeachment, **5:** 6–7
Imperialism
  American, **8:** 23, 26, 30
  of business expansion abroad, **8:** 30
  and capitalism, **8:** 20, 21, 23, 31
  costs and benefits of, **8:** 19
  economic and social explanations of, **8:** 15–33
  economic theory of, **8:** 17, 20–21, 22, 25, 28, 31, 32–33
  effects on imperialized nation, **8:** 19, 25, 27–28
  of England, **8:** 21, 25–26, 30
  and expenditures on armaments, **8:** 20
  of France, **8:** 21

  of free trade, **8:** 17–18, 22, 25–26, 30
  of great power, **8:** 23
  Hobson-Lenin theory of, **8:** 17, 18
  and industrialism, **8:** 22
  of Japan, **8:** 21, 27
  of monopoly capitalism, **8:** 22
  and multinational corporations, **8:** 24–25, 28
  and national level of advancement, **8:** 22
  neocolonialist theory of, **8:** 24, 25, 27, 31
  precapitalist, **8:** 21
  problems with, **8:** 20–21
  quality of, **8:** 20–21
  requirements for, **8:** 22
  of Russia, **8:** 21
  sociological theory of, **8:** 23, 24, 30, 32–33
  structural theory of, **8:** 26–28
  of swarming, **8:** 22
  and third-world poverty, **8:** 27–28
  and war, **8:** 17
Implementation of policy, **5:** 382–385
Impossibility theorems, **3:** 419–427
Inada, Ken-Ichi, **3:** 424, 430, 431, 438
Inanimate science, **5:** 11
Income redistribution, **6:** 195–199
Income supports, **6:** 125, 148, 190–195
  children's allowances, **6:** 151
  comparative perspective on, **6:** 199–203
  negative income tax, **6:** 151, 216–219
Incrementalism, **1:** 346
  rationality of, **3:** 594–595
Independence of irrelevant alternatives, **3:** 420
Index of decentralization, **5:** 139
  uses of, **5:** 140–141
Index of disharmony, **5:** 137–139
  in the United States from 1837 to 1967, **5:** 139
Index of injury, **8:** 121
Index of persecution, **8:** 120
Index of rejection, **8:** 121
Index of state-party independence, **5:** 137, 139
Indexes, to books and periodicals, **7:** 7–13
  Index to Legal Periodicals, **7:** 10
  International Political Science Abstracts, **7:** 10–11
  Public Affairs Information Service Bulletin (PAIS), **7:** 11
India, federalism of, **5:** 122–123, 150, 155
India, political acculturation in, **3:** 21–22, 25, 26, 58, 68–69
Indifference, **3:** 416

Indifference curves, **1:** 354; **8:** 155, 156, 157, 158
Indifference map, **8:** 156
Individual analysis
  life-history interviews, **2:** 35–36
  psychobiographies, **2:** 38, 39, 40
  single actors, **2:** 35
  single-case analysis, **2:** 37, 44
  validity, **2:** 44
Individual personalities, **2:** 28, 29, 32–33
Individual preferences, **7:** 355–358
Individual relevance, **1:** 347–348
Individualism, **1:** 252
Individualism, unregulated, **7:** 358–362
  social efficiency of, **7:** 362
Individualistic rationalism, **5:** 3
Indoctrination, **5:** 264
Indonesia, federalism of, **5:** 98, 126
Induction, **8:** 6–10
Inductive fallacy, **7:** 113
Inductive inference, **7:** 153
Inequalities, societal, **3:** 145–152
  in distribution of political resources, **3:** 145–147
  responses to by the disadvantaged, **3:** 149–152
  responses to by governments, **3:** 148–149
Inflation
  burdens of, **6:** 30
  "cost inflation," **6:** 30
  during Vietnam War, **6:** 56–57
Influence, **1:** 170, 299, 300, 301
Influences on politics, economic, **2:** 253
Informal structure, **2:** 350, 351
Information
  acquisition of, **4:** 96
  costs, **4:** 96–97, 98, 111, 121
  levels of public, **4:** 79, 81, 82–83, 93, 102, 156
Information theory, **2:** 332, 334
Inglehart, Ronald E., **2:** 101, 106, 111, 112, 115, 116, 120, 138, 165, 212; **8:** 371
Inkeles, Alex, **2:** 30, 60, 62, 68; **3:** 16, 27, 28, 34, 41, 97, 196, 203, 232; **4:** 22, 32; **7:** 289
Innovation, predicting the rate of, **7:** 419–420
Input variables in foreign policy
  domestic, **6:** 410–420
  external, **6:** 418–420
  governmental institutions as, **6:** 401–410
  individual psychological, **6:** 393–396
  issues as, **6:** 397–400
  role as, **6:** 402–403

Institut für Zeitgeschichte, **3:** 219
Institute for Behavioural Research Data Bank, **7:** 51
Institute for Social Research, **7:** 312
"Institutional completeness," **3:** 602
Institutional fact, **1:** 318
Institutional fallacy, **8:** 416
Institutionalization, **5:** 289
Instrumental rationality, **1:** 201
Insurrections, German, **3:** 530
Integration, political, **8:** 366–377
  attitudinal, **8:** 374–375, 388
  "cybernetic" approach to, **8:** 365
  definitions of, **8:** 366
  economic, **8:** 368–370
  evaluations of, **8:** 375–377
  institutional, **8:** 374–375
  monetary, **8:** 386
  perceptual conditions of, **8:** 381–382
  policy, **8:** 371–374
  process mechanisms, **8:** 382–387
  social, **8:** 370–371
Integration theory, **8:** 365
Intelligence
  alternatives, **6:** 14–15
  arenas, **6:** 7
  base values, **6:** 7
  criteria for, **6:** 11–13
  effects, **6:** 8
  external relations, **6:** 2
  functions and structures, **6:** 2–4
  goals of, **6:** 10–14
  internal relations, **6:** 2
  model, **6:** 2–3, 5
  outcomes, **6:** 8
  participants in process, **6:** 5–6
  perspectives, **6:** 6–7
  process of, **6:** 5–8
  projections, **6:** 14–15
  scientific task, **6:** 4–5
  strategies, **6:** 8
  trends, **6:** 14–15
Intentional action, **1:** 133, 155, 161, 164, 178
Intentionalist assessment, **7:** 167–199
  aggregative approaches, **7:** 167–180
  individual case, the, **7:** 188–199
  situational and structural measures, **7:** 180–188
Intentionality, **7:** 148, 157, 158, 196
  measurement of, **7:** 186–187
  relevant statistical practices, **7:** 140, 146

Intentions and inner states, 1: 165
Interaction, 2: 16–17
  contingent relationships, 2: 18, 35
  moderator variables, 2: 51
Interaction model, 8: 123, 124, 126, 177
Interchangeability of means, 2: 157
Interdependence, 8: 365, 366–377
  definitions of, 8: 366–367
  differential; 8: 397–398
  economic, 8: 368–370
  evaluations of, 8: 375–377
  policy, 8: 371–374
  sensitivity as dimension of, 8: 369–370
  social, 8: 370–371
  vulnerability, 8: 370
Interest, 1: 382
Interest groups, 2: 233; 3: 338–339; 5: 266, 375, 381, 391, 392, 393, 395, 396, 397, 401–403, 423
  benefits derived by members, 4: 184–185, 192
  catalytic groups, 4: 195
  categoric group, 4: 173
  as decision makers, 4: 180–181
  definitions, 4: 173–176
  elite interaction, 4: 210–211
  entrepreneurial theory, 4: 193
  expressive-benefit groups, 4: 195
  formal association, 4: 175
  growth within framework of law, 4: 198
  impact on society, 4: 219–223
  inferential group, 4: 173
  as input mechanisms, 4: 177–179
  interaction with government, 4: 206–209
  liberalism, 4: 221–222
  lobbyists, 4: 205–206, 209–213
  managerial groups, 4: 186
  membership density, 4: 199, 221
  mobilization, 4: 216–218
  opposition, importance of, 4: 218
  as organizations, 4: 181–182
  organizers, 4: 194–195
  origins and growth of, 4: 189–201
  pressure groups, 4: 176
  promotional groups, 4: 195
  representation, 4: 213–216
  role-based organizations, 4: 188–189
  role differentiation, 4: 202–206
  sectional groups, 4: 176
  strategies, 4: 183, 200, 212
  as system outputs, 4: 179–180

Intergovernmental relations, 5: 148–149, 151
Internal consistency, 1: 341
Internal party democracy, 3: 183
Inter-Nation Simulation (INS), 8: 95, 96
International "balances," 8: 204–208
International cooperation, 8: 364
International Council on Social Welfare, 6: 349
International Court of Justice, 8: 417, 429
International customary law, 8: 419, 420
International Data Library and Reference Service, 7: 50
International institutions, significance of, 8: 399–400
International Journal of Politics, 3: 320
International law, 8: 219, 415–435
  agreement in, 8: 418–420
  compared with domestic, 8: 416
  and consent, 8: 418, 421
  constitutional structure, 8: 416–418
  contextualism, 8: 432–434
  and individuals, 8: 420, 425
  institutions, 8: 415–416
  legality of, 8: 416
  and moralism, 8: 422–424
  perspectives on, 8: 420–424
  and positivism, 8: 421–422
  and realism, 8: 422
  and recognition of states, 8: 425–428
  Soviet theories, 8: 430–431
  states in, 8: 424–428
  and universalism, 8: 420
International Law Commission, 8: 429
International Monetary Fund (IMF), 8: 373, 391
International organizations, 8: 206–208, 217–218, 221, 223
International politics
  analysis of, 8: 93
  dynamics of, 8: 93
  models of, 8: 151–191
  and power, 8: 199–204
International politics, domestic factors in
  bureaucratic politics, 8: 230–231, 232
  public opinion, 8: 225
International politics, economic factors in, 8: 200, 201, 208, 209, 221, 223, 227, 237–240, 241
  ecology, 8: 233–234, 238
  economic models, 8: 203, 221, 231–232
  imperialism, 8: 226, 228–229, 230, 232, 240

multinational corporations, **8:** 227–228, 230, 234, 236
International proletariat, **3:** 213
International relations, theories of, **1:** 235–236; **8:** 1–85
  balance-of-power theory, **8:** 33–43
  reductionist theory, **8:** 15–33
  state of, **8:** 1
  systems approaches, **8:** 43–65
International Urban Research, **6:** 312
International Workers of the World, **3:** 570
Internationalism, **3:** 233
Interpolimetrics, **8:** 87, 99
Interpretations, testing of, **1:** 171–177
Interstate Commerce Commission, **5:** 399, 402
Inter-university Consortium for Political Research, **7:** 47, 49, 50, 51
Intrilligator, Michael, **8:** 191
Introspection, **1:** 165
Intuitionism, **1:** 319
Investment, foreign, in United States, **8:** 21
Ionescu, Ghita, **3:** 335, 337, 359
Ions, Edmund S., **1:** 31
Ippolito, Dennis S., **2:** 196, 197
Iron Guard, **3:** 285, 289, 291, 317
"Iron hand" theorem, **3:** 595
Iremonger, Lucille, **5:** 241
Irwin, Galen, **4:** 13
Isaacs, Harold R., **3:** 85; **6:** 267
Isaak, Alan C., **8:** 3, 5, 33
Isard, Walter, **6:** 16
Isenson, Raymond S., **6:** 86
Isolationism, **8:** 252
  attitudes toward, **2:** 52
Issue-area analysis, **8:** 395–396
Issue linkage, strategies of, **8:** 393–394
Issues in foreign policy, typology of, **6:** 397–398

Jäckel, Eberhard, **3:** 227
Jackman, Mary R., **2:** 131
Jackman, Robert W., **2:** 27; **3:** 6
Jackson, Don D., **8:** 78
Jackson, Douglas N., **2:** 48
Jackson, Elton F., **7:** 272, 335
Jackson, Gabriel, **3:** 363
Jackson, Henry M., **5:** 208, 223; **8:** 303
Jackson, John, **7:** 161
Jackson, Robert J., **5:** 228
Jacksonian democracy, **5:** 413
Jacob, Herbert, **2:** 67, 75, 161, 172, 179, 214; **5:**

157, 242, 329, 331; **6:** 16, 305, 341, 467
Jacobsen, Hans-Adolf, **3:** 215, 220, 359, 368
Jacobsen, Harold K., **6:** 93; **8:** 345, 391
Jacobson, Norman, **2:** 254
Jacoby, Neil H., **5:** 410
Jaffa, Harry A., **5:** 158
Jäger, Herbert, **3:** 221
Jahoda, Marie, **2:** 48, 73, 112; **3:** 619
Jakobson, Leo, **6:** 313, 334
James, Herman G., **5:** 119
James, Robert Rhodes, **3:** 337
Janda, Kenneth, **3:** 370; **7:** 53
Jänicke, Martin, **3:** 187, 241, 357
Janicon, F. M., **5:** 95, 103
Janis, Irving L., **5:** 378; **6:** 394, 395; **8:** 324
Janos, Andrew C., **3:** 84, 285, 286, 287, 290, 291, 336
Janowitz, Morris, **2:** 179; **3:** 363, 367; **6:** 16, 408, 414; **8:** 326
Jansen, M. B., **3:** 365
Japan
  political acculturation in, **3:** 20
  political opposition in, **3:** 126, 128
Jaros, Dean, **2:** 94, 100, 102, 106, 107, 111; **7:** 240
Jasper, Gotthard, **3:** 248
Jay, Martin, **1:** 217
J-curve phenomenon, **3:** 8, 528, 529
Jeffersonians, **5:** 152, 153
Jeffery, C. Ray, **5:** 329
Jencks, Christopher, **6:** 135, 196, 198
Jenkins, Peter, **5:** 195
Jenkner, Siegfried, **3:** 187
Jennings, M. Kent, **2:** 95, 106, 108, 119, 120, 123, 125, 126, 127, 128, 129, 130, 132; **4:** 143, 144, 162; **5:** 157; **7:** 278, 302
Jennings, W. Ivor, **5:** 179, 206, 219, 222, 281, 283
Jensen, Arthur R., **6:** 278, 279
Jensen, Richard, **4:** 148, 160
Jervis, Robert, **6:** 395; **8:** 316, 343
Jewell, Malcolm E., **2:** 203, 204; **4:** 205; **6:** 409
Jim Crowism, **6:** 246
Job Corps program, **6:** 284
Joffe, Ellis, **3:** 190
Johe, Werner, **3:** 222
Johns Hopkins University, **1:** 27
Johnson, Arlien, **6:** 165
Johnson, Chalmers, **1:** 193, 314; **3:** 488, 490, 491, 492, 493, 497
Johnson, Charles S., **7:** 309, 310

Johnson, Donald Bruce, **5:** 224, 226
Johnson, George E., **3:** 470
Johnson, Gerald W., **3:** 37
Johnson, John J., **3:** 367
Johnson, Lyndon, **2:** 2, 3, 32; **6:** 404
Johnson, N. B., **2:** 118
Johnson, Nevil, **5:** 231, 236, 238
Johnson, Peter A., **2:** 119
Johnson, Priscilla, **3:** 358
Johnston, Larry D., **5:** 224, 226
Johr, W. A., **6:** 75
Joint Chiefs of Staff, **5:** 212; **8:** 277, 323
Joint Committee on the Economic Report, **6:** 52
Joint Economic Committee, **6:** 24, 40, 53, 54
Joint War Games Agency/Joint Chiefs of Staff, **7:** 223
Jones, A. H. M., **3:** 74, 170
Jones, Arthur G., **6:** 403
Jones, Charles L., **7:** 176
Jones, Charles O., **5:** 286, 392
Jones, D. Caradog, **7:** 311, 312
Jones, Ernest M., **6:** 15
Jones, E. Terrance, **6:** 454
Jones, G. W., **5:** 184, 195, 206, 217, 224, 228, 231, 232; **6:** 362
Jones, H. G., **7:** 31, 32
Jones, Joseph M., **6:** 407
Jones v. *Mayer,* **6:** 291
Jones, Roy E., **6:** 383, 389
Jones, Susan D., **8:** 7
Jones, Victor, **7:** 14
Joravsky, David, **6:** 100
Jordan, Winthrop D., **6:** 250, 251, 252, 255, 256, 262
Jöreskog, K. G., **7:** 156
Jowitt, Kenneth, **3:** 233, 338, 344
Judaism, **4:** 232, 240
Judge of fact, **5:** 22
Judgmental probabilities, **2:** 336
Judicial attitudes, **5:** 342
Judicial behavior, **5:** 342
Judicial independence, **5:** 36–37, 334, 335, 340, 341, 343, 345–348
Judicial lawmaking, **5:** 335, 342–349, 353, 361
Judicial power, **5:** 42
Judicial recruitment, **5:** 346, 347
Judicial review, **5:** 6, 31, 34, 58, 69
"Judridical defenses," **5:** 4, 25
Jünger, Ernst, **3:** 177
Junker, Buford H., **7:** 309

Junta, **5:** 264
Jureen, Lars, **6:** 452
Jurisprudence, **5:** 18, 21, 35, 36, 45
Justice, **1:** 322–323, 364, 384–386

Kadushin, Charles, **3:** 239, 346
Kafoglis, M. L., **5:** 425
Kagan, Jerome, **2:** 11, 139; **8:** 342, 345
Kahin, Georg McTurnan, **3:** 365
Kahn, Alfred J., **6:** 143
Kahn, Herman, **6:** 391; **7:** 204, 419, 424; **8:** 263, 271, 298, 317, 318, 343, 344
Kaiser, Karl, **8:** 377, 395, 398
Kaldor, Mary, **6:** 98
Kalleberg, Arthur L., **1:** 310
Kaltefleiter, Werner, **3:** 248, 320
Kalven, Harry, Jr., **5:** 363
Kamien, M., **3:** 428
Kamin, Leon J., **7:** 235, 250
Kaminsky, Elijah Ben-Zion, **5:** 184, 185
Kanet, Roger E., **3:** 365
Kant, Immanuel, **1:** 230; **8:** 9
Kanter, Arnold, **5:** 375; **6:** 409; **8:** 322
Kantian phenomenology, **5:** 8
Kantor, Harry, **5:** 133
Kantor, Mildred B., **3:** 486
Kantorowics, E. H., **5:** 59
Kaplan, Abraham, **1:** 172, 284, 285, 292, 299, 309; **2:** 6, 22, 354; **7:** 213, 217, 218, 230; **8:** 61
Kaplan, Morton A., **6:** 419; **8:** 56, 57, 58, 59, 60, 61, 62, 63, 64, 69, 78, 79, 89, 94, 204, 331, 347, 424
Kariel, Henry S., **1:** 114; **2:** 245, 309; **7:** 330
Karol, K. S., **3:** 366
Karpat, Kemal H., **3:** 185, 365
Kase, Francis J., **3:** 335
Kasfir, Nelson N., **3:** 39
Kassof, Allen, **3:** 209, 229, 340, 343
Kast, Fremont, **6:** 81
Katona, George, **7:** 312; **8:** 78
Katz, Daniel, **2:** 9, 56; **4:** 248; **6:** 413; **7:** 303, 312
Katz, Elihu, **7:** 280, 329
Katz, F. E., **2:** 115
Katz, Irwin, **2:** 7; **7:** 299
Katz, Phyllis A., **2:** 118
Katzenbach, Nicholas, **8:** 424
Katzenstein, Peter J., **8:** 365
Katznelson, Ira, **6:** 277
Kaufman, A., **8:** 344
Kaufman, Arnold S., **1:** 292

Kaufman, Herbert, **1:** 80; **5:** 413, 418, 424, 425, 426, 429
Kaufman, Robert R., **3:** 97
Kaufman, Susan Beth, **3:** 268, 358
Kaufmann, H., **7:** 97
Kaufmann, William W., **5:** 408; **8:** 261, 284, 292, 297, 303, 323, 343, 345
Kautsky, John, **3:** 12, 240
Kavanagh, Dennis, **2:** 96, 113, 115, 136, 137
Kay, David A., **6:** 99
Kay, Hugh, **3:** 366
Kearney, Robert N., **3:** 79
Kecskemeti, Paul, **2:** 61; **8:** 315, 340
Kedward, H. R., **3:** 315
Kee, Woo Sik, **6:** 311
Keech, William R., **3:** 85; **6:** 295, 296
Keen, M. H., **5:** 304, 307
Kegley, Charles W., Jr., **6:** 381, 390
Keith-Lucas, Alan, **6:** 114, 161
Kele, Max H., **3:** 231, 317
Kelleher, Catherine McArdle, **3:** 367
Kelley, E. W., **7:** 396
Kelley, Harold H., **1:** 195
Kelley, Stanley, Jr., **4:** 22
Kelly, David H., **2:** 68
Kelly, E. Lowell, **2:** 130
Kelly, K. Dennis, **7:** 272
Kelsen, Hans, **3:** 358; **5:** 8; **8:** 428
Kemeny, J. G., **7:** 86
Kemp, M. C., **3:** 424
Kendall, Willimoore, **4:** 239; **6:** 97
Keniston, Kenneth R., **2:** 68, 69, 70, 75; **6:** 86
Kennan, George F., **5:** 376; **6:** 407, 408; **7:** 4; **8:** 278
Kennedy, John F., **2:** 2, 3, 32, 103–105
Kennedy, Robert F., **8:** 345
Kent, Sherman, **6:** 14; **8:** 347
Keohane, Robert O., **8:** 73, 227, 370, 377, 391, 399, 402
Kerlinger, Fred N., **7:** 248
Kern, Robert, **3:** 263
Kerner Commission, **6:** 280
Kerpelman, Larry C., **2:** 69, 76
Kershaw, Joseph A., **6:** 134, 173, 180, 181, 207
Kessel, John H., **2:** 307; **4:** 68, 159; **5:** 291
Kesselman, Mark, **6:** 313
Kevles, Daniel J., **6:** 83
Key, V. O., Jr., **2:** 103, 135, 137, 182, 308; **3:** 564, 576, 617, 618; **4:** 68, 77, 112, 119, 121–124, 133, 134, 137, 146, 158, 161, 183, 187, 191, 197, 240, 242, 257; **5:** 148; **6:** 113, 214, 257, 413; **7:** 1, 266, 267, 279, 280, 325, 331, 332

Keynes, John M., **8:** 76
Killingsworth, Charles C., **6:** 282, 283, 284
Kilpatrick, James J., **5:** 157
Kim, Jae-On, **1:** 217; **3:** 34, 97; **4:** 6, 13, 17, 22, 40, 42, 49, 50
Kim, Se-Jin, **3:** 367
Kim, Young C., **2:** 203, 204
Kimball, G. E., **8:** 344
Kinder, Donald R., **2:** 135, 140
Kindleberger, Charles P., **8:** 73
King, Anthony, **2:** 76; **4:** 269; **5:** 184, 187, 194, 195, 204, 219, 222, 224, 233, 235
King, David N., **6:** 339, 344, 362
King, Martin Luther, Jr., **2:** 291
Kingdon, John W., **4:** 148; **5:** 308
Kingship, principles of, **5:** 28, 56
  dual, **5:** 46
Kingsley, J. Donald, **5:** 423
Kintner, William R., **8:** 347
Kirchheimer, Otto, **3:** 333, 540; **4:** 268
Kirk, Russell, **5:** 157
Kirkendall, Richard S., **7:** 34
Kirkham, James F., **2:** 104
Kirkpatrick, E. M., **4:** 237
Kirkpatrick, Jeane, **3:** 78, 231
Kirkpatrick, Lyman B., Jr., **8:** 347
Kirlin, John J., **6:** 306, 332
Kirscht, John P., **2:** 47
Kish, Leslie, **7:** 311, 312
Kissinger, Henry A., **5:** 384; **6:** 384, 412; **8:** 219, 227, 237, 284, 302, 343, 345
Kistiakowsky, George B., **6:** 94
Kitzinger, Uwe, **6:** 415
Klahr, David, **3:** 428
Klapper, Joseph T., **2:** 131
Klarman, H. E., **6:** 16, 85
Klecka, William R., **2:** 132
Klein, Philip, **6:** 221
Klemperer, Victor, **3:** 360
Klevorick, Alvin, **7:** 378, 398
Kliman, G., **2:** 104
Kline, Paul, **2:** 45
Klineberg, Otto, **2:** 62, 97, 118; **6:** 278
Kling, Merle, **3:** 365
Klingberg, Frank L., **6:** 407; **8:** 226
Klingemann, Hans D., **4:** 102, 110, 159
Klönne, Arno, **3:** 209
Kluckhohn, Clyde, **2:** 26, 30, 31; **3:** 232
Kluke, Paul, **3:** 233
Knapper, Christopher, **7:** 236, 248
Kneese, Allan, **6:** 77
Knoke, David, **2:** 131
Knorr, Klaus, **6:** 412; **8:** 315, 318, 345

Knowledge, **1:** 253, 254
  practical, **1:** 253
  productive, **1:** 253
  theoretical, **1:** 253
Knutson, Jeanne N., **2:** 5, 129, 133, 136, 210, 211, 212, 233; **6:** 394
Kobielski, José, **6:** 340, 344
Koch, Howard E., Jr., **8:** 115, 116, 120
Kodane, Joseph B., **7:** 179
Koehl, Robert, **3:** 208, 237
Koenig, K. E., **2:** 115, 127, 128, 130, 131
Koenig, Louis W., **5:** 211, 222, 226
Koeppen, Sheilah R., **2:** 94, 96
Koestler, Arthur, **8:** 63
Koff, David, **2:** 157, 193, 201, 202
Kogan, Nathan, **2:** 75
Kogan, Norman, **6:** 414
Kohlberg, Lawrence, **2:** 133
Kohlmeier, Louis M., **5:** 398
Kohn, Hans, **3:** 619
Kolankiewicz, George, **3:** 344
Kolasa, Bernard D., **4:** 205
Kolko, Gabriel, **5:** 401, 407, 429; **6:** 399, 416
Kolkowicz, Roman, **3:** 210
Kolm, S., **2:** 330, 331
Kolodziej, Edward A., **8:** 322, 388
Kolson, Kenneth L., **2:** 106, 107, 111
Kool, Frits, **3:** 312
Korbell, J., **3:** 240, 335
Korean War, **8:** 282, 283–284, 321
Korn, Richard R., **6:** 273
Kornberg, Allan, **2:** 123, 176, 189, 190, 191, 192, 193, 196; **4:** 265; **5:** 295
Körner, Stephan, **1:** 216
Kornhauser, William, **3:** 208, 209, 247, 364, 569
Kort, Fred, **3:** 484
Kosheri Mahfouz, El, **3:** 369
Kothari, Rajni, **3:** 132
Kovel, Joel, **6:** 248
Kozol, Jonathan, **5:** 426
Krader, Lawrence, **3:** 364
Kramer, Gerald H., **3:** 439, 440, 443, 461, 468; **4:** 135, 161; **7:** 143, 147, 180, 202, 378, 398
Kramer, Ralph, **6:** 169, 176, 179, 180
Krasner, Stephen D., **5:** 375; **6:** 405
Krause, Lawrence B., **8:** 373
Krausnick, Helmut, **3:** 205, 215, 220, 225
Krech, David, **7:** 312
Kress, Paul F., **2:** 253, 254
Kriedler, Robert N., **6:** 93
Kriegel, Annie, **3:** 221, 225, 227
Krielkamp, Karl, **6:** 86

Krislov, Samuel, **4:** 211; **5:** 423; **6:** 467; **7:** 396
Kristol, Irving, **6:** 223
Kroeber, Alfred Louis, **2:** 26
Kronenberg, Philip S., **8:** 347
Kropotkin, Prince, **1:** 12
Ku Klux Klan, **6:** 245, 253, 267–268
Kubler, George A., **3:** 75
Kubota, Akira, **2:** 124, 126
Kuhn, Thomas S., **1:** 141, 195, 218, 219; **5:** 76; **7:** 147, 149; **8:** 11
Kühnl, Reinhard, **3:** 231, 233, 319
Kunkel, John, **3:** 603
Kuper, Hilda, **5:** 338
Kuper, Leo, **3:** 67, 75; **5:** 338
Kursunoglu, Behram, **6:** 86
Kurth, James R., **3:** 58, 94; **8:** 327
Kurtz, R. H., **6:** 221
Kutner, Bernard, **2:** 118, 134

Labedz, Leopold, **3:** 236, 358
Labor law, **5:** 356
Labor movement, destruction by fascism, **3:** 317
Labor violence, **3:** 516
Laboratory, **7:** 220
  design of, **7:** 221–229
Laboratory for Political Research, **7:** 50, 52
Labour Party, **1:** 177
La Cierva, Ricardo de, **3:** 363
Lacouture, Jean, **3:** 369
Lacouture, Simonne, **3:** 369
Lacy, Alex B., Jr., **5:** 223
Ladd, Everett Carll, Jr., **2:** 132, 202; **6:** 94, 95
Ladinsky, Jack, **7:** 239, 249
LaFeber, Walter, **6:** 399; **8:** 229
Lag models, **8:** 126
Lakatos, Imre, **1:** 141, 148, 150, 151, 152, 153, 154, 194, 207; **2:** 359; **7:** 147, 149, 152, 153, 180; **8:** 25, 75, 377
Lakoff, Sanford A., **6:** 80, 81, 94, 95
Lamare, Judith, **6:** 321, 322, 329, 340, 361
Lambert, W. E., **2:** 97, 118
Lambright, Henry W., **6:** 85, 88
Lamounier, Bolívar, **3:** 267
Lampman, Robert J., **6:** 130, 197
Landau, Jacob M., **3:** 365
Landau, Martin, **1:** 39; **2:** 332, 356, 357, 360; **5:** 344, 406; **8:** 72
Landé, Carl H., **3:** 97, 365
Landes, David S., **1:** 345
Landesman, Charles, **1:** 293
Lane, David, **3:** 344

Lane, Robert E., **2:** 18, 23, 36, 37; **3:** 38, 150; **4:** 5, 7, 27, 86, 87, 88, 89, 94; **6:** 80; **7:** 278, 287
Lang, Kurt, **3:** 367
Langdon, Frank, **2:** 112
Lange, M. G., **3:** 358
Langer, Walter C., **2:** 213
Langer, William A., **8:** 230
Langer, William L., **3:** 533
Langner, Thomas S., **2:** 213
Langton, Kenneth P., **2:** 95, 126, 127
Language politics, **3:** 69, 70, 71–72, 79, 85–87
Language of politics, **1:** 16–18
Lanning, Eldon, **3:** 180, 365
Lansdale, Robert T., **6:** 113
Lansing, John B., **7:** 312, 324
Lanternari, Vittorio, **3:** 82
Lanyi, Anthony, **8:** 370
La Palombara, Joseph, **2:** 308; **3:** 91, 159, 160; **4:** 172, 216, 233
LaPorte, Todd, **6:** 100
Lapp, Ralph, **6:** 86, 90, 91
Laqueur, Walter Z., **2:** 190; **3:** 236, 315
Larsen, J. A. O., **5:** 94
Lasch, Christopher, **1:** 274
Laski, Harold, **5:** 32, 160, 193, 222, 228; **8:** 19
Laslett, P., **5:** 178; **6:** 349
Lasswell, Harold D., **1:** 46, 66, 252, 284, 285; **2:** 6, 13, 22, 31, 39, 42, 44, 45, 46, 54, 68, 73, 74, 75, 157, 163, 178, 179, 199, 200, 211, 212, 354; **4:** 194; **5:** 242; **6:** 11, 14, 16, 17, 444; **7:** 54, 64, 142, 147, 184, 266, 336; **8:** 348
Latham, Earl, **4:** 172, 191
Latin America
    federalism of, **5:** 95–96, 118–119
    political acculturation in, **3:** 23, 26, 30
Latin American Data Bank, **7:** 50
Laurence, Joan, **2:** 102, 107, 116, 138
Laurenti, Luigi, **6:** 274
Law *(see also* Common law; Natural law; and Roman law)
    constitutional, 23–24, 33, 55, 67
    declarative, **5:** 28
    due process of, **5:** 25, 35
    English folk, **5:** 25
    feudal, **5:** 55
    fundamental, **5:** 23
    positive, **5:** 45
    and precedents, **5:** 23
    "unwritten," **5:** 21
Law-abidingness, **5:** 41
Lawley, D. N., **7:** 156

Law-like statements, **8:** 2, 10
Lawmaking, **5:** 258
    by proclamation, **5:** 263
Laws, **1:** 132, 133, 134
    "accidental" generalizations, **1:** 138
    counterfactual conditionals, **1:** 138, 139, 189
    as distinct from theory, **8:** 3
    vs. general statements, **1:** 137
    generalizations, **1:** 133, 136–138
    law-like statement, **8:** 2, 10
    "necessity" of, **1:** 138, 139
    of politics, **8:** 34
    probabilistic, **8:** 3
    subjunctive conditional, **1:** 138, 139, 189
    unrestricted universal statement, **1:** 138
Lawson Edwin D., **2:** 97, 106, 115, 118
Lawton, Raymond W., **8:** 101
Lawyers in politics, **2:** 203, 204–209
Layton, Christopher, **6:** 98
Lazarsfeld, Paul F., **2:** 60, 94; **4:** 3, 7, 112, 158, 159; **7:** 141, 147, 161, 168, 302, 308, 311, 318, 328, 329, 332, 335
Leacacos, John P., **6:** 409
Leach, Richard H., **5:** 151
Leader responsiveness, **4:** 60, 61, 63–68, 69
Leader, role of in totalitarian system, **3:** 195–196, 238–239
League of Communists, **3:** 346
League of Nations, **3:** 318; **8:** 48, 206–207, 263
Leagues
    early modern, **5:** 94–95
    primitive, **5:** 93–94
Learned, Henry B., **5:** 205
Lebanon, religious structure in, **3:** 68
Lebeaux, Charles, **6:** 143
Lebergott, Stanley, **6:** 455
Lebrun, François, **3:** 542
Ledeen, Michael Arthur, **3:** 233
Ledesma Ramos, Ramiro, **3:** 333, 357
LeDuc, Lawrence, Jr., **5:** 184
Ledyard, John O., **3:** 443; **7:** 377
Lee, J. M., **3:** 322
Lee, Mordecai, **5:** 399
Leeds, Anthony, **3:** 365
Leege, David C., **7:** 306
Lees, John D., **5:** 295
Lefcowitz, Myron J., **6:** 222; **7:** 239, 249, 321
Lefebvre, Georges, **3:** 499
Leff, Nathaniel H., **3:** 365
LeFur, Louis, **5:** 94, 160
Legal citation, **7:** 15–16
Legal institutions, **1:** 301–303

legal concepts, **1:** 303
legal system, **1:** 303, 322
Legal omnicompetence, **5:** 45
Legal order, horizontal, **8:** 418
Legal profession, **5:** 348–349
Legal realists, **5:** 21
Legal sovereignty, Austinian, **5:** 44–45
Legere, Laurence J., **5:** 208, 233; **6:** 402; **8:** 323
Legg, Keith R., **2:** 232; **3:** 97, 365
Legislative activity, **5:** 258
Legislative debates, **5:** 259
Legislative outputs, **5:** 277
Legislative reform, **5:** 296–297
Legislative supremacy, **5:** 58
Legislatures, **5:** 257–310
  accountability of, **5:** 260–262, 269
  African, **5:** 267
  Athenian Assembly, **5:** 272–273
  Belgium, **5:** 295
  classification, problems of, **5:** 262–263
  definition, problems of, **5:** 258–262
  dissolution of, **5:** 228
  and executives, **5:** 233–238
  folkmoot, **5:** 268
  France, **5:** 294–295
  functionalist orientation, **5:** 258
  Germany, **5:** 293
  Italy, **5:** 294
  modern democratic, constitutional variation in, **5:** 274–277
  as multipurpose organizations, **5:** 301–303
  the Netherlands, **5:** 292
  and obedience of subject population, **5:** 262
  powerless, **5:** 266–267, 268
  properties of, compared with other official bodies, **5:** 260, 261
  rubber-stamp, **5:** 264, 265, 266–267, 268
  of the Soviet Union (Supreme Soviet), **5:** 266
  status-ridden, **5:** 271–272
  structuralist approach, **5:** 258–259, 261
  Sweden, **5:** 293
  town meeting, **5:** 268–270
  transformative, **5:** 277–296
  tribal council, **5:** 268
  United States Congress, **5:** 275–276, 284–287, 288–291, 300–301
Legitimacy, **1:** 287, 321–322; **2:** 114, 116, 117; **5:** 259, 264
  distinguished from partisanship, **2:** 116
  of the judicial system, **5:** 327, 331, 338
  of a regime, **5:** 263–265
  sources of, **3:** 49, 197

Leibenstein, Harvey, **3:** 432, 453
Leibfried, Stephan, **2:** 307
Leif, Irving P., **6:** 307
Leighton, Alexander H., **2:** 23
Leiserson, Avery, **6:** 90
Leiserson, Michael, **3:** 125; **7:** 395, 396
Leiss, Arnold, **8:** 321, 340
Leites, Nathan, **2:** 9, 10, 61, 66; **3:** 221, 225, 363; **5:** 184, 309; **6:** 419
Lemarchand, René, **3:** 75, 97, 365
Lenin, V. I., **3:** 197, 202, 223, 226, 235, 244, 247, 360, 362, 524, 530, 531, 532; **8:** 17, 19, 20, 21, 22, 40, 76, 228, 230
Leninism, **3:** 235
Lenski, Gerhard, **1:** 285; **3:** 139, 147, 170; **6:** 172, 185; **7:** 272
Lentner, Howard H., **6:** 382, 385, 423
Leonard, Dick, **5:** 307
Leontief, Wassily, **8:** 78
Lepper, Mary M., **6:** 384
Lepsius, Rainer, **3:** 209, 248, 320, 364
Lerche, Charles O., **6:** 414
Lerner, Daniel, **2:** 178, 179; **3:** 2, 3, 32, 33, 40, 97, 98, 232, 619; **4:** 33; **6:** 15, 17
Lerner, Michael, **2:** 4, 37, 68, 70
Lessing, Lawrence, **6:** 89
Leuchtenburg, William E., **7:** 37
Lev, Daniel S., **5:** 342
Level of abstraction, **7:** 247
"Levels of analysis" problem, **6:** 386, 419
Levi, Carlo, **1:** 174
Levi, Edward H., **1:** 378
Levin, Henry M., **6:** 77
Levin, Martin A., **6:** 467
Levine, Donald N., **3:** 86, 159, 254
Levine, Robert A., **2:** 74, 75, 187; **6:** 90, 134, 135, 172, 173, 177, 178, 179, 180, 181, 207; **8:** 300, 347
Levinson, Daniel J., **2:** 18, 24, 60, 62, 67, 211; **3:** 16, 363; **7:** 289
Levi-Strauss, Claude, **6:** 249
Levitan, Sar, **6:** 134, 174, 178, 181, 221, 222
Levitt, Theodore, **6:** 98
Levy, Frank S., **6:** 306, 350, 357
Levy, Leonard W., **2:** 307
Levy, Marion J., Jr., **3:** 3
Levy, Sheldon, **2:** 104
Levytsky, Borys, **3:** 221, 238
Lewin, Kurt, **2:** 5; **7:** 281
Lewis, Bernard, **3:** 63
Lewis, David M., **7:** 289
Lewis, John Wilson, **3:** 239, 366; **6:** 310

Lewis, Oscar, **3:** 619; **6:** 221
Lewy, Guenter, **3:** 317, 359
Lexicographic hierarchy, **1:** 351–352
Liberal party (Canada), **5:** 190
Liberal-conservative ideology, **2:** 134
Liberalism, **1:** 246, 261; **3:** 422, 426
Liberia, political acculturation in, **3:** 24–25
Liberty, **1:** 379
Library of Congress, **7:** 35–36
Library reference sources, as data for political science *(See also listings for individual sources.)*
    aliases and fictitious persons, **7:** 5–6
    almanacs, **7:** 16
    anonymous authors, **7:** 3–4
    census figures, **7:** 5
    encyclopedias, **7:** 16–17
    errors and oddities in, **7:** 2–7
    hoaxes, **7:** 4–5
    United States government, documents by and about, **7:** 18–38
Lichtheim, George, **1:** 15
Liddell-Hart, Basil H., **8:** 283
Liebenow, J. Gus, **3:** 24, 25
Lieber, Francis, **1:** 25–26
Lieber, Robert J., **8:** 56, 57
Lieberson, Stanley, **6:** 87
Liebow, Elliot, **6:** 285
Liebschutz, Sarah, **2:** 102, 107, 138
Lieuwen, Edwin, **3:** 367
Lifton, Robert Jay, **3:** 224
Light, Richard J., **7:** 244
Lijphart, Arend, **2:** 308; **3:** 133, 171, 331; **4:** 240; **5.** 199, 292, 403, 404; **7:** 287
Likelihood Principle, **7:** 143, 148
Likert, Rensis, **7:** 311, 312
Likert scale, **2:** 49
Limited state, **5:** 31
Limited strategic war, **8:** 318
Limited war, **8:** 260, 279, 283–285, 317–321
Lincoln, Charles Eric, **6:** 296
Lind, Alden E., **2:** 96, 134, 135, 136, 137, 141; **4:** 117
Lindbeck, J. M. H., **3:** 366
Lindberg, L., **2:** 106, 112, 113, 115
Lindberg, Leon N., **8:** 370, 371, 373, 378, 383, 384, 385, 388, 395, 396, 398, 401
Lindblom, Charles E., **1:** 347, 363; **2:** 321, 322, 326, 332; **3:** 618, 619; **4:** 222; **5:** 304, 384, 407; **6:** 421, 447, 454; **7:** 267; **8:** 433
Lindsay, Alexander D., **5:** 2, 32, 45
Lindsay, Franklin A., **8:** 346

Lindzey, Gardner, **2:** 7, 10, 11
Linear programming, **2:** 335, 336
Lineberry, Robert L., **5:** 405; **6:** 305, 307, 309, 323, 336, 338, 339, 341, 342, 356
Lingoes, James C., **7:** 164, 165, 174
Link, Arthur S., **5:** 308
Linnemann, H., **3:** 370
Linz, Juan, **2:** 94, 159, 185; **3:** 51, 178, 197, 232, 239, 248, 264, 271, 274, 276, 288, 300, 316, 317, 320, 333, 336, 340, 354, 358, 361, 363, 364, 365, 367; **4:** 158, 232, 245
Lippmann, Walter, **4:** 4, 93, 96; **5:** 63
Lipset, Seymour M., **1:** 337; **2:** 26, 27, 46, 94, 132, 327; **3:** 3, 5, 16, 35, 77, 83, 84, 92, 96, 98, 171, 232, 316, 363, 364, 525, 576, 577–578, 584, 618, 620; **4:** 60, 148, 158, 160, 182, 194, 246, 269; **6:** 95, 223; **7:** 99, 121, 272, 273, 287, 288
Lipsky, Michael, **4:** 27; **5:** 157; **6:** 277, 305
Lipson, Leon, **3:** 218, 225, 342; **8:** 429, 431
Liska, Allen E., **7:** 296, 299, 301
Liska, George, **8:** 364
List, Friedrich, **8:** 77
Litigation, **3:** 30
Litt, Edgar, **2:** 202
Little, Graham, **2:** 38
Little, I. M. D., **2:** 329
Litwack, Leon F., **6:** 263
Livingston, William S., **5:** 103, 105, 106, 112
Llewellyn, Karl N., **5:** 339, 343
Lobbyists, **4:** 205–206, 209–213
Lockard, Duane, **4:** 243; **6:** 214, 223, 246, 276, 290, 291
Locke, Don, **1:** 166
Locke, John, **1:** 12, 230, 231, 241, 246, 248, 249, 252, 260, 264, 316; **5:** 31, 32, 34, 36, 63, 64, 65, 68, 74, 75, 87, 178
Lockwood, Lee, **3:** 366
Loewenberg, Gerhard, **2:** 163; **3:** 254; **5:** 184, 198, 199, 200, 237, 238, 263, 293, 303, 308, 309
Loewenstein, Karl, **5:** 177
Loewenstein, Louis K., **6:** 309
Logic of causation, **7:** 210–211
Logic of discovery, **7:** 211
Logic of verification, **7:** 211–213
Logical empiricism, **1:** 141
Logistic curve, **7:** 421
Logrolling, **3:** 444, 445, 470
Lonergan, Bernard J., **1:** 260
Long, Norton, **5:** 390, 424, 428; **6:** 205
Longitudinal studies, **2:** 128–130

Lopreato, Joseph, **2:** 131
Lopukhov, Boris R., **3:** 321, 369
Lord, Frederick M., **7:** 156
Lorenz curve, **8:** 104–105
Lorwin, Val R., **3:** 156, 171, 172; **5:** 295; **7:** 67
Lottery, use of in Athens, **5:** 273
Lotz, Joergen, **6:** 76
Louch, A. R., **1:** 295, 296
Louis Harris Political Data Center, **7:** 50
Lovejoy, Arthur O., **5:** 1
Lovrich, Nicholas P., Jr., **6:** 349
Lowe, K., **8:** 190
Lowell, A. Lawrence, **4:** 263
Lowenfeld, Andreas F., **8:** 422
Lowenthal, Abraham F., **3:** 367
Lowenthal, David, **5:** 126
Lowenthal, Leo, **2:** 46
Lowenthal, Richard, **3:** 341
Lowi, Theodore J., **2:** 247, 248, 252, 278, 279,
    280, 282, 283, 284, 285, 299, 300, 301, 302,
    303, 309, 310, 311, 312, 352; **4:** 221–222,
    223; **5:** 402, 409, 410, 425; **6:** 113, 167, 169,
    210, 383, 397; **7:** 97
  arenas of power typology, **2:** 247, 278–279,
    301–303
  on constraints on group activity, **2:** 283
  ethical view of American politics, **2:** 281
  as a group theorist, **2:** 279–282
  and judicial democracy, **2:** 283–284
  major political change, account of, **2:** 299–
    301
  on political process, **2:** 282
  on social movements, **2:** 284–285
  on stability-disruption-protest model, **2:** 280
Loyalties, ethnic and national, **3:** 599–616
  and racism, **3:** 606–607
Lubell, Samuel, **2:** 308
Lublinskaya, A. D., **3:** 542
Lubove, Roy, **6:** 220, 221
Luce, R. Duncan, **1:** 346; **2:** 321, 323, 335, 337,
    342; **3:** 424, 437, 438, 446, 456, 457, 458,
    464, 470; **5:** 307; **7:** 146, 182, 375, 379, 382,
    395, 396, 397, 398; **8:** 343
Lucena, Manuel, **3:** 289, 366
Luckman, Thomas, **1:** 216
Ludendorff, Erich, **3:** 177
Ludz, Peter Christian, **2:** 232; **3:** 344, 349
Lukács, Georg, **3:** 319, 363
Lumpenproletariat, **3:** 610–611
Lundberg, George A., **2:** 265
Luria, Z., **7:** 83
Lurie, Irene, **6:** 197, 198

Luther, Martin, **1:** 234
Luttbeg, Norman R., **4:** 158, 202; **7:** 286
Lyden, Fremont J., **6:** 444
Lynching, **6:** 260
Lyons, Gene, **6:** 465; **8:** 326
Lyons, Morgan, **6:** 463
Lyons, Schley R., **2:** 107, 108, 115
Lysenko affair, **6:** 99–100

Maass, Arthur, **5:** 141
Mabileau, Albert, **3:** 362
Mabry, Donald J., **3:** 358
Macartney, C. A., **3:** 286
Maccoby, E., **2:** 126, 127
MacCrimmon, K. R., **2:** 341, 354; **3:** 442
MacFarquhar, Roderick, **3:** 358
MacGaffey, Wyatt, **3:** 366
"Mach" scale, **2:** 50
Machiavelli, **1:** 12, 13, 230, 231, 236, 241, 246,
    248, 249, 252, 255, 260, 261, 264, 316; **8:** 2,
    34, 35, 77
Machine politics, **3:** 325
Machlup, Fritz, **6:** 14, 16
MacInnis, Donald E., **3:** 359
MacIntyre, Alasdair, **1:** 175, 217
MacIver, Robert M., **4:** 175
Mack, Ruth P., **6:** 16
Mackenzie, H. C., **7:** 302
Mackenzie, William J. M., **1:** 4, 38; **2:** 249, 262,
    307
Mackie, Thomas T., **7:** 67
Mackintosh, John P., **5:** 124, 157, 195, 198,
    200, 205, 208, 211, 214, 217, 219, 226, 227,
    228, 231, 232, 291
Maclear, Anne Bush, **5:** 269, 271
Macmahon, Arthur W., **6:** 402
Macpherson, Crawford B., **1:** 381
MacRae, Duncan, **3:** 617; **4:** 161, 162, 262; **5:**
    189, 195, 237; **7:** 159, 383
Macridis, Roy C., **4:** 172, 196; **6:** 382, 384; **7:** 82,
    83
Macroeconomic policy, **6:** 37–41
Macropolitics, **7:** 134
Madden, E. H., **1:** 216; **7:** 214, 216
Maddox, Robert James, **6:** 399
Madgwick, P. J., **5:** 231
Madison, James, **2:** 273
Magdoff, Harry, **8:** 24, 77, 228, 367
Maghreb, societies of, **3:** 255, 257, 321
Magistracies, **5:** 42
Magna Charta, **5:** 47
Maguire, Thomas O., **6:** 455, 467

Mahood, H. R., **2:** 307
Mahrer, Alvin R., **2:** 45
Mair, L. P., **3:** 83, 364
Maitland, Frederick W., **5:** 24, 29, 30, 32, 33, 45, 48, 87
Majority Decision, Method of (MMD), **3:** 425–426, 429–430, 431, 433, 438
Majority government, **5:** 235–237
Majority rule, **1:** 363–364, 383; **3:** 331, 427–444, 453, 454, 467: **7:** 368–373, 374
    multi-stage, **3:** 433–434, 436, 467
    Pareto-inclusive strict, **3:** 432, 433, 436
    strict, **3:** 432, 436, 438, 439
Majority winner, **7:** 369, 370
Majumdar, Tapas, **3:** 414, 461
Malaya, federalism of, **5:** 124
Malefakis, Edward E., **3:** 364
Malinowski, B., **7:** 118, 119
Malloy, James, **3:** 312
Malmgren, Harold B., **6:** 407; **8:** 392
Maloney, Joan, **3:** 366
Man, **1:** 238, 239–243, 245, 246, 248, 249, 253, 255, 257
    mature man, **1:** 240, 245
    political man, **1:** 242
Management science, **2:** 336
Mandelbaum, Maurice, **1:** 299, 302
Mandlebaum, David G., **2:** 34
Manis, Jerome G., **2:** 23
Manley, John, **5:** 234, 303, 308, 419; **6:** 212
Mann, Dean E., **5:** 183, 197, 202, 203
Mann, Irwin, **3:** 470; **7:** 396; **8:** 344
Mann, Leona, **7:** 235
Mannheim, Karl, **2:** 352
Manning, Thomas G., **6:** 83
Mannoni, O., **3:** 29
Manoïlesco, Mihail, **3:** 199, 306, 361
Manpower Development and Training Act, **6:** 132
Mansfield, Edwin, **6:** 87; **8:** 323
Mansilla, H. C. F., **3:** 320
Manuel, Allen D., **5:** 150
Manuscript collections, **7:** 27–28, 34–38
Manvel, Allen D., **6:** 77
Manzella, Andrea, **5:** 294
Mao Tse-tung, **3:** 219, 227, 342, 347, 360, 361, 366, 504; **8:** 77, 211, 302
"Map for the Analysis of Personality and Politics," **2:** 5
Marando, Vincent L., **6:** 343
Maranell, Gary M., **7:** 305
Maranini, Giuseppe, **3:** 170
Marascuilo, Leonard A., **6:** 467

March, James G., **1:** 285, 344; **2:** 319, 320, 322, 323, 349; **5:** 303, 429; **6:** 400, 403, 440
Marchetti, Victor, **6:** 406; **8:** 329
Marcus, George E., **2:** 213
Marcus, Grace F., **6:** 121
Marcuse, Herbert, **1:** 250, 259, 274, 327; **2:** 31; **3:** 242
Margenau, Henry, **7:** 211
Marginal rates of substitution, **1:** 353; **8:** 155
Marias, Julian, **7:** 17
Marine, Gene, **6:** 297
Marini, Frank, **1:** 114; **5:** 428
Maritain, Jacques, **1:** 249
Markov models, **8:** 130, 134
Markowitz, Harry, **3:** 446
Marks, Eli S., **7:** 298
Marks, John, **6:** 406; **8:** 329
Marmor, Theodore, **6:** 85, 151, 153, 200, 201, 448; **7:** 321
Marris, Peter, **6:** 168, 172, 221, 222, 351
Marschak, Jacob, **3:** 446, 448
Marsh, David, **2:** 96, 136, 137
Marshall, Andrew W., **7:** 54; **8:** 323
Marshall, Charles Burton, **6:** 408
Marshall, T. H., **3:** 148, 619; **4:** 3; **6:** 184, 211
Martin, Jane R., **1:** 217
Martin, Norman H., **5:** 183
Martin, P. C., **5:** 112
Martin, Robert E., **2:** 202
Martin, Roscoe, **5:** 149
Martinez-Alier, Verena, **3:** 24
Maruyama, Masao, **3:** 233, 315
Marvick, David, **6:** 221, 222
Marvick, Dwaine, **2:** 155, 180, 189, 196, 234
Marx, Karl, **1:** 12, 14–15, 230, 234, 235, 236, 239, 243, 247, 248, 250, 252, 254, 260, 261, 265, 275, 276, 381; **3:** 197, 234, 235, 236, 251, 290, 314, 362, 366, 525; **8:** 20, 31, 400
Marxism, **1:** 380; **3:** 235
Maschler, Michael, **7:** 395, 399
Maser, Werner, **3:** 362
Masland, John W., **8:** 326
Maslow, Abraham H., **2:** 75, 168, 212, 217, 233
Mason, Philip, **3:** 67; **6:** 246
Mason, T. W., **3:** 232
Masonry, **3:** 316
Masotti, Louis H., **6:** 327
Mass communications, **2:** 131
Massell, Gregory J., **6:** 287
Massing, Paul W., **3:** 316, 363
"Massive Retaliation" policy, **8:** 286–288, 289, 290, 292, 305
    and Eisenhower administration, **8:** 286

Masterman, Margaret, **1:** 141, 216
Masters, Nicholas A., **5:** 287
Materialism, **5:** 43
Mathiason, John R., **3:** 36
Matossian, Mary, **3:** 250
Matthews, Donald R., **2:** 162, 179, 182, 184, 205; **4:** 3, 162; **5:** 183, 184, 192, 308; **6:** 296
Matthews, Donald W., **6:** 296
Matthews, R. E., **2:** 126, 127
Matthews, Robert O., **3:** 89
Matthias, Erich, **3:** 248
Mau, Hermann, **3:** 216, 220
Maximin strategy, **7:** 381
Maxwell, A. E., **7:** 156
Maxwell, Grover, **1:** 216
Maxwell, James A., **5:** 149
May, Ernest R., **5:** 223; **6:** 399, 407, 414; **8:** 276, 347
May, John D., **3:** 350, 353, 363; **4:** 250
May, Kenneth O., **1:** 341; **3:** 421, 422, 425, 435, 437
May, R. J., **5:** 148, 150
Mayer, Jacob P., **1:** 14
Mayer, Lawrence, **5:** 142; **6:** 387
Mayer, Robert R., **6:** 205
Mayntz, Renate, **2:** 196
Mayo, Louis H., **6:** 15
Mazauric, Claude, **3:** 542
Mazlish, Bruce, **2:** 75; **6:** 83
Mazmanian, Daniel A., **5:** 399
McAlister, John T., Jr., **3:** 21, 98
McAlister, Lyle N., **3:** 367
McCamy, James L., **6:** 402
McCarthy, Philip J., **7:** 298
McClelland, Charles, **6:** 387; **8:** 5, 63, 106
McClelland, David C., **2:** 62
McClelland, M., **7:** 119, 135
McCloskey, Herbert, **2:** 20, 51, 52, 53, 125, 134, 182; **3:** 613; **4:** 1, 5, 84; **5:** 266, 426; **6:** 389; **7:** 265, 300, 301, 302, 330, 331
McClure, Robert D., **7:** 276; **8:** 126, 127
McConahay, John B., **2:** 102, 107, 110, 115, 131, 134, 138, 139, 140, 141
McConaughy, John B., **2:** 214
McConnell, Grant, **2:** 247, 248, 249, 252, 272, 273, 274, 275, 276, 277, 278, 281, 282, 283, 289, 290, 291, 301, 309; **4:** 180, 183, 208, 210; **5:** 220, 226, 228, 229, 393, 409, 425
on constituency theory, **2:** 247, 276–278
ethical view of American politics, **2:** 274–275, 276–277
as a group theorist, **2:** 273
on public interest, **2:** 275

on regime norms, **2:** 275
on stability-disruption-protest model, **2:** 274
on subjective interest approach, **2:** 273–274
McCorkle, Lloyd W., **6:** 273
McCoy, Charles A., **1:** 114; **7:** 330
McCrone, Donald J., **2:** 106, 112, 113, 115, 120, 124, 140; **3:** 5, 65; **4:** 2, 32, 33; **6:** 223
McCurdy, Howard E., **5:** 429
McDermott, John, **6:** 86
McDonald, Ronald H., **3:** 365
McDougal, M. S., **6:** 11, 14; **8:** 430
McFarland, Andrew S., **2:** 307; **5:** 214
McGarvey, Patrick J., **6:** 406; **8:** 329
McGowan, Patrick J., **6:** 382, 398
McGuire, William, **2:** 16, 130; **7:** 274
McIlwain, Charles H., **5:** 2, 3, 6, 24, 26, 28, 29, 32, 33, 34, 35, 36, 58, 66, 87
McKean, Roland, **2:** 359; **6:** 81, 96; **8:** 323, 344
McKenzie, R. T., **5:** 184, 195
McKenzie, Robert, **4:** 245, 251, 256, 268
McKinnon, Victor S., **5:** 145
McLemore, S. Dale, **2:** 75; **7:** 306
McMurty, C. Allen, **2:** 133
McNamara, Robert S., **8:** 346
McNeill, William H., **1:** 5
McPhail, C., **2:** 141
McPhee, John, **8:** 333
McPhee, William N., **4:** 3, 7, 159, 248; **7:** 302, 332, 335
McRae, Kenneth D., **3:** 331
McWhinney, E. W., **5:** 145
Mead, Margaret, **2:** 61
Meaning, openness of, **1:** 309
Meaning of action, **1:** 178, 180, 191, 207
Meaning structures, **7:** 157, 190
Means, Gardiner C., **5:** 304, 410, 411
Measurement
of conflict of interest, **7:** 183–184
error in, **7:** 159
nonmetric, **7:** 167
representational, **7:** 157–167
structural, **7:** 159–165
by technique, **7:** 161
theory, **7:** 159
Mecham, J. Lloyd, **3:** 78; **5:** 112, 119
Mechanistic model, **2:** 358
Medawar, P. B., **5:** 244
Medhurst, Kenneth N., **3:** 367; **5:** 267
Media, effect on political attitude, **7:** 276, 328, 329
Mediation, **5:** 323–325, 328–333
Medicaid, **6:** 137–138, 143
Medvedev, Zhoros A., **3:** 358; **6:** 100

Meehan, Eugene J., **1:** 276–277
Meehl, Paul E., **1:** 220; **8:** 75
Meekison, J. Peter, **5:** 150, 151, 161
Megapolitics, **7:** 134
Mehr, Hjalmar, **6:** 344
Mehta, Usha, **5:** 150
Meier, Kenneth J., **7:** 276
Mein Kampf, **3:** 201, 212, 362
   changes in, **3:** 207
Meisel, James H., **1:** 393
Meldrum, James A., **4:** 161
Mellos, Koula, **7:** 383
Melman, Seymour, **5:** 375; **6:** 86, 417; **8:** 328
Melnik, Constantin, **5:** 184, 309
Melson, Robert, **3:** 13, 68, 84
Meltsner, Arnold J., **6:** 306, 330, 350, 357
Membership market, **4:** 196–197
Mendenhall, William, **7:** 252
Menges, Gunter, **2:** 321, 348
Menon, V. P., **5:** 123
Mental states, **1:** 299–300
Mentschikoff, Soia, **5:** 130
Mercantilism, **7:** 141
Mercantilist economy, **5:** 59
Merelman, Richard, **2:** 73; **4:** 248
Merkl, Peter H., **3:** 237, 317; **5:** 121, 140, 196
Merriam, Charles E., **1:** 47, 48–49, 252; **2:** 94;
   4: 112; **5:** 407
Merritt, Anna J., **7:** 315
Merritt, Richard L., **3:** 87, 97; **6:** 16; **7:** 54, 315
Merry, Henry J., **1:** 14
Merryman, John Henry, **5:** 339, 346
Merton, Robert K., **7:** 82, 328, 329, 333, 334
Mesa-Lago, Carmelo, **3:** 366
Mesarovich, Mihajlo D., **6:** 331
Messerschmidt, Manfred, **3:** 238
Messick, Richard E., **8:** 371
Messick, Samuel, **2:** 48
metastasis, **1:** 243, 250
Metatheory, **2:** 334, 347
Method artifacts, **7:** 222
"Methodism," **7:** 153
Methodological controversies, **7:** 147–153
   and issue of quantification, **7:** 139
   issues in, **7:** 147–148
Methodological holism, **1:** 299
Methodological individualism, **1:** 299
Methodological problems, **2:** 136
Methodology
   hermeneutical model, **1:** 133
   interpretive model of inquiry, **1:** 132, 133,
      135, 155, 175, 177, 206, 207

model of political and social inquiry, **1:** 132
   "naturalist" model, **1:** 132, 133, 155, 175,
      206, 207
   and political philosophy, **1:** 211–212
   "positivist" model, **1:** 132
   scientific model of inquiry, **1:** 134, 135
Metricization, **7:** 140
Mexican Porfiriato, **3:** 263
Mexico, political institutions in, **3:** 62–64
Meyer, Alfred G., **3:** 200, 236, 245, 246, 349,
   350, 370; **5:** 266
Meyerhoff, Hermann, **3:** 363
Meyers, Jerome L., **7:** 231
Meyerson, Martin, **6:** 467
Meynaud, J., **5:** 182
Meyriat, Jean, **7:** 66
Mezey, Michael L., **2:** 223, 224; **5:** 295
Micaud, Charles, **3:** 364, 365
Michelena, José A., **6:** 17
Michels, Robert, **2:** 264; **3:** 177, 206, 241, 358,
   364, 367; **4:** 201, 238, 268; **5:** 411; **7:** 118,
   119
Michigan model of proximal orientations, **4:**
   115–118
Mickiewicz, Ellen Propper, **3:** 204
Microeconomic policies, **6:** 42–44
   coordination of, **6:** 43
   role of economist in, **6:** 43
Micropolitics, **7:** 134
Middleton, John, **3:** 364
Middleton, Margaret R., **2:** 118
Middleton, R., **2:** 123, 126
Midlarsky, Manus, **8:** 371
Migratory farm workers, **6:** 279–280
Miguel, Amando de, **2:** 185
Mikulak, Robert, **6:** 98
Mikulas, William L., **2:** 75
Milbrath, Lester W., **2:** 137, 162; **3:** 33, 35, 40;
   4: 1, 5, 7, 27, 32–33, 46, 205, 206, 211; **6:**
   413
Milenkovitch, Deborah, **3:** 346
Miles, Rufus E., Jr., **6:** 208
Milgram, Stanley, **2:** 20
Militants, **3:** 565, 568
Militarism, **2:** 65
Military authority in totalitarian systems, **3:**
   189–190, 211
Military coups, **3:** 10, 298, 299, 325, 355, 539,
   569, 576
   Latin American palace, **3:** 493
   public opinion and, **3:** 304–305
   success of, **3:** 304

in Third World, 3: 321–322
Military expenditures, 8: 254–255, 328, 334, 335–336
Military forces, control of, 3: 538
Military history, United States, 8: 252–253
Military-industrial complex, 5: 4, 375, 395; 6: 86–87; 8: 264, 326, 327
Military intervention in politics, 3: 301–306
  moderating pattern, 3: 303–304, 305
Military powers, major, 8: 255, 275
Military professionalism, 3: 305
Military regimes, 3: 65, 186, 275
  national security doctrines in, 3: 297
Military rule
  attentivism, 3: 303
  civilian control of, 3: 303
  foreign influences on, 3: 302
  models of, 3: 303
  stages in, 3: 302
Military science, 8: 251
Military technology, 8: 258, 262, 264–265, 268
  major sources of, 8: 274
  proliferation of exotic "conventional" technology, 8: 333–335
  technological uncertainty, 8: 258
  United States–Soviet competition in, 8: 273–274
  worldwide technological competition in, 8: 274–275
Mill, John Stuart, 1: 12, 14, 135; 4: 4; 5: 258, 281, 282, 411; 7: 220, 221, 223
Miller, Arthur H., 2: 110, 140; 4: 147, 162
Miller, Arthur R., 7: 61, 65, 278
Miller, Arthur S., 5: 36
Miller, Delbert, 7: 306
Miller, Ernest G., 6: 444
Miller, Herman P., 6: 223
Miller, Howard S., 6: 82
Miller, J. D. B., 5: 135
Miller, Loren, 6: 275
Miller, S. M., 6: 185
Miller, Warren E., 1: 231; 2: 9, 49, 103, 124, 125, 127, 131, 134, 137, 184, 332; 4: 60, 64, 85, 90, 94, 98, 99, 100, 113, 133, 147, 149, 150, 152, 153, 154, 157, 158, 159, 160, 162, 248; 7: 45, 47, 146, 218, 277, 286
Miller, William, 2: 206
Millett, John H., 4: 213
Milliken, Max, 6: 15
Mills, C. Wright, 2: 273; 3: 67, 81, 246, 370; 5: 388
Mills, Harvey, 2: 179, 320, 322

Milne, R. S., 3: 255; 5: 206; 7: 302
Milstein, Jeffrey S., 7: 179
Milward, Alan S., 3: 232
Minar, David W., 6: 335
Miner, Horace, 6: 313, 334
Mineral resources, dependence of industrial world on, 8: 249–250, 255
Minimal winning coalition, 5: 137
Minimax, 1: 364–365
Minimax strategy, 7: 381
Minimax theorem, 7: 382–383
Minimum deterrence, 8: 299–300
Ministerial responsibility, collective, 5: 6, 197
Ministers, recruitment of, 5: 196–205
  in Australia and New Zealand, 5: 197
  tenure and turnover, 5: 203–204
Minnesota Data Archive, 7: 50
Minnesota Multiphasic Personality Inventory, 2: 26
Minority governments, 5: 189, 198
Mintz, Morton, 5: 400
MINUTEMAN program, 8: 296, 297, 308
MIRV (Multiple Independently-targetable Re-entry Vehicle), 8: 269, 308–309
Mischel, Walter, 2: 17, 133, 137, 140, 141
Mishan, E. J., 6: 76
Mishkin, Saul J., 5: 348
Missile accuracy, 8: 257
"Missile gap," 8: 294–295, 296
Mitchell, Edward J., 1: 187
Mitscherlich, Alexander, 2: 31, 230
Mixed government, 5: 43, 64
Mixed-state doctrine, 5: 33, 34
  and the separation of powers, 5: 41–44
Mobilization
  defensive, 3: 528
  limitations on, 3: 504
  organizational structure limiting, 3: 505
  power contention and, 3: 503–506
Mobilization model, 4: 33
Mobilization system, 3: 31–32, 357–358, 569
Mobocracy, 5: 41, 43
Model
  "parity-fluidity," 8: 13
  "preponderance-stability," 8: 13
  as a representation of reality, 8: 8
  as a representation of theory, 8: 9
  state-centric, 8: 9
Model Cities program, 6: 133, 146, 166, 177–178, 181
Model platonism, 7: 152, 153
Models of man, 1: 192–195, 204, 208, 209, 210

Models for study of political recruitment, **2:** 171–177
Modelski, George, **6:** 389
Modern political man, **3:** 27–29
Modern political systems, **3:** 47
Modernization, of South America, **3:** 295
Modernization theory, limits of, **6:** 334
Mogi, Sobei, **5:** 94, 160
Moira, concept of, **5:** 15
Mokken, Robert J., **7:** 161
Molleman, Henk, **4:** 13, 16
Monarchial constitution, **5:** 68
Monarchial presidency, **5:** 37
Monarchy, mixed, **5:** 35, 41
Monetary policy, **6:** 41–42, 47–49; **8:** 386
Money and credit, **6:** 47–49
Money-Kyrle, Roger E., **2:** 31
Monnet, Jean, **8:** 395
Monroe, Michael J., **6:** 332
Montagu, Ashley, **6:** 243, 279
Montegranesi society, **1:** 173
Montesquieu, **1:** 13, 14, 230, 325
Montgomery, John D., **3:** 97, 186
Montgomery, William D., **5:** 429
Montgomery Bus Boycott, **2:** 290–292, 295–296, 301
Montgomery Improvement Association, **2:** 291
Montias, John Michael, **3:** 347, 348
Montross, Lynn, **8:** 341
Monypenny, Philip, **2:** 307
Moon, Bruce E., **6:** 418
Moon, J. Donald, **7:** 140, 142, 143, 149, 168, 169, 180, 184, 189, 196, 197, 201, 330
Moore, Barrington, Jr., **1:** 274, 345; **3:** 3, 12, 227, 242, 251, 252, 298, 370, 496, 497, 532, 539, 543, 544; **8:** 40
Moore, Clement H., **3:** 54, 180, 274, 365, 369
Moore, David W., **6:** 418; **8:** 99
Moore, Wilbur E., **6:** 206
Moos, Malcolm, **5:** 183
Moral principles, **1:** 315, 316
Moralism, **8:** 422–424
More, Sir Thomas, **1:** 244
Morehouse, Sarah M., **6:** 223
Morey, Roy D., **6:** 467
Morgan, James N., **6:** 130; **7:** 324
Morgan, Lewis Henry, **5:** 94
Morgenstern, Oskar, **2:** 336, 346; **3:** 446, 447, 448, 449, 450, 451, 458; **7:** 382, 389, 399; **8:** 343

Morgenthau, Hans J., **1:** 252; **6:** 389; **8:** 35, 36, 38, 39, 58, 69, 89, 91, 199, 200, 201, 202, 203, 363, 399
Moriyama, Iwao M., **7:** 323
Morley, Felix, **5:** 157
Mörner, Magnus, **3:** 69
Morocco, monarchy in, **3:** 255–258
Morris, Alfred, **5:** 236
Morris, Clarence, **5:** 348
Morris, Cynthia Taft, **3:** 13, 62, 171
Morris, Ivan, **3:** 233, 315
Morris, Robert, **6:** 349
Morrison, Donald George, **3:** 325
Morrison of Lambeth, Lord (Herbert Morrison), **5:** 211, 214, 219
Morse, Arthur D., **6:** 260
Morse, Edward L., **6:** 381, 382, 384, 411, 419; **8:** 390
Morse, P. M., **8:** 344
Morse, Richard M., **3:** 24, 30
Morsey, Rudolf, **3:** 248
Morss, Elliott, **6:** 330
Morton, A. S., **2:** 126, 127
Mosca, Gaetano, **2:** 178; **5:** 4, 25, 28, 29, 411
Mosca's theory of the ruling class, **2:** 177
Moscow trials, **3:** 223
Moser, C. A., **6:** 327
Moses, Bernard, **1:** 38
Moses, E., **7:** 179
Mosher, Frederick C., **6:** 409
Moskos, Charles C., Jr., **8:** 326
Mosley, R. K., **5:** 194, 224
Moss, Howard A., **7:** 11
Mossawir, Harve, **3:** 363
Mosse, George L., **3:** 235, 315, 316, 319, 358, 363
Mossin, Jan, **2:** 336
Mosteller, Frederick, **6:** 467; **7:** 3, 142, 146, 283, 298, 321, 322
Mote, Max E., **3:** 362
Mousnier, Roland, **3:** 542
Moy, Roland F., **3:** 252
Moynihan, Daniel P., **6:** 114, 149, 150, 152, 153, 154, 158, 163, 168, 169, 171, 184, 189, 215, 221, 284, 307, 335, 467; **7:** 320, 321, 322
MPO ratio, **6:** 343
Mueller, John E., **2:** 103, 104, 115, 116; **5:** 225; **6:** 413; **7:** 282, 325; **8:** 221
Muir, William K., Jr., **2:** 271

Mukerjee, Tapan, **8:** 76
Muller, Edward N., **3:** 8
Muller, Steven, **5:** 135, 136
Multibureaucratic decisionmaking, **8:** 398
Multicollinearity, **7:** 215
Multidimensional scaling, **7:** 164, 176–177, 179
Multiethnic democracies without consensus, **3:** 330–332
Multinational corporations, **5:** 373; **8:** 391, 398
Multinational state, **3:** 330
Multiparty systems, choice of leaders in, **5:** 187
Multiple regression, **7:** 215; **8:** 130
Multiple sovereignty, **3:** 519, 520, 521, 522, 523, 527, 530, 533, 542
Multipolarity, **8:** 204, 213, 214, 215, 222, 223, 230
Multivariate estimation procedures, **7:** 215
Mumford, Lewis, **6:** 86, 361
Mundel, David S., **7:** 146
Municipal budgets, **6:** 356
Municipio, **6:** 312
Murakami, Yasusuke, **3:** 421, 424, 434, 435, 467
Murdock, Clark A., **8:** 348
Murphy, Russell D., **6:** 343
Murphy, Walter F., **2:** 116; **5:** 321
Murray, Henry A., **2:** 13, 30, 31
Mus, Paul, **3:** 21, 98
Musgrave, Alan, **2:** 359; **8:** 377
Musgrave, Richard A., **6:** 333
Mushkin, Selma J., **6:** 357
Mutchler, David E., **3:** 78
Mutual veto, **3:** 133–134
Myrdal, Gunnar, **1:** 338; **2:** 106; **6:** 184, 332, 335
Myth, **1:** 234, 248

Nadel, Mark V., **5:** 392, 410, 421
Nadel, S. F., **8:** 39, 46, 78
Nader, Ralph, **5:** 407
Nagel, Ernest, **1:** 138, 139, 140, 216, 284, 315; **7:** 211, 221, 397; **8:** 3, 11, 75, 76
Nagy-Talavera, Nicholas M., **3:** 231, 290
Nakane, Chie, **3:** 96
Namenwirth, Gvi, **6:** 11
Namier, Lewis, **5:** 278, 281, 306
Napoleonic Wars, **8:** 261–262
Nardin, Terry, **3:** 513; **6:** 87
Narroll, Raoul, **7:** 54
Nash, Gerald D., **6:** 83

Nash, John F., **3:** 419, 455, 456, 457, 458, 464, 470; **7:** 386, 395
Nash bargaining solution, **7:** 395
Nash equilibrium point, **7:** 385–386, 392, 395
Natanson, Maurice, **1:** 216
Nathan, N. M. L., **1:** 384
Nathan, Richard P., **5:** 150; **6:** 77
Nation building, **3:** 322–323
National Academy of Sciences, **6:** 86, 97, 100
National Advisory Commission on Civil Disorders, **6:** 268
National Aeronautics and Space Administration, **5:** 393; **8:** 273
National Archives and Records Service, **7:** 63, 65
National Assembly, French, members of, **5:** 199, 237–238
National Association for the Advancement of Colored People (NAACP), **6:** 260, 290, 291, 293; **7:** 326
National Association of Real Estate Boards Code of Ethics, **6:** 269–270
National Association of Social Workers, **6:** 119, 125, 165
National character, **2:** 36
    modal personality, **2:** 60
    studies of, **7:** 288–289
National Commission on Technology, Automation, and Economic Progress, **6:** 283
National Committee against Discrimination in Housing, **6:** 274
"National data center," **7:** 66
National front governments, **3:** 335
National identity, **3:** 14, 29, 32
National interests, **8:** 249
    of the United States, **8:** 249
    and values, **8:** 249
National Journal Reports, **7:** 23
National Labor Relations Board, **5:** 400
National liberation, **8:** 423–424
National Liberation Council of Ghana, **5:** 264
National Opinion Research Center, **7:** 50, 284, 296, 312, 324
National Science Foundation, **6:** 86
National security
    as an ambiguous symbol, **8:** 250
    decision making for, **8:** 321–324
    national interests, **8:** 249
    organization for, **8:** 321–324
    original sense of citizen protection, **8:** 248

as preservation of reigning political structure, **8:** 248
primacy of, **8:** 247–252, 256
and the "security dilemma," **8:** 250
and sources of insecurity, **8:** 250
and values, **8:** 249
National Security Act, **8:** 277
National security affairs, **8:** 251, 256–260
and Congress, **8:** 281
contemporary context of, **8:** 268–275
developing context of, **8:** 260–268
evolution of, **8:** 275–313
first phase, **8:** 282, 287
second phase, **8:** 303–304
and technology, **8:** 256–257, 266
topic areas of, major, **8:** 314–335
National Security Council, **5:** 378, 417; **6:** 405, 422; **8:** 277, 281, 323
National security "culture," **8:** 324–330
National security, United States, **8:** 252–256
during the 1950s, **8:** 281–296
during the early 1960s, **8:** 296–305
in the 1960s and early 1970s, **8:** 305–313
post-World War II, **8:** 276–281
National Socialism, **3:** 319, 368
National Technical Information Service, **7:** 63
National urban policy
measures of international differences in, **6:** 314–315
polar variables in, **6:** 314
National Welfare Rights Organization, **6:** 141, 149, 212
Nationalism, **3:** 295, 331–332, 599–616; **8:** 202, 203, 205, 226
Nationalsozialistische Deutsche Arbeiterpartei (NSDAP), **3:** 200, 201, 203, 211, 324, 351
Nation-state, **8:** 73
NATO, **8:** 251–252, 258, 290, 299, 331, 373
creation of, **8:** 278
evolution of, **8:** 282, 302
and SALT, **8:** 331
Natural law, **5:** 1, 7–8, 9, 17, 19–20, 23–24, 32, 36, 37, 44, 75, 76, 81
obligations of, **5:** 8
Naturalism, **1:** 319
Nazi Germany, **4:** 232
Nazism, **3:** 207–208, 231, 235–236, 252, 608–609
conflict with Christianity, **3:** 317
feudal characteristics of, **3:** 237
foreign policy, **3:** 359

ideological roots, **3:** 363
Neal, Fred W., **3:** 346
Neale, J. E., **5:** 306, 307
Needleman, Carolyn, **3:** 358
Needleman, Martin, **3:** 358
Needler, Martin C., **3:** 3, 9, 10, 358, 365, 367; **4:** 2; **5:** 305
Nef, John U., **8:** 341
Negandhi, Anant R., **2:** 319, 320
Negative income tax, **6:** 60, 151, 216–219
Negro Front, **3:** 71–72
Neisser, Ulric, **2:** 11
Nelson, Joan M., **3:** 6, 66, 97, 486; **6:** 349, 358
Nelson, Richard R., **6:** 16, 99
Nelson, Stephen D., **8:** 341, 347
Nelson, William R., **6:** 93
Neoclassical liberalism, **5:** 25
Neofascism, **3:** 236
Neofunctionalism, **8:** 383–384
Nerlove, Sara B., **7:** 156, 167
Nesbitt, Paul D., **7:** 235
Nesselroade, John R., **2:** 129
Nesvold, Betty A., **3:** 8, 9
Netherlands, federalism of, **5:** 95, 100, 117–118
Netherlands Social and Economic Council, **5:** 403, 404
Nettl, J. P., **3:** 503; **4:** 2; **6:** 223
Neubauer, Deane F., **1:** 313; **3:** 6, 171, 363; **4:** 33
Neumann, Franz, **3:** 188, 318, 321, 334, 361, 363, 368; **4:** 232; **5:** 157
Neumann, Sigmund, **3:** 187, 195, 364; **4:** 237
Neurath, Otto, **1:** 174
Neustadt, Richard E., **2:** 74; **5:** 110, 208, 209, 211, 213, 215, 216, 217, 219, 220, 221, 222, 223, 224, 225, 226, 227, 229, 230, 234, 243, 375, 378, 417; **6:** 384, 404, 409, 418; **8:** 231, 324, 331, 399
Neutralism, **8:** 155, 160
New Deal, **1:** 50–51
New Jersey income-maintenance experiment, **6:** 457
"New politics," **2:** 165
New York Mayor's Advisory Panel on Decentralization of the New York City Schools, **6:** 294
New York Times, **6:** 266, 268, 275, 276, 468; **8:** 338, 348
New Zealand, federalism of, **5:** 120
Newcomb, Theodore M., **2:** 127, 128, 130, 131
Newell, Allan, **2:** 320
Newhouse, John, **6:** 396; **8:** 331, 347

Newing, R. A., **3**: 439
Newman, J. R., **7**: 116
Newton, Isaac, **7**: 213; **8**: 3, 17, 23
Newton, Kenneth, **6**: 349
Nicholas, Ralph W., **5**: 305
Nichols, David, **6**: 95
Nichols, Lee, **7**: 318
Nicholson, Michael, **3**: 428, 459
Nicholson, Norman K., **2**: 233
Nicholson, R. J., **6**: 321, 339, 342, 344, 362
Nicolaevsky, Boris I., **3**: 228
Nie, Norman, **2**: 95; **3**: 33, 34, 35, 36, 41, 97; **4**:
    6, 11, 13, 16, 17, 22, 32, 33, 34, 35, 39, 40,
    41, 42, 49, 50, 58, 62, 64, 66, 68, 70, 76, 77,
    91, 99, 101, 103, 104, 105, 107, 109, 118,
    126, 149, 150, 151, 152, 153, 154, 155, 158,
    159, 162; **7**: 286, 296
Nieberg, Harold L., **6**: 86
Niebuhr, Reinhold, **8**: 343, 363
Niemi, Richard G., **2**: 95, 102, 106, 107, 108,
    119, 120, 123, 124, 125, 126, 127, 128, 129,
    132, 138; **3**: 428, 470; **4**: 144, 162; **7**: 278,
    302
Nigerian Labor party, **3**: 83–84
    traditional, **3**: 286
Nimmo, Dan, **7**: 248
Nisbet, Robert A., **6**: 17, 169
Niskanen, William A., **5**: 422, 423, 427
Nitze, Paul H., **8**: 281, 284, 343
Nixon, Charles R., **2**: 180, 189, 196
Nixon, Richard, **2**: 32, 40
Noakes, Jeremy, **3**: 368
Noel, Robert, **7**: 225, 241, 246
Noelle-Neumann, Elisabeth, **7**: 295
Noetic thought, **1**: 256
Nogee, Joseph L., **8**: 278, 345
Noll, Roger, **5**: 407
Nolte, Ernst, **1**: 380; **3**: 235, 315, 316, 319, 368,
    369
Non-attitudes, **2**: 121
Noncausal formalisms, **7**: 190
Non-decision making, **5**: 384–385
Nondecisions, **2**: 352
Nondemocratic regimes
    conditions for in modern societies, **3**: 247–
        251
    succession of leaders in, **3**: 360
    variety and prevalence of, **3**: 175–182
Noneconomic objectives of government policy
    alleviation of plight of disadvantaged
        groups, **6**: 35
    fair distribution of national income, **6**: 35

federal system, **6**: 35–36
free enterprise system, **6**: 36
national security, **6**: 35
Nonpartisan politics, **2**: 228, 229
Nonzero-sum game, **7**: 180–181
Nordlinger, Eric A., **3**: 14, 65, 85, 87, 88, 171,
    302; **4**: 245
Norling, Richard, **3**: 180, 352
Normalization, **7**: 183
Norman, H., **3**: 365
Normative order, **3**: 558
    creative principles of, **3**: 559
Normative political inquiry, **1**: 314–328
Normative resources, **3**: 503
Norris, Clarence, **5**: 328
North, Liisa, **3**: 367
North, Robert C., **1**: 186; **6**: 412; **7**: 248; **8**: 113,
    115, 116, 120, 121, 122, 123, 124, 127, 128,
    193
Northedge, F. S., **6**: 382
Northrop, F. S. C., **1**: 262; **5**: 75
Nossiter, T. S., **2**: 112, 113, 116
Notestein, Wallace, **5**: 308
Nourse, Edwin G., **6**: 24, 75
Nove, Alec, **3**: 228
Novick, David, **6**: 95; **8**: 292, 323
Novick, Melvin R., **7**: 156
Nozick, Robert, **1**: 212
NSC-68, **8**: 281–282, 286, 288, 305
NSDAP, Reichsorganisationsleiter, **3**: 361
Nuclear explosion, first by Soviet Union, **8**:
    281–282
Nuclear Nonproliferation Treaty, **8**: 222–223,
    301–302, 332, 333
Nuclear proliferation, **8**: 222–225, 230, 332–
    333
Nuclear war
    and China, **8**: 270
    controlled, **8**: 318–319
    and the Soviet Union, **8**: 269
Nuclear weapons, **8**: 199–201, 203–204, 207,
    210, 212, 214, 219, 220, 221, 233, 269,
    305–313, 317–321, 335–339
    atomic bomb, **8**: 199, 201, 208, 254
    effect of early United States monopoly of, **8**:
        279
    nonuse of to date, **8**: 269
    power of, **8**: 281
    proliferation of, **8**: 332–333
    strategic and tactical use of, **8**: 270
Nugent, Jan, **5**: 404
Null hypothesis, **7**: 124

Nun, José, **3:** 288, 367
Nuremberg judgments, **8:** 421
Nuremberg racial laws, **3:** 213
Nye, Joseph, **5:** 125; **8:** 73, 217, 227, 366, 368, 370, 371, 373, 375, 377, 378, 379, 380, 381, 383, 387, 391, 396, 399, 402
Nyomarkay, Joseph, **3:** 215, 239, 362

Oakeshott, Michael, **1:** 236, 273
Oates, Wallace E., **5:** 148, 149
Oberschall, Anthony, **7:** 324
Objective interest approach, **2:** 251–252, 263, 277, 295–297, 300, 301–303, 306–307
Objective probability, **2:** 344
Obligations, **1:** 371
Observation, **1:** 298; **7:** 216
Observer judgments about group interest, **2:** 251–252
O'Connell, D. P., **8:** 428, 429
O'Connor, Dennis M., **3:** 225
O'Connor, James, **8:** 76
October Revolution, **2:** 29; **3:** 524
Odegard, Peter H., **1:** 47; **2:** 245; **4:** 176, 209
O'Donnell, Guillermo, **3:** 293, 294, 295, 299, 300, 367
Odumosu, O. I., **5:** 124
Office of Economic Opportunity, **5:** 425; **6:** 44, 73, 457
Office of Management and Budget, **5:** 403, 404, 416; **6:** 24, 38, 39, 40
Office of Science and Technology, **6:** 91
Office of War Information, Surveys Division, **7:** 312
Official Language Commission, **5:** 151
Ogburn, William F., **1:** 46; **4:** 112, 159
Oglesby, Carl, **6:** 407
O'Hara, Rosemary, **2:** 182
Ohlin, Goran, **7:** 54
Ohlin, Lloyd, **6:** 221
Okamura, Tadao, **2:** 112
Okner, Benjamin A., **6:** 78
Okun, Arthur M., **6:** 75, 76, 77
O'Leary, Thomas J., **3:** 224
Oligarchic democracies, **3:** 265, 332
Oligarchy, **5:** 40
    competitive, **3:** 128
Oliver, F. R., **6:** 339, 344, 362
Olsen, John, **2:** 349
Olsen, Marvin E., **4:** 32
Olson, David J., **6:** 277

Olson, Mancur, Jr., **1:** 195, 200; **2:** 198, 248, 288, 289, 290; **3:** 465, 466, 467, 580; **4:** 7, 69, 182, 186, 189, 192, 195, 196; **5:** 143; **7:** 249, 250, 363; **8:** 66, 221
Olympianism, **5:** 13
Ombudsman, **2:** 333; **5:** 420–421
O'Neil, Robert P., **2:** 193
Ong, Walter J., **5:** 61
"Open Skies" proposal, **8:** 299
Open society, **1:** 233, 256, 258
"Operational code," **6:** 419–420
Operationalism, **1:** 293–294, 297–298, 299, 311–313
Operationalization, **8:** 91, 95, 99, 102, 103, 119, 120
Operations research, **2:** 336; **7:** 147; **8:** 291
Operative ideals, **1:** 176
Opinion formation, **4:** 79–83
Opinion poll, **3:** 558
Oppenheim, Felix E., **1:** 212, 217, 218, 273, 284, 287, 290, 300, 311, 314, 317, 319
Oppenheim, L., **8:** 424
Oppenheimer, Joe A., **2:** 248, 289; **4:** 193
Oppenheimer, Mary, **3:** 370
Opportunity set, **8:** 156, 159, 160
Opposition
    in authoritarian regimes, **3:** 271–273
    competitiveness, **3:** 162–163
    concentration, **3:** 161–162
    in Czechoslovakia, **3:** 126
    definition of, **3:** 116–117
    distinctiveness, **3:** 166
    goals, **3:** 166, 167
    in hegemonic regimes, **3:** 126–127
    in Japan, **3:** 126
    in polyarchies, **3:** 161–169
    and regimes, **3:** 117–133
    site for encounters with government, **3:** 163–165
    strategies, **3:** 166–169
    suppression of by governments, **3:** 137
    in Tanzania, **3:** 127
Opposition parties, influence of, **5:** 236
Optimal behavior, **7:** 358
Optimal-control theory, **8:** 191
Oral history, **7:** 37
Orbell, John M., **3:** 43
Ordeshook, Peter C., **1:** 202; **3:** 441, 442, 443, 444, 466, 468; **4:** 68, 113, 125, 160; **7:** 179, 354, 377, 384, 396, 398
Oren, Nissan, **3:** 221, 335, 344

Orfield, Gary, **6:** 292
Organic democracy, **3:** 184, 307
Organic model, **2:** 358
Organic statism, **3:** 281, 306–313
Organization of African Unity, **8:** 218
Organization costs, **2:** 288–289
Organization for Economic Cooperation and
   Development, **6:** 84, 98; **8:** 373, 390, 391
"Organization man," **5:** 83
Organization of Petroleum Exporting Coun-
   tries (OPEC), **8:** 250
Organization theory, **2:** 319, 320
Organizational behavior, **2:** 335, 361
Organizational conservatism, **2:** 300, 303
Organizational survival, **2:** 334
Organski, A. F. K., **3:** 357, 369; **8:** 37, 89, 91
Orlow, Dietrich, **3:** 201, 202, 203, 204, 207,
   209, 210, 211, 239, 361, 362, 368, 370
Ornati, Oscar, **6:** 184
Orr, Larry L., **6:** 222; **7:** 321
Orren, Karen K., **2:** 124; **5:** 410
Orum, Anthony M., **2:** 107, 108, 115; **3:** 35
Orvik, Nils, **6:** 407
Orwell, George, **3:** 619
Osanka, Franklin M., **8:** 346
Osborn, Robert, **6:** 335
Osgood, Charles E., **2:** 140; **7:** 83
Osgood, John Field, **6:** 323, 340, 341
Osgood, Robert E., **2:** 63; **8:** 199, 282, 321, 331,
   341, 345
OSIRIS III, **7:** 49–50
Osofsky, Gilbert, **6:** 269
Ostracism, **5:** 272
Ostrogorski, M., **4:** 238
Ostrom, Elinor, **5:** 151, 427; **6:** 463, 465
Ostrom, Vincent, **2:** 358; **5:** 151, 160, 427
Ozbudin, Ergun, **3:** 63; **4:** 259, 265

Pace v. *Alabama*, **6:** 272
Paci, Enzo, **1:** 250
Pacifist movements, **3:** 597
Packard, Vance, **6:** 413
Packenham, Robert A., **3:** 97; **5:** 267, 268, 303
Pacta servanda sunt, **5:** 8; **8:** 418, 428
Padgett, Vincent, **3:** 358
Page, Benjamin I., **4:** 68, 106, 126
Pahl, Ray E., **6:** 306, 349
Paige, Glenn D., **6:** 389, 399; **8:** 94, 231
Paige, Jeffrey M., **2:** 107, 110
Paine, Thomas, **1:** 398

Pakistan
   federalism of, **5:** 122–123
   political parties in, **3:** 80–81
Palamountain, Joseph C., Jr., **4:** 211
Palmer, David Scott, **3:** 312
Palumbo, Dennis, **2:** 323, 325, 337, 357, 359
Pammett, Jan H., **2:** 99, 106, 112, 115
Pantin, C. F. A., **8:** 69
Pap, Arthur, **1:** 290
Papal absolutism, **5:** 30–31
Papandreou, A. G., **3:** 437
Paradigmatic society, **1:** 243–248, 258
Paradox of voting, **7:** 373
Paramilitary organizations, **3:** 215–216,
   237–238
Paranzino, Dennis, **1:** 187
Parenti, Michael, **2:** 37
Parents, politically active, **2:** 189–190
Pareto, Vilfredo, **2:** 155
Pareto criterion, **2:** 330
   strict, **3:** 419–420, 426, 432, 438, 447, 448
   weak, **3:** 419, 427
Pareto-Extension Rule, **3:** 426, 433
Pareto optimality, **1:** 362–363, 365; **3:** 420; **7:**
   367
Parham, Iris A., **2:** 129
Parity in strategic power, **8:** 305, 306
Parkin, F., **4:** 211, 217
Parkinson, G. H. R., **1:** 289
Parliament, British, **5:** 185–186, 190, 199,
   282–283
   choice of party leader by, **5:** 185–186, 187
   private bills procedure of, **5:** 180
Parliament, Canadian, **5:** 190
Parliamentarianism, **5:** 29, 189
Parliamentary committees, **5:** 281
Parliamentary parties, **5:** 291–292
Parliamentary procedure, **5:** 270
Parry, Hugh J., **7:** 297
Parsimony, **7:** 89–90
Parsons, Talcott, **2:** 63, 70; **3:** 3, 619; **6:** 211, 223
Parten, Mildred, **7:** 268, 269, 271, 307
Partial goods, **1:** 371, 375
Participatory mechanisms, adequacy of, **4:** 4–5
Partisan attachment
   formation of, in the population, **3:** 569–571
   and party competition, **3:** 562–564
   utility of, **3:** 561–569
Partisan ideologies, **2:** 114–115
Partisan predispositions, **2:** 117–127
   childhood beginnings, **2:** 118

nationality, **2:** 118
parental transmission, **2:** 123–127
party identification in Europe, **2:** 120–121
party identification in United States, **2:** 119–120
racial attitudes, **2:** 118–119
social class, **2:** 119
strength of early party identification, **2:** 121–123
Partisanship, **2:** 105–106
Party affiliations, **4:** 49–50
Party of Color, **3:** 71
Party identification, **2:** 9, 119–121, 124, 137
Party leaders, British, **5:** 193
Party officials, relation to society, **3:** 205
Party organization, **2:** 166, 220
Party politics, internal **3:** 568–569
Party, relative strength of, **2:** 181, 220
Party support, social bases of, **4:** 53–55
Party system, **2:** 325
Pasanella, Anna K., **2:** 60
Pateman, Carole, **7:** 330
Path analysis, **2:** 27; **8:** 130, 131, 138
biometric, **7:** 154, 215
Patrimonial bureaucracy, **3:** 287
Patrimonial rule, **3:** 253, 256
Patronage, **3:** 263
Patron-client relations, **3:** 44–45
Pattanaik, Prasanta K., **3:** 415, 420, 421, 424, 430, 431, 432, 433, 436, 437, 438, 440, 452, 467
Patterson, James T., **5:** 148
Patterson, Samuel, **2:** 115, 116, 179, 180, 184, 189, 196, 197, 203, 204, 223, 225, 233; **4:** 205; **5:** 235, 287; **6:** 458, 467, 468
Patterson, Thomas E., **7:** 276
Patterson, William L., **6:** 260
Pauker, Guy J., **3:** 302, 367
Pavitt, Keith, **6:** 98
Paxton, Robert O., **3:** 368
Payne, James L., **2:** 75, 217, 218, 233; **3:** 78; **4:** 252; **6:** 395
Payne, Stanley G., **3:** 303, 367; **7:** 290
Payoff matrix, **2:** 338; **7:** 183
Peabody, Robert L., **5:** 286, 287, 288, 303, 408
Peace research, **8:** 315–316
Peaceful coexistence, **8:** 430–432
Peak, G. Wayne, **4:** 197
Peak, Helen, **7:** 313
Peak association, **4:** 187–188
Pear, R. H., **7:** 302
Peasant parties, **3:** 288

Peasant rebellions, **3:** 497–498
Peasantry and political development, **3:** 251–252
Pechman, Joseph A., **6:** 77, 78
Peck, Merton J., **6:** 88; **8:** 303, 323
Peel, Roy V., **4:** 249
Pegis, Anton C., **1:** 264
Pelczynski, Zbigniew, **3:** 362
Peltason, Jack W., **4:** 174
Pempel, T. J., **5:** 405
Pen, Jan, **3:** 459
Pendley, R. E., **7:** 241
Penniman, Howard R., **3:** 363
Pennock, J. Roland, **5:** 154
Pepper, Stephen C., **8:** 11, 78
Per capita income, **6:** 319
Perception, **2:** 7
Perelman, Chaim, **1:** 384
Perham, Margery, **3:** 254
periagogē, **1:** 239
Perillo, Joseph M., **5:** 339
Peripheralized governments, **5:** 102, 157
Perkins, Dexter, **6:** 413
Perlmutter, Amos, **3:** 367
Perlmutter, Arnold, **6:** 86
Perloff, H. S., **5:** 146, 147; **6:** 307, 351
Peronism, **3:** 292, 299
Perrow, Charles, **2:** 320, 322, 323, 325, 353
Perry, George L., **6:** 76
Perry, Robert L., **6:** 87, 89
Personality, **2:** 1, 11, 13
affect, **2:** 8, 15
aversive characteristics, **2:** 52
character formation, **2:** 39
cognitions, **2:** 8, 9, 12, 22, 26, 34, 60
cognitive balance, **2:** 15
cognitive styles, **2:** 11
conations, **2:** 8
conscious psychological orientations, **2:** 8, 9, 13, 22, 26
dynamics of, **2:** 41–42
ego, **2:** 10
ego defenses, **2:** 10, 11, 12, 13, 22–23, 34, 36, 42, 57, 59, 60, 63, 74
id, **2:** 10
ideological orientations, **2:** 52
isolationist attitudes, **2:** 52
mediation of self-other relations, **2:** 9–10, 22, 34, 73
political orientations, **2:** 13, 52
reference group identifications, **2:** 52
self-esteem, **2:** 53, 74

situational determinants, 2: 39, 73
social attitudes, 2: 52
superego, 2: 10, 73
syndromes, 2: 1
traits, 2: 1, 41, 59
unconscious forces, 2: 39
Personality and politics, 2: 1–92
  classification of the literature, 2: 30–31
  contingent connections, 2: 13, 16
  functional approach to study of, 2: 9, 11
  interactive connections, 2: 13, 16
Personalization, 2: 112–113
"Perversity hypothesis," 5: 145–147
Petchesky, Rosalind, 6: 86
Peters, R. S., 1: 167, 284
Peterson, Edward N., 3: 200, 214, 239, 245, 363
Peterson, Paul E., 2: 297, 311, 313; 6: 338
Peterson, Phyllis, 5: 133
Peterson, Richard E., 2: 70, 124
Petras, James, 3: 97
Petrie, Charles, 5: 224
Pettigrew, Thomas F., 2: 12, 60
Petty, William, 7: 141
Pfaltzgraff, Robert, 6: 389; 8: 347
Pfautz, Harold W., 2: 202; 6: 467
Phelan, James, 5: 410
Phenomenology, 2: 41, 43, 57, 58, 59
Philadelphia Convention of 1787, 5: 73, 94, 95, 108, 109
Philadelphia Plan, 6: 277
Philip, Kjeld, 5: 148
Phillips, Harlan B., 7: 37
Philosophers, 1: 236, 238, 239, 241, 242, 244, 248, 254, 255, 257
Philosophy, 1: 235, 236, 248, 249, 250–256, 258, 261
  classical, 1: 240
  Greek, 1: 241
  history of, 1: 235, 260
  meaning of, 1: 235
  practical, 1: 234–235
  study of, 1: 256, 257
  uses of, 1: 235
Pickles, Dorothy, 5: 199
Pierce, John C., 4: 90, 100, 102, 158, 159; 7: 286, 304
Pierce, Roy, 4: 27, 158, 159; 5: 309; 7: 288
Pierson, Donald, 3: 70
Pike, Douglas, 8: 346
Pike, Frederick B., 3: 306
Pinard, Maurice, 3: 617
Pincus, J., 6: 464

Pinney, Edward L., 5: 140, 145
Pipes, Richard, 3: 358, 363
Pipping, Knut, 3: 209
Piret, R. V., 2: 115
Pirker, Theo, 3: 369
Pi Sigma Alpha, 1: 55
Pitcher, George, 2: 5
Pitkin, Hanna F., 1: 212, 322; 2: 297; 4: 162; 5: 298, 424
Pitt-Rivers, Julian, 3: 69
Piven, Francis F., 5: 426; 6: 148, 173, 279
Planning
  administration of, 3: 586, 591–594
  politics of, 3: 586–591
  technology of, 3: 586
Planning-Programming-Budgeting System (PPBS), 5: 406, 417; 6: 44, 96, 130, 144, 208, 440, 444, 462, 465–466; 8: 292, 303, 323
Plantation economy, 3: 262
Plato, 1: 9, 210, 231, 233–234, 235, 237, 239–240, 243, 244, 245, 248, 249, 252, 255, 258, 260, 261, 262, 263, 322; 5: 19, 24, 25, 26, 39, 40, 41, 42, 43
Platt, Gerald M., 2: 31
Platt, John, 6: 89; 7: 91, 125; 8: 4
Platt, Washington, 6: 14
Plausibility probes, 7: 108–113
Playford, John, 1: 114; 7: 330
Plea bargaining, 5: 329, 331
Plessner, Helmuth, 3: 363
Plessy v. *Ferguson*, 6: 270, 272
Ploss, Sidney I., 3: 336
Plott, Charles R., 3: 428, 439, 440, 442, 454
Plumb, J. H., 6: 255
Plural societies, 3: 67
Pluralism, 4: 172–173, 192; 5: 45; 7: 267
  in authoritarian regimes, 3: 265, 270–271, 277–278
Pluralist-elitist controversy, 6: 307
Pluralistic ignorance, 7: 280
Plutchik, Robert, 7: 243
Plutocratic democracies, 3: 318
Poincaré, Henri, 8: 4
Poisson distribution, 2: 337, 338
Polak, F. L., 7: 408
Poland, polyarchy in, 3: 157
Polanyi, Michael, 1: 169
POLARIS program, 8: 289, 292, 296, 308
Polarity, 8: 14
Polarization, 3: 131
Police socialism, 3: 583

Policy
  administrative reaction to, **6:** 444
  defined, **6:** 441–442
  enactment of, **6:** 444
  feedback, **6:** 445
  goals of, **6:** 442–443
  primary contact, **6:** 444
  primary impact, **6:** 444
  secondary impact, **6:** 444–445
  systemic impact, **6:** 445
Policy analysis, **6:** 382–384, 423
Policy coherence, difficulties of, **8:** 392–393
Policy domain, **4:** 184
Policy evaluation, **7:** 334
Policy-impact research
  applied, **6:** 460–461
  data requirements, **6:** 462–463
  organization of, **6:** 463–465
  political science, relation to, **6:** 458–460
  scientific, **6:** 460–461
  scope and conceptualization of, **6:** 441–448
Policy implementation, **6:** 444
Policy output, neglect of, **6:** 382–383
Policy process, **7:** 333–334
  concentration on, **6:** 383
Policy space, **3:** 439, 441
Policymakers, perceptions and intentions of, **6:** 388–389
Policymaking, **5:** 273
  scientific approach to, **6:** 95–97
Policy-sciences approach, **6:** 15
Polimetrics, **7:** 139–203
  alternate names for, **7:** 146
  branches of, **7:** 139–140
  definition of, **7:** 139
  foundation of, **7:** 141–157
Polis, **1:** 241, 244, 245, 252, 261
Politbureau, **3:** 200, 238
Political acculturation, **3:** 18–26, 29, 67–68, 72; *see also* Political culture
  and adaptation to Christianity, **3:** 19–20, 24
  and China, **3:** 20–21
  and communism, **3:** 21
  consummatory cultures, **3:** 18–19, 20, 31
  of Cuba, **3:** 31
  donor political culture, **3:** 22–25
  Fon of Dahomey, **3:** 19, 21
  and France, **3:** 19
  Ganda of Uganda, **3:** 19–20
  Ibo of Nigeria, **3:** 20
  and India, **3:** 21–22, 25–26
  and Japan, **3:** 20
  and Latin America, **3:** 23, 26, 30

  and Liberia, **3:** 24–25
  mixed cultures, **3:** 19
  patterns of response, **3:** 22, 23
  recipient political culture, **3:** 18–22
  through syncretism, **3:** 19
  and Vietnam, **3:** 21, 89
  Westernization, **3:** 30
Political activists, beliefs of, **3:** 158–161
Political activity
  consequences of, **4:** 60–68
  incentives for, **2:** 166
  rationality of, **4:** 68–70
Political actors, case studies of individual, **2:** 32–44
Political anthropology, **3:** 253, 364
Political apathy, **5:** 83
Political behavior, **7:** 275, 277, 278, 282–285
  differences in style of, **2:** 163–164
  empirical theories of, **7:** 333
Political beliefs, **4:** 56–59
Political campaigns, financing of, **4:** 254–255
Political careers
  commitment to, **2:** 166
  and mobility, **2:** 201–204
  typology of, **2:** 162
Political commissars, **3:** 210
Political community, **2:** 114
Political competition, **3:** 119
Political conflict, **3:** 130–131
  fallacies in study of, **3:** 487–488
Political culture, **2:** 61; **3:** 15–32
  and change, **3:** 29–30
  and modern man, **3:** 27–28
  modernization within, **3:** 27–29
  and political acculturation, **3:** 18–26
  political change within agglomerative political culture, **3:** 25–26
  and political planning, **3:** 31–32
  and political structures, **3:** 16–18
  types of, **3:** 16, 17
Political decay, **3:** 4
Political "decompression," **3:** 6
Political democracy, **3:** 5–6
  and feudalism, **3:** 12
  relationship to economic development, **3:** 5–6
  role of communications in, **3:** 5, 6
  and totalitarian or authoritarian regimes, **3:** 12
Political design, **8:** 400–401
Political development in political science, **3:** 1–11
  derivative, **3:** 4, 48

and environments, **3:** 13
factors of, **3:** 12–13
functional, **3:** 4–5, 48
future of, **3:** 90–96
geographical, **3:** 3–4
goals of, **3:** 4
influences on, **3:** 11–15
institutionalization of political organizations and procedures, **3:** 4
phases of, **3:** 11–12
political modernization, **3:** 4
rates of change in, **3:** 15
sequences of, **3:** 14–15
teleological, **3:** 4
and timing, **3:** 14
Political economy, **5:** 343, 344; **7:** 354–378
Political efficacy, **3:** 34, 36, 41
Political evaluation, **1:** 209, 213–214
Political experimentation, control dimensions
  in, **7:** 236–244
Political families, **2:** 188–189
Political freedom, **3:** 183
Political identity, **3:** 32
Political inactives, **4:** 40, 61
Political instability, **3:** 48
Political institutionalization, **3:** 14, 47, 57, 59
Political institutions, **1:** 4–7; **3:** 47–66
  administrative, **3:** 51–53
  analysis of, **7:** 376–378
  ancient empires, **1:** 5
  and economic development, **3:** 59–66
  governing, **3:** 49–50
  Greek experience, **1:** 5
  medieval influence, **1:** 6–7
  modern state system, **1:** 7
  neolithic revolution, **1:** 5
  participatory, **3:** 50–51
  and political change, **3:** 53–59
  Roman experience, **1:** 6
  and socioeconomic modernization, **3:** 47–48
Political integration, **3:** 66–90
  definitions of, **3:** 66
  patterns of stratification, **3:** 67–68
  and religious politics, **3:** 75–83
Political intelligence, **3:** 558
  and social structure, **3:** 584–599
Political interest group, definition of, **2:** 244–
  245, 252–253, 264, 266–267, 295
Political interests, **3:** 124
Political involvement, **2:** 162
  commitment, **2:** 162
  continuity of service, **2:** 162
  time, **2:** 162

Political judgments, **7:** 281–282
Political justice, in totalitarian regimes,
  3: 222
Political leadership, **5:** 259
Political legitimacy, **2:** 96
Political man, **2:** 327, 331
Political mobilization, **2:** 269; **7:** 278
Political model, **2:** 321, 322, 326
  and accessibility, **2:** 324
  bargaining, **2:** 325
  conflict, **2:** 321
  consensus, **2:** 325
  and criterion of evaluation, **2:** 324
  and goals, **2:** 324, 325
  and ideology, **2:** 324
  power, **2:** 321, 322
  ruling elites, **2:** 325
Political modernization, **3:** 4, 5, 27–29
  phases of, **3:** 13
Political office, full-time, **2:** 168
Political organizations, **2:** 164
Political orientations, **4:** 17–22
Political participation, **2:** 167, 213; **3:** 9, 10, 14,
  33–47
  activists, **4:** 39–40, 42, 60–61
  amount of, **4:** 23
  autonomous participation, **3:** 33
  black-white participation, **4:** 56–59
  campaign activity, **4:** 10, 13, 18, 50–52
  ceremonial, **4:** 2
  citizen-initiated contacts, **4:** 10–11, 13
  "departicipation," **3:** 39
  evidence from cross-national study, **4:** 1
  forms and bases of, **3:** 43–47
  frequency distributions in various coun-
    tries, **4:** 24–25
  group consciousness, **3:** 36
  importance of, **4:** 4
  leader responsiveness, **4:** 63–68
  mobilized participation, **3:** 33
  nature of, **3:** 33; **4:** 1–3
  neighborhood participation, **3:** 45
  and organizational involvement, **3:** 35–36
  "participation explosions," **3:** 39
  particularized contacting, **4:** 21–22, 69
  partisan identification, strength of, **4:** 17, 41
  political beliefs, **4:** 56–59
  and political parties, **4:** 49–53, 54–55
  protests, **4:** 26–27
  reasons for, **4:** 4
  reasons for increase in, by socioeconomic
    modernization, **3:** 33–38
  rural and urban, differences between, **3:** 40

and social conflict, **3:** 37
and socioeconomic level, **4:** 40–41
and socioeconomic status, **3:** 34–35
and socioeconomic status in cross-national
  perspective, **4:** 41–45, 62
study of, **4:** 5–6
unitary model of, **4:** 7, 28
and urbanization, **4:** 32–33
voting, **4:** 9–10, 13, 19–20, 53
voting participation, urban and rural, **3:**
  40–41
Political parties, **3:** 28, 46, 50–51, 306; **4:**
  49–53, 54–55
activists, **4:** 262
African, **3:** 325–326
antisystem party, **4:** 240
authoritarian or totalitarian party, **4:** 232
in Britain, **4:** 231, 233, 237, 238, 239
in Canada, **4:** 245
candidate-centered organizations, **4:** 254
candidate selection, **4:** 257–260
catchall parties, **4:** 251
caucuses, **4:** 249, 260
centralized, **5:** 137
Christian democratic parties, **3:** 77–78
class-based voting in Britain, **4:** 245
cohesion, **4:** 263, 266
Communist, **3:** 203, 215–216, 360–361; **4:**
  232–233
competition between, **3:** 441–444, 468,
  562–564
conservative authoritarian, **3:** 320
decentralized, **5:** 133–136
electoral system, **4:** 234
emergence of, **3:** 50
Fascist party, **3:** 215–216, 316–320, 361
freedom for, **3:** 184
Hindu, **3:** 79–80
individual's choice of, **3:** 558
issue differentiation, **4:** 92, 99, 105, 111, 118,
  134
mass-membership party, **4:** 237, 249–250,
  251, 263
multiparty competition, **4:** 234, 240
one-party domination, **4:** 242
one-party ideology, **3:** 31, 60
organization, **4:** 248–256
parliamentary system, **4:** 264–265
party identification, **4:** 117, 125, 126, 127,
  129–130, 132, 134, 141, 142, 145
patronage in America, **4:** 238, 250, 257

in Poland, **4:** 233
primary election, direct, **4:** 239, 242, 258,
  259
with religious links, **3:** 76
responsible-party school, **4:** 237
single-party noncompetitive systems, **3:** 30
social base, its choice of, **3:** 558
"splinter," **5:** 136
statutory party, **4:** 252–253
third parties, **4:** 241–242
totalitarian, **3:** 198–216
trade unions, **4:** 251, 253
two-party competition, **4:** 234, 239–240
two-party systems, **3:** 162
in the United States, **4:** 231–232, 237, 239
and voting behavior, **7:** 282–283
working-class party, **4:** 244, 249, 260
Political personality, **2:** 209–219, 230
Political phenomena, explanation of, **1:** 131
Political philosophers, **1:** 230, 231, 233
Political philosophy, **1:** 209, 233, 235, 236, 241,
  248, 251, 252–253, 254, 255, 257, 258, 260,
  262
analytic, **1:** 317, 321
classics of, **1:** 229–230, 231, 237, 248, 252,
  254, 257, 259–260, 261
Greek, **1:** 232
history of, **1:** 233, 236–237, 252–253
relevance of, **1:** 256–262
uses of, **1:** 230, 233–236, 256
Political power, **7:** 273
Political process, **2:** 258–260, 268–269, 282,
  322
group activity as, **2:** 254–255
Political promotion, **2:** 161
Political protests, **4:** 26–27
Politcal psychology, **2:** 211, 215–217, 218–219
Political reality, **1:** 231, 232, 236, 253, 257, 261
Political recruitment, **2:** 155–233
apprenticeship, **2:** 174, 177, 187, 195–199,
  202, 219, 228–230
candidacy, **2:** 171
class-determined, **2:** 184
concepts, **2:** 160–169
contextual variables, **2:** 174
cooptation, **2:** 228–229
crisis recruitment, **2:** 232–233
definition of, **2:** 155, 156
developmental model, **2:** 159
eligibility for candidacy, **2:** 171, 220
group-oriented, **2:** 176, 221, 227

initial, **2:** 161, 167–168, 171, 195–199, 215
interelection probability model, **2:** 176–177
ladders, **2:** 156, 161
lawyers in politics, **2:** 203, 204–209
as link between polity and society, **2:** 156
and minorities and immigration groups, **2:** 202
models, **2:** 171–177, 216
motivations, **2:** 209–219
occupation as cluster of variables, **2:** 200–209, 230
occupational role-profile analysis, **2:** 207
"open" vs. "closed," **2:** 172
operational definition, **2:** 160–169
organizational model of congressional recruitment, **2:** 175
pathways of, **2:** 174
and personality, **2:** 209–212
perspectives, **2:** 169–171
and political socialization, **2:** 186–195
preoccupations with, **2:** 160
risk involved, **2:** 172–173
selection, **2:** 171–173, 219–229
sponsorship, **2:** 222, 228
variables in local non-partisan recruitment, **2:** 174
Political resources, distribution of, **3:** 145–147
inequalities in, **3:** 145–147
Political roles, **2:** 155
Political science, Americanization of, **1:** 30–32, 44–45
Political science, definition of, **1:** 1–2
by David Easton, **1:** 1
Political science, development of in the United States, **1:** 18–23
American political experience, **1:** 20
citizen literature, **1:** 20–21
industrialization, **1:** 21–22
political knowledge, codification of, **1:** 19
specialization, **1:** 21–22
urbanization, **1:** 21–22
university, rise of, **1:** 22–23
Political science, as discipline, **1:** 117–118
Political science, as enterprise, **1:** 123–124
Political science, as profession, **1:** 118–122
Political science, rise of university-based, **1:** 26–29
Political science, as science, **1:** 122–123
Political science, tradition of, **1:** 4–18, 116–117
political institutions, **1:** 4–7
political thought, **1:** 7–16
politics, languages of, **1:** 16–18

Political science, before World War I, **1:** 23–41
academic political science before 1880, **1:** 24–25
historical-comparative method, decline of, **1:** 29–30
Lieber, Francis, **1:** 25–26
reformism, **1:** 32–34
rise of university-based political science, **1:** 26–29
Political science, from World War I to World War II, **1:** 41–50
Americanization and "re-Europeanization," **1:** 44–45
interwar matrix, **1:** 41–42
quantitative and organizational factors, **1:** 42–44
scientism, **1:** 47–50
Political science, since World War II, **1:** 50–73
behavioral movement, **1:** 58–62
comparative method, expansion of, **1:** 68–69
historical factors, **1:** 50–54
professional-disciplinary developments, **1:** 54–58
public-oriented activities and responsibilities, **1:** 62–67
scientific philosophy and methodology, rise of, **1:** 71–73
theory, revitalization of, **1:** 70–71
voting and opinion studies, expansion of, **1:** 69–70
Political Science Quarterly, **1:** 27
Political scientists, **1:** 37–38, 231, 232, 254, 255, 258
Political socialization, **2:** 183–184, 186–195; **4:** 143; **7:** 278
adult behavior, **2:** 137
age range, **2:** 95, 138
attachment to political system, **2:** 94, 96–117, 127–128
conservative political bias, **2:** 138
cross-national comparisons, **2:** 111–112
definition of, **2:** 95
early, **2:** 187
evaluations of the field, **2:** 96
in the family, **2:** 187–194
field as a whole, **2:** 136–139
methodology, **2:** 136, 138
minority children, **2:** 102, 106–111, 112–113, 138
"New Urban Blacks," **2:** 110
in nonpartisan settings, **2:** 194–195
participatory orientations, **2:** 127

partisan attitudes, **2:** 94
partisan predispositions, **2:** 117–127, 128
persistence of residues from preadult, **2:** 127–136
political participation, **2:** 94
and recruitment, **2:** 186–195
resocialization, **2:** 110–111
specificity of early socialization, **2:** 132–135
Political society, **1:** 233
Political stability, **3:** 6–11; **7:** 273
and civil violence, **3:** 8
and continuity, **3:** 7
and military intervention, **3:** 9
and socioeconomic modernization, **3:** 7–8, 9–10
Political systems
characteristics of, **2:** 156
persistence of, **2:** 99, 114
typologies of, **3:** 357
Political thought, **1:** 7–16
Athenian thinkers, **1:** 8–9
categorization, problems of, **1:** 15–16
Christian church, rise of, **1:** 11
experiment with democracy, Athenian, **1:** 9
feudalism, influence of, **1:** 11
Great Dialogue, **1:** 8–11
during medieval period, **1:** 10–11
modern period, **1:** 11–15
"natural law," **1:** 10
Roman contribution to, **1:** 10
"state of nature," **1:** 10
Stoics, **1:** 9–10
Political tradition, American, **5:** 2
Political trust, **2:** 137
Political union, **5:** 51
Political variables in foreign policy, **6:** 414–416
participation characteristics of, **6:** 415
structural characteristics of, **6:** 414
substantive characteristics of, **6:** 415–416
Political violence, **3:** 10
Politicians
amateur, **2:** 161–162, 163–164, 165, 166–167
"gain," **2:** 163
"game," **2:** 163
professional, **2:** 161–162, 163–164, 165, 167, 215, 226
rewards for, **2:** 163
semiprofessionals, **2:** 163
student leaders, **2:** 165
Politicization, **8:** 387, 397; **4:** 30–38; 45–48

analysis of, **4:** 45, 47
communal participation, **4:** 20–21, 53
and communication of preferences, **4:** 60–63
community context and, **4:** 34–36
concentration of, **4:** 27–30
cooperative activity, **4:** 11–12
decline-of-community model, **4:** 33–38
dimensions and modes of, **4:** 6–22
as educational device, **4:** 4
empirical structure of, **4:** 12–17
institutional constraints, **4:** 47
of the masses, **3:** 208
mobilization model, **4:** 33
and modes of activity, **4:** 48
and socioeconomic status, **4:** 46
Politics, **1:** 246, 252–254, 257
American, **1:** 230
electoral, **1:** 230
history of, **1:** 230
international, **1:** 230
military intervention in, **3:** 301–306
Polity, operation of, affecting collective violence, **3:** 502
Polity, specialized
and closed regime, **5:** 266–268
and open regime, **5:** 274–277
Polity, unspecialized
and closed regime, **5:** 263–265
and open regime, **5:** 268–274
Pollack, Jonathan D., **3:** 190
Pollock, Frederick, **1:** 4
Pollock, Ross, **5:** 183, 197
Polsby, Daniel D., **6:** 468
Polsby, Nelson, **1:** 131, 132; **2:** 164, 245; **3:** 569; **4:** 162, 260; **5:** 183, 187, 234, 288, 290, 291, 310; **6:** 172, 307, 335, 361
Polyarchy, **1:** 306
conditions favoring, **3:** 133–161
conflicts in, **3:** 130–131
definition of, **3:** 118–119, 122
and education and literacy, **3:** 144
and foreign domination, **3:** 155–158
inauguration of, **3:** 136
inequalities in, **3:** 130
legitimacy of, **3:** 159
mutual security in, **3:** 134
opposition in, **3:** 161–169
paths to, **3:** 133–137
polarization in, **3:** 130–133
segmentation in, **3:** 130–133
and socioeconomic development, **3:** 142
sources of discontent in, **3:** 129–133

and subcultural pluralism, **3**: 153
  in the United States, **3**: 143
Polybius, **5**: 43, 44, 94
Polycentrism, **3**: 360
Pomper, Gerald, **2**: 180, 196, 197, 327; **4**: 68, 91,
  92, 98, 101, 105, 107, 118, 119, 126, 159; **5**:
  183, 188, 192; **7**: 286
Pondy, Louis, **2**: 322, 347
Pool, Ithiel de Sola, **2**: 332; **4**: 162, 207; **5**: 287;
  6: 407, 413, 417; **7**: 223
Poor Law tradition, **6**: 115, 153
Pope, John, **5**: 237
Popkin, Samuel, **7**: 223
Popper, Karl R., **1**: 218; **7**: 86, 119, 211
Popular courts, **5**: 362–365
Population growth, **7**: 424–425
Population sampling, **7**: 230
Populism, **7**: 287
Populist coalition, **3**: 295–296
Populist democracy, **3**: 282
"Populist totalitarianism," **3**: 229
Porchnev, Boris, **3**: 542
Porter, John, **5**: 183, 202
POSEIDON, **8**: 308
Positivism, **7**: 140, 142, 188, 201; **8**: 421–422,
  428
Positivity, **2**: 105–106
Positivity bias, **2**: 117
Pospisil, Leopold, **5**: 323, 326, 334
"Post bourgeois" values, **2**: 165
Postindustrial society, **6**: 80
  new patterns of politics among, **8**: 389–
  394
Posttotalitarian authoritarian regimes, **3**:
  336–350
Potash, Robert A., **3**: 367
Potholm, Christian P., **3**: 322, 327, 369, 370
Potter, Allen, **4**: 206
Poulton, Helen J., **7**: 67
Poussaint, Alvin F., **6**: 253, 254
Poverty, **6**: 130–136
  cultures of, **6**: 131
  documentation of, **6**: 130–131
  identification and measurement, **6**: 183–186
  and income redistribution, **6**: 195–199
  and welfare policy, **6**: 182–203
Powell, Charles A., **7**: 241, 247, 248
Powell, G. Bingham, Jr., **1**: 141, 194; **2**: 308; **3**:
  3, 33, 35, 36, 41, 180, 274, 357; **4**: 32, 33,
  177, 178, 179, 180
Powell, John Duncan, **3**: 15, 36, 97, 365
Power, **1**: 285, 287, 288, 289, 304, 305, 308; **2**:
  321, 324, 353, 357

centralization of, **3**: 53
as coercion, **2**: 354
consolidation in, **3**: 250
dispersion of, **3**: 53, 470
expansion of, **3**: 53
instability of, **3**: 596
as legitimate, **2**: 354, 355
personalistic use of, **3**: 260
and political institutions, **3**: 53–54
relationships, **2**: 324
and social structure, **3**: 560–584
struggle, **2**: 324, 325
takeover of, **3**: 239–240
transfer of, **3**: 538–539
utility of, **3**: 595–597
Power assessment, **7**: 180
Power contention, **3**: 502, 503–506
  associational, **3**: 505, 506, 507
  communal, **3**: 505, 506, 507, 508
  organizational structures of, **3**: 508
Power deflation, **3**: 490
Power index, **5**: 137–138
Power politics, **7**: 171; **8**: 92–93
Pozen, Robert, **5**: 410
Practical inference, **1**: 163, 164, 166, 184–185,
  189, 191, 192, 208; **7**: 168, 170–171, 190,
  196, 202
Practical syllogism, **1**: 162; **7**: 179
Practices, interpretation of, **1**: 168–171,
  172
Praetorian society, **3**: 57–58, 61
Praetorianism, **3**: 297
Prakash, Ved, **6**: 313, 334
Prandi, Alfonso, **6**: 340
Pratt, John W., **7**: 204
Pratt, Raymond B., **3**: 97
Precision-guided munitions (PGM), **8**: 333
Prediction, **7**: 431–433; **8**: 4
  concrete, **7**: 89
  experimental, **7**: 89
Predisposition, **2**: 6, 7, 13, 15, 16, 19, 20, 26, 27,
  30, 69, 76
Preemption, **8**: 200, 203, 205, 206, 209, 210–
  211, 217, 229, 238
Preferences
  acyclic, **3**: 417
  collective, **3**: 417
  complete, **3**: 416
  individual, **3**: 414, 416–417, 439, 469
  intensities of, **3**: 420, 424, 444–451
  intransitive, **3**: 437–438
  lexicographic, **3**: 438, 440, 442
  quasitransitive, **3**: 417

reflexive, **3:** 416
single-peaked, **3:** 429
social, **3:** 424
strict, **3:** 416
transitive, **3:** 416
variable, **3:** 414
weak, **3:** 416
Preference maps, **7:** 202
Preference ordering, **1:** 197; **7:** 356
    constraints on, **1:** 198
Prejudice, racial and ethnic, **2:** 134, 137
Prerogative
    absolute, **5:** 48, 49, 50, 56, 57, 59, 63, 70
    ordinary, **5:** 48, 54, 57, 59, 63
Prescott, William H., **6:** 258
Prescriptions, **1:** 314–315
Prescriptive theory, **2:** 352
Presidency, **2:** 277–278
    idealization of, **2:** 97–99
    personalizing of, **2:** 97–99
President, American, **5:** 173, 193, 195, 196,
    198, 199, 200, 208, 211, 216, 221, 222, 228,
    230, 240–241
    "clerkship" of, **5:** 221
    "natural" enemies of, **5:** 220
President, French, **5:** 198–199
Presidential candidates, American, **5:** 193
Presidential libraries, **7:** 29–31
Presidential papers, **7:** 29
Presidentialism, **5:** 189
President's Commission on Income Main-
    tenance Programs, **6:** 77
President's Science Advisory Committee, **6:**
    90
Press, Charles, **7:** 67
Pressman, Jeffrey L., **6:** 87, 90, 350
Pressure groups, **4:** 176; **5:** 3
Pretheories, **8:** 89
"Pretotalitarian" regimes, **3:** 332–336
Prewitt, Kenneth, **2:** 94, 112, 127, 172, 173,
    179, 184, 187, 188, 189, 190, 191, 193,
    194–195, 198, 199, 201, 228; **3:** 33, 35, 36,
    41; **4:** 32, 33
Price, David, **5:** 308
Price, Don K., **5:** 223, 403, 405; **6:** 81, 84, 90,
    101, 403
Price, H. Douglas, **3:** 92; **4:** 145; **5:** 288
Price, Jacob M., **5:** 306; **7:** 67
Price, Miles O., **7:** 12, 27
Price indexes, **6:** 31
Price stability, **6:** 25, 30–31
Pride, Richard A., **3:** 98
Pridham, Geoffrey, **3:** 368

Priestley, Joseph, **7:** 216
Primack, Joel, **6:** 91
Primary elections, **2:** 220, 222; **5:** 188
Prime minister, British, **5:** 183, 193, 195, 196,
    198, 199, 200, 211, 222, 228, 230, 240–241
    Private Office of, **5:** 223–224
Prime minister, French, **5:** 195
"Prime ministerial" government, debate
    about, **5:** 232–233
Primordial loyalties, **3:** 324
Principle of unanimity, **7:** 374, 375
Pring, David, **5:** 235
Prisoner's Dilemma, **3:** 466, 467; **7:** 152, 180–
    187, 203, 241, 387, 392–394; **8:** 200, 201,
    209
Private goods, **7:** 355
Private organizations, **2:** 322
Private ownership of economy, **3:** 141, 232
Private and public goals, **2:** 157
    intended consequences, **2:** 157
    observed consequences, **2:** 157
Probabilistic individual choice, **3:** 438
Probability
    judgmental, **2:** 336
    objective, **2:** 336, 345
    personal, **2:** 346
    relative, **7:** 430–431
    subjective, **2:** 335, 336, 345, 346
Process theory, **7:** 199
Proctor, Charles H., **2:** 75
Professional associations, **5:** 409
Professional revolutionaries, **3:** 236
Professionalism, **5:** 425–426
    in welfare, **6:** 117–119, 121, 122, 127, 133,
    162–163
Professionalization, **2:** 162, 166, 167
Profile analysis, **2:** 53
Programmatic appeals, **2:** 166–167
Programmatic consensus, **3:** 268
Programmatic research, **7:** 236
Programmed decisions, **2:** 356
Progress, **1:** 252
Progressive-Conservative party (Canada), **5:**
    190
Progressivism, **5:** 413
Projective tests, **2:** 35
Proletarian nation, **3:** 316
Proliferation of exotic "conventional" technol-
    ogy, **8:** 333–335
Pronk, J. P., **3:** 370
Propaganda campaigns, **5:** 264, 265
Property, private, **1:** 385
Property concepts, **1:** 286–287

Property law, **5:** 339
Propositional inventories, **8:** 94, 99
Proshansky, Harold, **2:** 118, 134
Prospective procedure, **3:** 485, 491, 494
Prothro, J. W., **2:** 115; **4:** 3, 162; **6:** 296; **7:** 300, 301, 330, 331, 332
Prouty, L. Fletcher, **8:** 329
Proxmire, William, **6:** 86
Prussian Army, **8:** 262
Pryor, Frederic L., **5:** 304; **6:** 199, 200, 316, 324; **8:** 376
Przeworski, Adam, **1:** 175; **6:** 387; **7:** 133, 288
Pseudoconstitutional parliamentary forms, **3:** 287
Pyschoanalysis, **2:** 39
Psychoanalytic ego psychology, **2:** 10
Psychological involvement in politics, **4:** 17
Psychometrics, **7:** 158
Public administration, **1:** 230
Public assistance, **6:** 60–61, 113, 114, 193
  administration of, **6:** 117–119, 128
  Aid to the Blind (AB), **6:** 116, 150
  Aid to Dependent Children (ADC), **6:** 116, 123
  Aid to Families with Dependent Children (AFDC), **6:** 126–127, 135, 136, 148, 150, 157
  eligibility determination, **6:** 116, 123, 142, 143, 144
  federal development of, **6:** 118
  food stamps, **6:** 138
  Medicaid, **6:** 133, 137–138, 143
  Medicare, **6:** 137
  and 1962 amendments, **6:** 126–127, 129, 139, 147, 151, 162, 166
  and 1965 amendments, **6:** 139
  and 1967 amendments, **6:** 139–141, 166
  Old Age Assistance (OAA), **6:** 116, 150
  Social Service Amendments of 1974, **6:** 147
  work-incentive plan, **6:** 140, 150
Public-choice analysis, **5:** 427
Public choice theory, **2:** 320, 328, 331, 361
Public contestation, **3:** 119–120
  conditions favoring, **3:** 133–161
Public good, **3:** 465, 466, 467; **6:** 34
Public goods, optimal allocation of, **5:** 143
Public-health services, **6:** 116
Public interest, **1:** 347, 382–384, 389, 394; **2:** 275–276, 328
  search for the, **5:** 412–415
Public-interest groups, **5:** 399, 422, 427
Public opinion, **7:** 280; *see also* Attitudes

character of, variation in, **4:** 89–93
  ideology, **4:** 83–89
  nature of, **4:** 77–111
  opinion formation, **4:** 79–83
  psychology of, **4:** 78–89
  representation of, **4:** 148–156
Public Order of the World Community, **8:** 430, 432–433
Public Papers of the President, **7:** 24
Public policies, **2:** 276–277, 278, 328
  categories of, **5:** 410
Public policy analysis, **7:** 306
  criminal procedure, **7:** 325–326
  Depression years, **7:** 307–311
  education, **7:** 320
  GI Bill, **7:** 316
  health services, **7:** 323
  income maintenance, **7:** 320
  postwar years, **7:** 319–324
  poverty, **7:** 320
  race, **7:** 317
  troop integration, **7:** 317
  world war and cold war, **7:** 311–319
Public welfare
  and race, **6:** 149
  since Social Security Act, **6:** 115–157
  and work, **6:** 136–148
Publicity, administrative, **5:** 391
Puchala, Donald J., **7:** 315; **8:** 371, 388
Pugwash conferences, **8:** 300–301
Puhle, Hans-Jürgen, **3:** 367
Pulzer, P. G. J., **3:** 316, 363
Pumphrey, Murial, **6:** 221
Pumphrey, Ralph, **6:** 221
Punishment, **1:** 299
Punnett, R. M., **5:** 184, 236
Purges, **3:** 221–222, 224
Puryear, Paul L., **6:** 467
Pusić, Eugen, **3:** 346; **6:** 335
Putnam, Robert D., **3:** 9, 10, 302, 367; **4:** 221; **7:** 303; **8:** 371
Putney, S., **2:** 123, 126
Pye, Lucian W., **2:** 187; **3:** 3, 16, 29, 30, 91, 97, 357, 363, 365; **7:** 99, 105
Pylee, M. V., **5:** 123

Q techniques, **7:** 248
Quade, E. S., **6:** 95; **8:** 303, 323, 344
Quadriad, **6:** 38, 42
Quanbeck, Alton, **8:** 347
Quandt, William B., **3:** 369
Quantification of data, **7:** 139, 161, 165, 167

Quantitative data, **7:** 43–68
Quantitative international politics (QIP), **8:** 87, 99
Quantitative measurement, **7:** 288
Quasi-pluralistic authoritarianism, **3:** 345
Quasi-totalitarianism, **3:** 344
Quester, George H., **6:** 389; **8:** 222, 269, 333, 341, 342, 344, 345
Quine, Willard van Orman, **1:** 147
Quirk, James, **3:** 424; **7:** 397

RA index, **8:** 110
Raab, Earl, **3:** 525
Rabinovitz, Francine F., **6:** 309, 312, 313, 321, 322, 329, 333, 334, 335, 340, 361
Rabinowitz, George Burt, **4:** 161
Rabushka, Alan, **2:** 321
Rabushka, Alvin, **3:** 13
Race
  Aryan, **6:** 243–244, 252
  genetics, **6:** 243
  and immigration policies of the United States and Great Britain, **6:** 256
  and intelligence, **6:** 278–279
  meaning of, **6:** 242–245
Race policy
  and the American Indian, **6:** 247–248, 254, 259
  apartheid, **6:** 275
  in Australia, **6:** 242, 254, 256
  in Brazil, **6:** 242, 245
  in Canada, **6:** 242
  in China, **6:** 252
  concept of, **6:** 241–258
  covert, **6:** 246
  by default, **6:** 246–248
  detention camps, **6:** 255
  in Great Britain, **6:** 242
  in India, **6:** 242, 246, 252
  in Kenya, **6:** 242
  meaning of, **6:** 244, 245–248
  in New Zealand, **6:** 242, 254, 266
  and perception of injustice, **6:** 258
  pervasiveness of, **6:** 241–242
  school desegregation, **6:** 257
  sources of, **6:** 249–258
  in South Africa, **6:** 241, 242, 245, 246, 254, 255, 257, 268, 275–276
  types of, **6:** 258–297
  in Uganda, **6:** 242
  in United States, **6:** 242, 268
  in Vietnam, **6:** 261

Race policy, types of, **6:** 258–297
  domination of subject races, **6:** 266–285
  extermination of subject races, **6:** 258–261
  liberating, **6:** 285–297
  racial enslavement, **6:** 261–266
Racial discrimination
  and the criminal code, **6:** 273–274
  in housing, **6:** 274–275, 291
  in jobs, **6:** 270, 280
  in public accommodations, **6:** 270
Racial domination, **6:** 266–285
  by physical coercion, **6:** 266–268
  through segregation, **6:** 268–269
Racial enslavement, **6:** 261–266
Racial or ethnic democracies, **3:** 281, 326–332
  Republic of South Africa, **3:** 326–329
Racial extermination, **6:** 258–261
  American Indians, **6:** 259
  Australian aborigines, **6:** 259, 260
  Incas, **6:** 258
  in Nazi Germany, **6:** 260–261
Racial injustice, perception of, **6:** 249, 258
Racial liberating policies, **6:** 285–297
  in Brazil, **6:** 285, 286
  in New Zealand, **6:** 286
  in United States, **6:** 285
Racial supremacy, **6:** 260
Racial war, **6:** 267
Racism, **3:** 319, 327, 565
  in attack on lumpenproletariat, **3:** 610–611
  and avarice, **6:** 249, 254
  and the Bible, **6:** 250
  and capitalism, **6:** 252, 280–282
  and cultural factors, **6:** 249
  defined, **6:** 245
  and ethnic loyalty, **3:** 606–607
  and expectation of political reward, **6:** 249, 257
  and fear, **6:** 249, 255–257
  and ingroup-outgroup, **6:** 249
  and intellectual "superiority," **6:** 278–279
  as justification of exploitation, **3:** 611–612
  Ku Klux Klan, **6:** 245, 253, 267–268
  in Nazi Germany, **6:** 244
  and politics, **6:** 295
  populist, **3:** 611
  as product of xenophobia, **6:** 249
  and self-respect, **6:** 285
  and sexual factors, **6:** 253
  unconscious, **6:** 248
  and psychological factors, **6:** 249, 253–254

Radicalism, **1:** 235
Radicalization, **3:** 525
Radnitzky, Gerard, **1:** 171, 217
Radojkovic, Milos, **8:** 430
Radway, Laurence I., **8:** 323, 326
Rae, Douglas W., **1:** 138, 205, 214, 215, 221,
    391; **2:** 321, 334, 348; **3:** 415, 440, 454, 470;
    4: 240
Rafuse, Robert W., Jr., **5:** 146, 147
Rai, Kul B., **6:** 386
Raiffa, Howard, **1:** 346; **2:** 321, 323, 335, 337,
    342, 346, 348; **3:** 424, 446, 456, 457, 458,
    464, 471; **7:** 142, 143, 144, 146, 147, 204,
    375, 379, 382, 395, 396, 397, 398, **8:** 343
Raine, Alden S., **2:** 110, 140; **4:** 147, 162
Rainwater, Lee, **6:** 149, 184, 221
Rakoff, Stuart H., **6:** 305, 330
Rämisch, Raimund, **3:** 310
Ramo, Simon, **6:** 89
RAND Corporation, **6:** 463–464; **8:** 278, 291,
    292
Randomization, **7:** 243–244
Ranney, Austin, **2:** 183, 221, 225, 234; **4:** 60,
    229, 239, 258, 259, 261; **6:** 383, 467
Ransom, Harry Howe, **6:** 406; **8:** 324, 347
Rapacki Plan of 1957, **8:** 299
Raphael, David D., **1:** 375
Raphaeli, Nimrod, **5:** 373
Rapoport, Anatol, **1:** 200, 305; **2:** 343; **3:** 458,
    466, 470; **7:** 182, 184, 379, 398; **8:** 15, 45,
    99, 193, 200, 315, 343, 347
Rappard, W. E., **5:** 113
Raske, Winfried, **6:** 330
Rational choice, **2:** 319, 320, 321, 326, 350, 360
    assumptions of, **2:** 323
    axioms of, **2:** 327
    multiple goals, **2:** 326
    optimal choice, **2:** 323
    process of action, **2:** 327
    single goal, **2:** 326
Rational choice paradigm, **1:** 195–204, 206
Rational choice research program
    negative heuristic, **1:** 202
    positive heuristic, **1:** 198–200, 202
Rational model, **6:** 387, 395, 410, 418, 421
"Rationale," explanations, **1:** 166
Rationale structures, **7:** 169
Rationalism, **1:** 252; **5:** 78–79, 82
Rationality, **2:** 334; **4:** 115, 118–125, 153
    conflict between individual and collective, **7:**
        362–363, 387
    individual, **3:** 464–467

individualistic theories, **7:** 182
    rational voting, **4:** 118, 121, 122
    of science, **1:** 207
    substantive, **2:** 352, 357
    as success in achieving goals, **2:** 327
Rationality, of action, **1:** 158, 192
    as dispositional concept, **1:** 158
Rationalization, **2:** 12, 73
Rationalized totalitarianism, **3:** 340
Raup, Ruth, **6:** 113
Raupach, Hans, **3:** 248
Raven, Berthran, **2:** 354
Rawls, John, **1:** 273, 276, 323, 364; **2:** 333, 360;
    3: 451, 452, 453, 455
Ray, David, **5:** 289
Ray, John L., **2:** 65
Raz, Joseph, **1:** 303, 308, 321
Read, Thornton, **8:** 318
Reading, Reid R., **2:** 99, 106, 112
Reagan, Michael D., **1:** 307; **5:** 149; **6:** 84
Realism, **8:** 422
Realpolitik, **8:** 33–43, 202, 203
Reason, **1:** 249
Reason analysis, **7:** 146, 168–175, 179
Reasons for action, **1:** 156, 160, 163, 165, 207
Reback, Gary L., **7:** 235
Rebellion, against Castile, **3:** 530
Recessions
    1948–49, **6:** 52
    1953–54, **6:** 53
    1957–58, **6:** 53
    1960–61, **6:** 55
    1969–70, **6:** 58
Rechtstaat, **3:** 177, 353
Reciprocal causation, **6:** 451–452
Recognition of states, **8:** 425–428
    constitutive or declaratory, **8:** 426
    criteria for, **8:** 427
    duty of, **8:** 426–427
Recruitment process, **2:** 159, 169
    operational definition, **2:** 159
    perspectives on, **2:** 159
Recruitment studies, **2:** 155–159, 169–171,
    229–233
    centrality of in political science, **2:** 156
    of crisis recruitment, **2:** 232–233
    importance of, **2:** 156
    and political-elite studies, **2:** 155
    purpose of, **2:** 156
    as sequence of screenings, **2:** 177
    short-term situational studies, **2:** 171
    sociological approach, **2:** 209

specialization, **2:** 230–231
strategies of research, **2:** 170–171
theoretical controversies over, **2:** 158
UNESCO study, **2:** 179
Redford, Emmette S., **5:** 385, 407, 413
Reductionist theory, **8:** 15–33, 50
  and the cause of war, **8:** 66
Reed, John Shelton, **7:** 325
Reed, Roy, **6:** 293
Reed, Thomas H., **1:** 48–49
Reedy, George, **5:** 379
Rees, Anthony M., **6:** 362
Rees, Ioan Bowen, **6:** 344
Rees, W. J. **1:** 212
Reese, Hayne W., **2:** 129
Referent system, in simulation, **7:** 224–225,
  228, 246
Reformism, **1:** 32–34
Regan, Opal G., **7:** 270, 271
Regier, C. C., **5:** 421
Regimes, **2:** 114; *See also* Authoritarian re-
  grimes; Nondemocratic regimes; Totalitarian regimes
  breakdown of, **3:** 247–248
  competitive, **3:** 135–137
  hegemonies, **3:** 118, 126–129, 273
  military, **3:** 65, 186, 275
  mixed, **3:** 127–129
  "mobilization," **3:** 241, 246
  and opposition, **3:** 107–113
  parliamentary, **5:** 275
  "personal control," **3:** 365
  presidential, **5:** 275
  reequilibration of, **3:** 354
  satellite, **3:** 371
  "sultanistic," **3:** 179, 259–263
  syncratic, **3:** 357
  threats to, **3:** 126–133
  transformation to democracy, **3:** 184–185,
    333, 337
  types of, **3:** 122
Regimes, closed
  and specialized polity, **5:** 266–268
  and unspecialized polity, **5:** 263–265
Regimes, open
  representation in specialized, **5:** 298–301
  and specialized polity, **5:** 274–277
  and unspecialized polity, **5:** 268–274
Region, concept of, **8:** 215–216
Regional integration, **8:** 364–365
  conflict and concordance in, **8:** 388–389
  dynamics of, **8:** 365, 377–389

structural conditions of, **8:** 379–381
Regionalism, **3:** 131–132
Regression analysis, **7:** 164, 167
Regulators, and international systems, **8:** 48
Regulatory agencies, independent, **5:** 385–387,
  393, 398, 401, 407
Reich, C. M., **7:** 188, 196
Reich, Charles A., **1:** 274; **5:** 400; **6:** 185, 222
Reichenbach, Hans, **8:** 75
Reid, Gordon, **5:** 235
Reid, Ira DeA., **7:** 309
Rein, Martin, **6:** 153, 168, 172, 201, 221, 222; **7:**
  240
Reinemer, Vic, **5:** 404
Reis, Fabio Wanderley, **3:** 44
Reischauer, Edwin O., **3:** 20, 97
Reisman, Arnold, **6:** 331
Reisman, W. M., **6:** 11, 14
Reitlinger, Gerald, **3:** 219
Relational concepts, **1:** 287
Relative deprivation, **7:** 281, 328, 336
Relativism, **1:** 350
Reliability, **2:** 44, 74
Religious politics, **3:** 75–83
  ahistorical religions, **3:** 76, 82–83
  Christianity, **3:** 76–77
  clericalism, **3:** 76
  ecclesiastical religions, **3:** 76
  Hinduism, **3:** 79–80
  historical religions, **3:** 75–76
  Islam, **3:** 80–81
  Theravada Buddhism, **3:** 78
Remak, Joachim, **3:** 368
Remington, Robin A., **3:** 337, 362
RePass, David E., **4:** 116, 119, 128, 129, 132,
  160; **7:** 286
Representation, **1:** 170, 176–177, 231, 232; **1:**
  390; **5:** 3–4, 70
  elemental, **1:** 231
  existential, **1:** 231
  proportional, **1:** 381
  in specialized, open regimes, **5:** 298–301
  transcendental, **1:** 231
Representative assembly, **5:** 258
Representative bureaucracy, **5:** 423–424
Representative democracy, **3:** 427–444
Repression costs, **2:** 289–290, 299
"Reproductive fallacy," **1:** 179
Republicanism, **5:** 40, 59, 68
Rescher, Nicholas, **7:** 171
Research and development allocations
  basic research, support of, **6:** 83, 86

corporate interest in, **6:** 85
for defense, **6:** 84, 86
by federal government, **6:** 80, 82, 84, 85
in health, **6:** 85
political requirements, **6:** 83
Research methodology, **6:** 448–458
decisional research, **6:** 448
experimental, **6:** 453, 455–456
"interrupted time-series analysis," **6:** 454
multiple-regression analysis, **6:** 448–449, 452
nonexperimental, **6:** 453, 454
path analysis, **6:** 452
quasi-experimental, **6:** 453–454
Research paradigms, **7:** 147–153, 168–169, 180, 197; **8:** 93–94, 96, 98
Research procedures, **7:** 148, 157
Research program, **7:** 149
Researcher, "traditional," **8:** 88, 89
Resocialization, **2:** 110–111, 131
Resource allocation, **8:** 290
Response, **2:** 6
Response-set controversy, **2:** 51
Response triviality, **7:** 250
Restoration of 1815, **3:** 543
Restrictive covenants, **6:** 274
Retrospection prediction strategy, **2:** 170
Retrospective procedure, **3:** 485, 493
Reuss, Henry, **5:** 149
Revelation, **1:** 249
Revenue sharing, **5:** 150
Revisionism, **8:** 229
Revolution, **3:** 519–541, 570–571
Aristotle's theory of, **3:** 483, 484
causes of, **3:** 490–491; **7:** 100–103
class theory of, **5:** 42
colonial, **3:** 520
conditions of, **3:** 521–541
crime rate as predictor of, **3:** 491
Egyptian, **3:** 533
estimating probability of, **3:** 483
European of 1848, **3:** 533
French, **1:** 379
ideal sequence for, **3:** 536–537
intellectuals, role of, **3:** 526
and national unity coalition structures, **3:** 582–583
of 1789, **3:** 542
Turkish, **3:** 533
Revolutionaries, evolution of, **3:** 571–573
Rhinelander, John B., **8:** 347

Ribbich, Thomas I., **6:** 184
Riccards, Michael P., **2:** 94
Rice, Stuart, **1:** 46, 47; **7:** 308
Richards, Peter G., **5:** 200, 235, 236, 306
Richardson, John M., Jr., **1:** 220; **7:** 86
Richardson, Lewis F., **1:** 184, 186; **3:** 489; **8:** 98, 99, 101, 142, 150, 163, 164, 165, 166, 167, 168, 169, 170, 171, 172, 173, 174, 175, 176, 177, 178, 179, 185, 189, 190, 191, 192, 193, 316, 340
Richmond, Mary, **6:** 120, 204, 221
Rickert, H., **7:** 122
Rickman, John, **2:** 61, 62
Ridgeway, Marian E., **5:** 151
Ridley, Clarence E., **6:** 355, 357
Ridley, F. F., **5:** 237
Ries, John C., **8:** 323
Rieselbach, Leroy N., **1:** 277; **4:** 162; **6:** 414
Riesman, David, **2:** 33, 46; **7:** 278
Riessman, Frank, **6:** 185
Rigaudias-Weiss, Hilde, **7:** 324
Rigby, T. H., **3:** 202, 210, 229, 246, 360, 362
Riggs, Fred, **3:** 3, 255; **4:** 188; **5:** 304, 373; **6:** 332, 409
Rights, **1:** 320–321, 379
minority, **1:** 393
Riker, William H., **1:** 195, 202, 285; **2:** 321; **3:** 88, 466, 469, 470; **4:** 68, 113, 160; **5:** 95, 99, 101, 102, 104, 106, 110, 111, 113, 114, 116, 117, 118, 124, 127, 129, 132, 134, 137, 139, 140, 144, 145, 154, 157, 158; **6:** 242; **7:** 86, 241, 354, 376, 395, 396, 397; **8:** 58, 65, 221
Riksdag of Sweden, **5:** 293
Riley, John, **7:** 312
Riley, Matilda White, **2:** 129; **7:** 3, 81, 105
Risk, **1:** 345–347; **2:** 328, 331
decision making under, **2:** 332, 337, 343, 347
and uncertainty, **2:** 331, 357
Rivlin, Alice M., **6:** 15, 77, 96, 97, 207; **7:** 204, 319, 320, 322, 323, 334
Robbins, Lionel, **8:** 228
Roberts, Adam, **3:** 337
Roberts, Harry V., **7:** 54, 134
Roberts, Henry L., **3:** 286, 288
Robins, Robert S., **2:** 179
Robinson, Edgar E., **4:** 231
Robinson, James A., **3:** 65; **5:** 157, 287; **6:** 17, 223, 398, 409; **8:** 94
Robinson, John P., **7:** 306
Robinson, Michael J., **7:** 239
Robinson, Richard D., **3:** 64

Robinson, Ronald, **8:** 26
Robinson, Thomas W., **3:** 360
Roche, John P., **2:** 307
Roche, T. W. E., **6:** 256
Rockefeller, Nelson A., **5:** 157
Rodgers, Harrell R., Jr., **2:** 94, 102, 106, 107, 113, 115, 138
Rodwin, Lloyd, **6:** 313
Roethlisberger, F. J., **2:** 351; **6:** 457
Rogers, David, **6:** 16, 293
Rogers, Lindsay, **5:** 307
Rogers, W. C., **2:** 115
Roggemann, H. **3:** 346
Rogger, Hans, **3:** 315
Rogin, Michael Paul, **2:** 308; **4:** 201
Rogow, Arnold A., **2:** 40, 74, 163; **3:** 470; **5:** 239; **6:** 391
Rogowski, R., **7:** 125, 135
Rohde, David, **7:** 396
Roherty, James M., **6:** 97
Rohrer, John H., **7:** 310
Roig, Charles, **2:** 99, 100, 112, 113, 115, 116, 120
Rokeach, Milton, **2:** 50, 211; **7:** 299
Rokkan, Stein, **1:** 183; **3:** 35, 77, 84, 98, 165, 312, 364, 544, 576, 577–578, 584; **4:** 3, 31, 148, 160, 246, 269; **6:** 16, 223; **7:** 45, 66, 99, 121, 287, 288
Role, **2:** 4, 21, 24
Role behavior, **2:** 355
Role expectations, **1:** 192
Role of laws and generalizations in explaining actions, **1:** 156–161, 166
Role theory, **2:** 24
Röling, B. V. A., **8:** 430
Roll, Charles W., Jr., **7:** 282
Roman law, **1:** 10; **5:** 29, 325, 339, 361
Rome, origins of dictatorship in, **3:** 185
Romney, A. Kimball, **7:** 156, 167
Ronall, Juachim O., **3:** 64
Ronfeldt, David, **3:** 367
Roosevelt, Franklin, **2:** 32
Roper, Elmo, **2:** 189; **7:** 325
Roper Public Opinion Research Center, **7:** 48–49, 50, 51, 316, 325
Ropp, Theodore, **8:** 341
Rorty, Richard, **1:** 218
Rosberg, Carl G., Jr., **3:** 322, 324
Rose, A. M., **3:** 437
Rose, Arnold, **4:** 179
Rose, Douglas D., **4:** 158; **6:** 223; **7:** 304

Rose, H. J., **5:** 15
Rose, Leo E., **3:** 254
Rose, Richard, **3:** 331, 363; **4:** 162, 208, 245, 266; **5:** 184, 196, 199, 200, 201, 203; **7:** 67
Rosecrance, Richard N., **8:** 48, 49, 50, 52, 56, 69, 78, 205, 215, 222, 223, 238, 347, 363
Rosen, Steven, **6:** 87
Rosenau, James N., **3:** 94, 371; **6:** 382, 383, 384, 385, 386, 387, 390, 391, 397, 398, 410, 413, 418; **8:** 10, 89, 94, 395
Rosenberg, Milton J., **7:** 188
Rosenberg, Morris, **2:** 17, 60, 74, 119; **7:** 214
Rosenstock, Irwin M., **6:** 440
Rosenthal, Alan, **5:** 297, 308; **8:** 281
Rosenthal, Donald B., **6:** 319, 341, 343, 361
Rosenthal, Howard, **4:** 148
Rosenthal, Robert, **6:** 467; **7:** 235, 248
Rosenweig, James, **6:** 81
Rosenzweig, Robert M., **2:** 200
Rosi, Eugene J., **8:** 346
Ross, D. Scott, **7:** 204
Ross, H. Laurence, **6:** 454, 455, 467
Ross, Irwin, **3:** 64
Ross, Philip, **3:** 516
Ross, Stanley R., **3:** 358
Ross, Thomas **6:** 406; **8:** 329
Rossi, Alice, **7:** 328
Rossi, Peter, **4:** 158; **6:** 181; **7:** 240
Rossiter, Clinton, **3:** 92, 186; **5:** 109, 192, 211, 222, 417; **7:** 10
Rostow, Walt W., **8:** 211, 340
Rotberg, Robert I., **3:** 261; **5:** 125
Roth, Guenther, **3:** 253, 259, 287, 364
Rothchild, Donald S., **5:** 124
Rothenberg, Jerome, **2:** 329, 331; **3:** 420, 421, 446, 447, 470; **5:** 143; **6:** 16
Rothman, David, **5:** 288
Rothman, Stanley, **2:** 248, 292, 307; **3:** 544; **5:** 309
Rothstein, David A., **2:** 11
Rothstein, Robert L., **6:** 408
Rothwell, C. Easton, **2:** 178, 179
Rourke, Francis E., **5:** 174, 375, 391, 394, 408
Rousseau, André, **3:** 78
Rousseau, Jean-Jacques, **1:** 215, 230, 242–243, 247, 252, 254, 260, 264, 324, 390; **8:** 54, 78, 340, 375
Rowat, Donald C., **5:** 420
Rowe, L. S., **5:** 112
Rowntree, B. Seebohm, **7:** 265, 268
Roy, Naresh, **5:** 150, 151

Royal Commission on Bilingualism and Bicul-
turalism, **5:** 151
Royal Commission on the Constitution, **5:** 297
Royal Commission on Dominion Provincial
Relations, **5:** 150
Royal Commission on Local Government in
England, **6:** 320, 327, 349, 363
Royal Commission on Taxation, **5:** 150
Rubenstein, Albert, **2:** 319
Rubenstein, Richard E., **3:** 516, 517
Rubison, Richard, **8:** 191
Ruchames, Louis, **6:** 263
Rudé, George, **3:** 499, 500
Rudner, Richard S., **1:** 179, 181, 218
Rudolph, Frederick, **6:** 83
Rudolph, Lloyd, **3:** 21, 22, 25, 30, 46; **5:** 337; **6:**
329; **7:** 105
Rudolph, Susanne Hoeber, **3:** 21, 22, 25, 30, 46;
5: 337; **6:** 329; **7:** 105
Rudwick, Elliott M., **6:** 280
Ruggie, John Gerard, **8:** 402
Ruiz, Ramón E., **3:** 86
Rule adjudication, **5:** 177
"Rule of anticipated reactions," **3:** 214
Rule application, **5:** 177
Rule-following, **1:** 169
Rule of law, **5:** 1, 4, 24, 25, 26, 31, 33, 36, 44, 59,
64
Rule-making, **5:** 177
Rules of evidence, **5:** 354
Ruling class, **5:** 4
Rummel, Rudolph J., **6:** 327; **7:** 146, 153, 156; **8:**
100, 101, 113, 130, 131, 132, 133, 134, 135,
136, 137, 139, 140, 141
Runciman, W. G., **3:** 150; **6:** 195, 245
Rundquist, Barry Spencer, **5:** 291
Rush, Gary B., **7:** 272
Rush, Michael, **5:** 306
Rush, Myron, **3:** 360; **8:** 294, 331, 345
Rusk, Jerrold G., **4:** 158, 161, 162; **7:** 306
Russell, Bertrand, **1:** 288
Russell, Robert W., **8:** 391
Russett, Bruce M., **1:** 187; **3:** 5, 9, 61, 74, 97,
142, 170; **6:** 16, 98; **7:** 54, 64; **8:** 75, 204,
216, 218, 221, 316, 318, 323, 326, 365, 380
Rustow, Dankwart A., **3:** 3, 14, 32, 91, 92, 98,
122, 180, 181, 357, 360, 365; **5:** 305
Rutherford, Brent M., **2:** 23, 45, 74, 212,
213
Ryan, Cornelius, **7:** 37
Ryle, Gilbert, **2:** 5

SA oath, **3:** 359
Sabine, George H., **1:** 8, 11, 47; **3:** 177
Sacks, Seymour, **6:** 312, 330, 363
Saddle point, **7:** 381
SAFEGUARD, **8:** 258, 306
Safran, William, **5:** 238
Salamon, Lester M., **3:** 92
Salamore, Steven, **8:** 113
Salisbury, Robert H., **2:** 190, 191, 197, 233,
289, 307, 310; **4:** 184, 189, 193, 198, 199,
200, 202, 204; **6:** 210, 448
Saloma, John S., **4:** 270; **5:** 419
Salomon, Jean-Jacques, **6:** 100
Saloutos, Theodore, **4:** 194
SALT I, **8:** 308, 309–310
SALT II, **8:** 312, 313
SALT III, **8:** 313
Salvemini, Gaetano, **3:** 315
Samberg, Robert, **5:** 157
Samelson, Franz, **2:** 48, 49, 50
SAMOS reconnaissance satellites, **8:** 296, 297
Sample space, **2:** 344–345
Sampling, **7:** 251–253
Sampson, Anthony, **8:** 371
Samuel, William, **7:** 249
Samuelson, Paul, **3:** 421, 446; **6:** 15, 76
Sanders, Ralph, **6:** 97
Sanders, Thomas G., **3:** 78
Sanford, R. Nevitt, **2:** 46, 47; **3:** 363
Sanford, Terry, **5:** 149
Sankoff, David, **7:** 383
Sanskritization, **3:** 22, 25
Santos, C. R., **5:** 184
Sapin, Burton M., **5:** 212, 222, 223, 234; **6:** 389,
402, 421; **8:** 89, 94, 231
Sapolsky, Harvey M., **6:** 85, 87, 88, 93; **8:** 323
Saposnik, Rubin, **3:** 424; **7:** 397
Sarbin, Theodore R., **6:** 402
Sargent, Thomas J., **3:** 428
Sarkesian, Sam C., **8:** 327
Sarlvik, Bo, **4:** 159
Sarmiento, D. F., **5:** 96, 112
Sarti, Roland, **3:** 367
Sartori, Giovanni, **2:** 162, 163, 167, 204, 208; **3:**
176, 184, 185, 243, 244, 274, 294, 358; **4:**
235, 240, 248
Sastri, K. V. S., **5:** 150
Satellite regimes, **3:** 371
Satisficing, **1:** 344; **2:** 332, 333, 347, 348; **3:** 443
Sauer, Wolfgang, **3:** 248, 336, 362, 369
Saunders, Charles B., **6:** 464

Saunders, Robert J., **6**: 330
Savage, E., **8**: 343, 347
Savage, Leonard J., **2**: 323
Savage, Richard, **8**: 110
Savage, Robert L., **7**: 248
Savigny, Friedrich Karl von, **5**: 29
Sawyer, Jack, **7**: 383
Sayeed, Khalid B., **3**: 81
Sayre, Wallace S., **6**: 335, 361
Scalapino, Robert A., **3**: 239, 248, 336, 366
Scarrow, Harold A., **1**: 311, 312, 315
Scarrow, Howard A., **4**: 258; **6**: 458, 467
Scelle, Georges, **8**: 417
Scenarios
    "business-as-usual," **7**: 427–428
    "context," **7**: 431
    defined, **7**: 427
    "surprise-free," **7**: 428–430
    "what-if," **7**: 430
Schaar, John H., **2**: 51, 52
Schaefer, Elma, **2**: 329, 330, 348
Schaefer, Guenther, **6**: 305, 330
Schäfer, Wolfgang, **3**: 361, 362, 370
Schaie, K. Warner, **2**: 129, 139
Schaller, Howard G., **6**: 307
Schanberg, Sidney H., **6**: 246
Schanck, Richard, **7**: 146, 190, 191, 196, 197, 203, 280
Schapiro, Leonard, **3**: 187, 206, 236, 247, 336, 362
Schapiro, Meyer, **2**: 26
Schaps, Ronald, **5**: 137, 139
Schattschneider, E. E., **1**: 47; **2**: 244, 291, 309; **4**: 180, 192, 222, 237, 250; **5**: 288, 392; **6**: 172; **7**: 14, 20, 266
Scheffer-Van der Veen, Maria, **5**: 183, 199, 201, 202, 203
Scheffler, Israel, **1**: 218; **8**: 75
Scheiber, Harry N., **5**: 104, 140; **6**: 83
Schein, Edgar H., **3**: 224
Scheingold, Stuart A., **8**: 377, 378, 383, 384, 385, 395, 398, 401
Scheinman, Lawrence, **8**: 384, 385
Scheler, Max, **1**: 257
Schelling, Thomas, **2**: 320, 349; **6**: 389, 395; **7**: 387, 393, 395; **8**: 200, 284, 285, 300, 315, 318, 343, 345, 396
Scherer, Frederick M., **6**: 87, 88; **8**: 303, 323
Scheuch, Erwin K., **2**: 186; **7**: 53, 54, 284
Schick, Allen, **5**: 406
Schick, Frederick, **3**: 424, 438

Schild, E. O., **7**: 241
Schilling, Warner R., **5**: 377, 384, 403; **6**: 91, 390, 409; **8**: 303, 323, 331
Schindler, Margaret C., **7**: 6
Schlaifer, Robert, **2**: 321, 346, 348; **7**: 204
Schlesinger, Arthur, Jr., **5**: 36, 232, 239, 377, 383; **6**: 220, 395, 404
Schlesinger, G., **1**: 293, 294
Schlesinger, James R., **6**: 96; **8**: 344
Schlesinger, Joseph A., **2**: 170, 198, 204, 205, 207; **4**: 234, 249; **5**: 200, 202
Schlesinger, Rudolph, **5**: 100, 122, 126, 361
Schlick, Moritz, **1**: 291
Schmandt, Henry J., **6**: 222, 312, 256
Schmeckebier, Laurence F., **7**: 22
Schmidhauser, John, **4**: 243; **5**: 110, 145, 160
Schmidt, Carl T., **3**: 367
Schmitt, Carl, **3**: 177, 185, 186, 220
Schmitt, Hans O., **8**: 386
Schmitter, Philippe C., **2**: 308; **3**: 51, 65, 235, 285, 289, 291, 302, 306, 307, 311, 312, 366, 367, 618; **8**: 379, 380, 381, 383, 384, 385
Schneider, Anne L., **3**: 9, 10
Schneider, Herbert W., **3**: 367
Schneider, Jeanne, **3**: 97
Schneider, Peter R., **3**: 9, 10
Schneider, Ronald M., **3**: 248, 367
Schnore, Leo F., **6**: 309
Schoenbaum, David, **3**: 231, 232
Schofield, Norman, **3**: 454
Scholtz, Harold, **3**: 204
Schonfield, Andrew, **5**: 403
School desegregation, **6**: 257, 263, 287, 292–293
    Roberts v. *City of Boston*, **6**: 263
School Desegregation Cases, **6**: 273
Schooler, Dean, Jr., **6**: 93
Schöpflin, George, **3**: 337
Schorn, Hubert, **3**: 222
Schorr, Alvin L., **6**: 143, 220
Schram, Stuart R., **3**: 366
Schrodt, Philip A., **8**: 191
Schubert, Glendon, **3**: 342, 414; **7**: 396
Schueller, George K., **3**: 238
Schulberg, Herbert C., **2**: 75
Schuler, Edgar, **5**: 123
Schuler, Kathryn, **5**: 123
Schultz, Theodore W., **6**: 77, 135
Schultze, Charles L., **6**: 77, 207, 223
Schulz, Gerhard, **3**: 248, 336, 362
Schulz, John E., **6**: 467

Schuman, Howard, **2:** 102; **6:** 349, 357; **7:** 289, 290, 291, 295, 299, 300
Schumann, Hans-Gerd, **3:** 232
Schumpeter, Joseph A., **3:** 358; **8:** 23, 24, 31, 76, 226, 230
Schurmann, Franz, **3:** 190, 201, 204, 205, 206, 209, 212, 240, 342, 361, 366
Schutz, Alfred, **1:** 216, 295
Schuyler, Robert L., **5:** 66
Schwartz, Anna Jacobson, **6:** 77
Schwartz, Barry A., **6:** 254, 280
Schwartz, Bernard, **5:** 400
Schwartz, David C., **2:** 54, 214
Schwartz, Herman, **5:** 409
Schwartz, Joel J., **2:** 96, 134, 135, 136, 137, 141; **4:** 117
Schwartz, Mildred A., **4:** 258, 265
Schwartz, Richard D., **7:** 222
Schwarz, Fredrick, **5:** 124
Schwarz, John E., **3:** 72
Schweitzer, Arthur, **3:** 232, 362
Schwödiauer, Gerhard, **3:** 470
Science policy, American
  in comparative perspective, **6:** 97–100
  in historical perspective, **6:** 82–86
"Scientific" ideal, **1:** 134–154
  explanation, scientific, **1:** 135–140
  theories, choice and testing of, **1:** 145–153
  theories, scientific, **1:** 140–145
Scientific management, **2:** 332, 351, 353
Scientific method, **7:** 211
  plausibility principle, **7:** 213
  plausible hypotheses, **7:** 213
  rules of, **7:** 213
Scientific progress, **1:** 195, 200–204
Scientific research programs, **1:** 151–153, 194–195, 196, 208
  positive heuristic, **1:** 198–200
Scientific study of international politics (SSIP)
  definition of, **8:** 88–92
  evolution of research, **8:** 92–99
  use of indices in, **8:** 101–111
Scientific task, **6:** 4–5
Scientific theory, **7:** 351, 353, 354
Scientism, **1:** 47–50
Scientists as advisors, **6:** 90–95
Scioli, Frank P., Jr., **7:** 235, 240, 242, 248, 249
Scoble, Harry, **4:** 3, 186, 203, 217; **6:** 327, 328
Scott, Andrew M., **6:** 392, 400, 404
Scott, James C., **3:** 97
Scott, Joseph W., **2:** 70
Scott, Robert, **3:** 30, 312, 358

Scott, Robert, **7:** 321
Scott, William A., **6:** 395; **7:** 274, 305
Scott, Wolf, **6:** 327
Scriven, Michael, **1:** 218; **2:** 6
Searing, Donald D., **2:** 96, 134, 135, 136, 137, 141, 185, 186, 189; **4:** 117; **5:** 202, 203
Searle, John R., **1:** 167–168, 180, 301, 318, 319
Sears, David O., **2:** 8, 23, 94, 96, 97, 99, 102, 106, 107, 110, 115, 116, 117, 121, 122, 123, 124, 125, 126, 127, 128, 131, 133, 134, 135, 136, 137, 138, 139, 140, 141; **4:** 158, 160; **7:** 278, 279, 302
Secession, **3:** 131
"Secession-potential" of a state, **5:** 142
Secher, H. Pierre, **4:** 243
Sechrest, Lee, **7:** 222
Second Continental Congress of 1776, **5:** 95
Second-strike capability, **8:** 282, 288
Secondary analysis, **7:** 45–46, 56, 60
Secord, P. F., **7:** 174
Secrecy, bureaucratic, **5:** 378, 380
Secret police, **5:** 264
Secretary of state, American, **5:** 214
Secretary of the treasury, **6:** 39
Sectionalism, state control and, **3:** 510
Sects, **3:** 81–82
Securities and Exchange Commission, **5:** 400
Security, **3:** 123–124
  in polyarchies, **3:** 134
"Security dilemma," **8:** 250, 314, 337, 339
Seddig, Robert G., **2:** 307
Seidel, Bruno, **3:** 187
Seidenberg, Bernard, **2:** 49
Seiler, John A., **2:** 320
Self, Peter, **4:** 215
Self-determination, **8:** 423
Self-understandings, **1:** 132
Seligman, Lester G., **2:** 171, 172–173, 220, 221, 222, 231; **4:** 179; **5:** 207, 223
Sellars, W. F., **1:** 220, 397
Sellers, Charles G., **4:** 161
Selten, Reinhard, **3:** 458, 461
Selznick, Philip, **2:** 245, 309, 324, 350; **3:** 586, 589; **5:** 386, 397
Semantic concepts, **7:** 190, 197
Semantic differential scales, **7:** 83, 276
Semiconstitutional monarchies, **3:** 264
Sen, Amartya K., **1:** 341, 397; **2:** 321; **3:** 415, 418, 419, 420, 421, 422, 423, 424, 425, 426, 430, 431, 432, 446, 450, 451, 452, 457, 469
Sen, Subrata, **3:** 442
Senate, **2:** 62

Senate Committee on Government Operations, Subcommittee on National Security Staffing and Operations, **6:** 403
Senate Finance Committee, **6:** 40
Senate Foreign Relations Committee, **6:** 401
SENTINEL system, **8:** 306
Separate-but-equal doctrine, **6:** 263, 272
Separation-of-powers, **4:** 243, 260, 264, 265; **5:** 6, 33, 34, 35, 37–40, 55, 73–76, 176, 234, 275, 341, 344
and the classical mixed state, **5:** 41–44
Separatism, **6:** 296–297
Servan-Schreiber, Jean-Jacques, **6:** 98
Seton-Watson, Hugh, **3:** 239, 286, 288, 335, 359
Settlement-house movements, **6:** 120, 164
17-hydro-oxycorticosteroid, **2:** 64
Sessions, Vivian S., **7:** 52
Sewell, William H., **6:** 467; **7:** 322
Shabad, Goldie, **4:** 13, 16
Shackleton, Robert, **1:** 14
Shaffer, Harry G., **3:** 236, 366
Shaffer, Jerome A., **1:** 297, 300
Shanks, John Merrill, **4:** 161
Shannon, Wayne, **5:** 288
Shapere, Dudley, **1:** 218
Shapiro, Barbara J., **5:** 355
Shapiro, Gilbert, **7:** 56
Shapiro, Howard B., **6:** 382, 398
Shapiro, Martin, **5:** 321, 330, 342, 345, 360, 420; **6:** 467
Shapiro, Michael, **4:** 68, 160, 161, 162; **7:** 189
Shaplen, Robert, **7:** 5
Shapley, L. S., **2:** 358; **3:** 458, 470; **5:** 137; **7:** 396
Shapley value, **7:** 396
Sharan, Parmatma, **5:** 123
Sharkansky, Ira, **2:** 248; **3:** 65; **4:** 2; **6:** 223, 305, 309, 323, 329, 330, 342, 356, 363, 447, 467, 468
Sharp, Gene, **8:** 315
Sharpe, L. J., **6:** 335, 344, 362
Shaull, Richard, **6:** 407
Shaver, Phillip R., **7:** 306
Shaw, Albert, **6:** 345
Shaw, J. C., **2:** 320
Shaw, Malcolm, **5:** 295
Shaw, Marvin E., **7:** 306
Shaw, Paul C., **5:** 161
Sheahan, John, **6:** 77
Sheatsley, Paul B., **2:** 25, 104, 115, 116, 131; **7:** 311, 312, 325
Sheehan, Neil, **6:** 400

Sheffield, James, **7:** 242
Sheldon, Eleanor, **6:** 206, 462
Shelley v. *Kraemer,* **6:** 274
Shepard, Roger N., **7:** 156, 167
Shepard, W. J., **5:** 273, 303
Shepsle, Kenneth A., **2:** 321; **3:** 13; **7:** 384
Sherbenou, Edgar L., **6:** 341
Sherif, Muzafer, **2:** 216
Sherman, Richard B., **6:** 278
Sherman Anti-Trust Act, **5:** 343
Sherwin, Charles W., **6:** 86
Shils, Edward, **1:** 390; **2:** 18, 50, 69; **3:** 178, 180, 274, 286, 287, 357; **6:** 86, 100
Shively, Phillips W., **4:** 160
Shonfield, Andrew, **4:** 216; **5:** 423; **6:** 76
Shore, Arnold, **7:** 239, 249, 321
Shoup, Paul, **3:** 365; **5:** 100, 126, 133
Shubik, Martin, **2:** 358; **3:** 443, 464, 470; **5:** 137; **6:** 17; **7:** 384, 389, 395, 396, 398, 399; **8:** 78, 343, 347
Shulman, Marshall D., **6:** 396
Shultz, George P., **6:** 77
Sibley, Mulford Q., **1:** 293
Sica, Morris G., **2:** 102, 111, 140
Sicinski, Andrzej, **2:** 104
Sidgwick, Henry, **1:** 398
Siegel, Barry N., **6:** 324, 325
Siegel, Sidney, **3:** 470
Siegfried, Andre, **3:** 617; **4:** 112, 159
Siffin, William J., **5:** 429
Sigal, Leon V., **5:** 396, 421; **6:** 409
Sigel, Roberta S., **2:** 11, 94, 102, 104, 107, 116; **5:** 225
Silent revolution, **3:** 239
Sills, David, **4:** 176
Silva, Umberto, **3:** 359
Silver, Allan, **4:** 245
Silver, Brian, **3:** 97, 98
Silverman, Corinne, **4:** 207
Silvert, Kalman, **3:** 367
Simaan, Marwan, **8:** 191
Simandjuntak, B., **5:** 124
Simeon, Richard, **5:** 136, 150
Simmel, Georg, **5:** 322
Simmons, Ernest J., **3:** 358, 363
Simmons, Robert H., **5:** 428
Simmons, Roberta G., **2:** 119
Simon, Herbert A., **1:** 216, 284, 285, 305, 344; **2:** 320, 322, 323, 328, 331, 332, 345, 349, 351, 355, 358, 359; **3:** 442; **5:** 303, 376, 386; **6:** 355, 357, 400, 403, 421; **7:** 171; **8:** 400
Simon, Yves, **1:** 274

Simons, John, **5:** 59
Simons, William R., **6:** 419
Simpson, Paul B., **3:** 441
Simpson, Smith, **6:** 391, 404
Simulation, **8:** 95–96
  all-analog, **7:** 223, 241
  all-deductive, **7:** 227
  and availability of measurement
    techniques, **7:** 227–228
  and computers, **8:** 97, 101
  inter-nation, **7:** 225, 228, 241
  laboratories, **8:** 95, 96
  man-computer, **8:** 95, 97
  "manned," **7:** 241
  of political phenomena, **7:** 221–229
  referent system in, **7:** 224–225, 228
  and theory, **7:** 223
Sindler, Allan P., **4:** 239
Singer, Eleanor, **7:** 328
Singer, H. W., **6:** 75; **8:** 77
Singer, J. David, **6:** 386, 418, 419; **7:** 56, 64,
    115; **8:** 6, 7, 9, 13, 112, 113, 143, 144, 145,
    146, 148, 149, 150, 212, 215, 223, 231
Singer, Marshall R., **2:** 159
Singer, Milton, **2:** 30, 61
Single-member district, **5:** 299–300
Single party, **3:** 324–326
  in authoritarian regimes, **3:** 291
  and corporativism, **3:** 310
  government-sponsored, **3:** 285
  internal democracy within, **3:** 282
  preselection of candidates, **3:** 326
  social equality in, **3:** 194
Single-peakedness, **7:** 370, 371
Sino-Soviet conflict, **8:** 268
SIOP (Single Integrated Operations Plan), **8:**
    298, 320
Situational control, **7:** 230
Six Day War of 1967, **8:** 265
Sjoberg, Gideon, **5:** 423
Skidmore, Max J., **6:** 448
Skilling, H. Gordon, **3:** 126, 157, 229, 238, 245,
    277, 336, 337, 338, 339, 340, 341, 343, 344,
    345, 346, 347; **4:** 204
Skinner, B. F., **1:** 277; **2:** 6; **7:** 218
Skolnick, Jerome, **3:** 515; **4:** 27; **5:** 385, 426
Skolnikoff, Eugene B., **6:** 93, 99
Skurnik, W. A. E., **6:** 386, 396, 418
Slater, Jerome, **6:** 86
Slavery
  ancient, **6:** 250–251
  in Brazil, **6:** 264–265
  and capitalism, **6:** 250–251, 264
  in the Caribbean, **6:** 255–256

  in England, **6:** 254–255
  in Latin America, **6:** 242, 263
  in United States, **6:** 241, 259–260
SLBM (Submarine-Launched Ballistic Mis-
    sile), **8:** 269, 270, 289
Small, Melvin, **7:** 56, 64; **8:** 143, 146, 149, 150
Small group theory, **2:** 320
Smallwood, Frank, **6:** 349
Smart, J. J. C., **1:** 218
Smelser, Neil J., **2:** 5, 56; **3:** 488, 525, 526, 614;
    6: 392
Smelser, William T., **2:** 5; **6:** 392
Smith, Adam, **1:** 382
Smith, Arthur K., Jr., **3:** 9
Smith, Bruce L. R., **6:** 94, 95, 463; **8:** 344
Smith, Constance, **4:** 203
Smith, David **2:** 254; **3:** 97; **4:** 172; **6:** 166, 169,
    211
Smith, Donald E., **3:** 75, 79, 80
Smith, Joel, **2:** 123, 190, 191, 192, 196
Smith, K. Wayne, **6:** 81, 406, 422; **8:** 323
Smith, Katherine Archer, **7:** 288
Smith, M. Brewster, **2:** 1, 5, 9, 13, 27, 34, 35, 51,
    58, 69, 70; **4:** 84; **7:** 278, 287
Smith, M. G., **8:** 78
Smith, Marshall S., **7:** 322
Smith, Michael, **3:** 67, 79; **5:** 424
Smith, Paul E., **1:** 132
Smith, Perry M., **6:** 84
Smith, T. V., **1:** 252
Smith, Trevor, **6:** 362
Smith v. Allwright, **6:** 273, 288
Smithies, Arthur, **3:** 442
Smoke, Richard, **6:** 419; **8:** 316, 343
Smoker, Paul, **8:** 190
Smookler, Helene V., **2:** 107
Sniderman, Paul M., **2:** 1, 12, 51, 52, 53
Snow, C. P., **5:** 378; **6:** 91
Snowden, Frank M., Jr., **6:** 250
Snowiss, Leo M., **2:** 174, 220; **5:** 287
Snyder, Frank Gregory, **3:** 324, 369
Snyder, Glenn H., **6:** 395; **8:** 204, 278, 344
Snyder, Richard C., **6:** 17, 389, 421; **7:** 211, 225,
    241, 246; **8:** 89, 94, 231, 303
Soboul, Albert, **3:** 499
Social background variables, **2:** 26–27
Social change, **1:** 175, 183, 191, 210
Social choice, methods of, **7:** 373–376
Social cleavages, **7:** 287–288
Social contract, theory of, **5:** 64, 74
Social control, **5:** 333–341, 347, 353, 359–360
Social Decision Function (SDF), **3:** 418, 425,
    426, 431, 433, 436, 437, 468
Social deference, **5:** 265

Social Democratic Party **3:** 531, 532; **4:** 238
Social efficiency, **7:** 363–368
Social engineering, **3:** 83
Social equity, **2:** 360; **7:** 363–368
Social groups
  and group politics, **2:** 285–287
  and the stability-disruption protest model, **2:** 287–288
Social mobility, **2:** 131; **7:** 271–272, 273, 274
Social mobilization, **3:** 12–13, 14, 25–26, 27, 68–75
Social movements, **2:** 284–285, 299–301
Social orders, **3:** 138–139
  centrally dominated, **3:** 138
  pluralistic, **3:** 138, 144–145
Social-process approach to political development analysis, **3:** 3; **6:** 4
Social Science Data and Program Library Service, **7:** 50
Social Science Research Archive, **7:** 51
Social Science Research Council, **7:** 308
Social Science Research Council's Committee on Governmental and Legal Processes, **6:** 383
Social Science Research Council Survey Archive, **7:** 51
Social sciences, **1:** 251
  behavioral, **1:** 251
Social Security Act, **6:** 113, 121, 133, 137
  public welfare since, **6:** 115–157
Social services, **6:** 137, 140, 141, 144, 147, 156, 186–195
  casework, **6:** 127–128, 129
  vs. financial relief, **6:** 122–130
Social stratification theory, **2:** 177–178, 179, 219
  social background characteristics, **2:** 177–186
Social structure
  and authoritarian regimes, **3:** 295
  and political intelligence, **3:** 584–599
  and posttotalitarian regimes, **3:** 340
  and the utility of power, **3:** 560–584
Social Welfare Function (SWF), **3:** 417, 423, 425, 426, 431, 436, 449, 468
Social work, **6:** 121, 128
  community organization, **6:** 170–171
Societal variables in foreign policy, **6:** 412–414
  participation characteristics of, **6:** 413
  structural characteristics of, **6:** 412–413
  substantive characteristics of, **6:** 413–414
Socialism, Maximalist, **3:** 315
Socialist legality, **3:** 339
Socialization, **2:** 15

environmental, **2:** 16
Socialization, preadult and adult, **2:** 190–194
  adult experiences, **2:** 192
  initial interest in politics, **2:** 190–191
  predispositions characteristic of, **2:** 193
  as residual category, **2:** 195
  school politics, **2:** 191
Socialization residues, persistence of early, **2:** 113–114
Society, **1:** 243, 244, 247, 255
  agrarian, **3:** 139–140, 141
  class, **1:** 248
  closed, **1:** 245, 258, 262
  commercial and industrial, **3:** 140–141
  communist, **1:** 248
  free-farmer, **3:** 139
  traditional peasant, **3:** 139
Socio-demographic background data, comparisons of, **2:** 180–181, 183, 185, 209, 215
Socioeconomic development, **3:** 142–145
  and polyarchy, **3:** 142
Socioeconomic modernization
  and increase in political participation, **3:** 33–38
  and political institutions, **3:** 47–48
  and political stability, **3:** 7–10
  rates of change in, **3:** 15
Sociology of knowledge, **8:** 276
Socrates, **1:** 9, 232, 244, 261, 263
Sofer, Elaine G., **2:** 46
Solaún, Mauricio, **3:** 263, 304, 367
Solomon, Richard H., **2:** 61; **3:** 363
Solomon Four Group Design, **7:** 238–239
Solow, Robert M., **6:** 76, 77, 99
Solzhenitsyn, Aleksandr I., **3:** 217
Somit, Albert, **1:** 27, 35, 38, 39, 42, 48, 67, 72, 124; **2:** 30
Sonderbund, **5:** 117
Sonquist, John A., **2:** 17, 27
Sontag, F. H., **4:** 270
Sontheimer, Kurt, **3:** 319, 363; **5:** 196, 237
Sorauf, Frank J., **2:** 182; **4:** 162, 236, 252; **5:** 415
Sorensen, Theodore O., **5:** 219
Sorenson, Theodore, **2:** 355; **6:** 404; **8:** 345
Sorokin, Pitirim A., **3:** 370
Sosnovy, Timothy, **6:** 335
Soule, John W., **2:** 104, 164, 193
South Africa, Republic of
  caste system in, **3:** 326
  political development of, **3:** 72–73, 183
"Southern Manifesto," **6:** 293
Sovereignty, **5:** 38, 41, 56, 64; **8:** 418, 421, 424
  legislative, **5:** 64

in the Middle Ages, **5:** 46
parliamentary, **5:** 55, 64
state **5:** 7
Soviet Union
  federalism of, **5:** 102, 122, 151
  leadership of, **3:** 232
  party in, **3:** 199–200
  party membership, **3:** 362
  revitalization of the party in, **3:** 342
Spacensky, Alain, **3:** 369
Spaeth, Joe L., **2:** 128, 130
Spanier, John W., **8:** 278, 342, 345
Spatial modelling, **7:** 377
Spatial models of collective choice, **3:** 438–441
  equilibrium in, **3:** 438–441
Spear, Allan H., **6:** 269
Special Tribunal for the Defense of the State, **3:** 219
Spector, Bertram, **8:** 130, 134, 136
Spector, Marshall, **1:** 144, 145, 216
Speculation decision maker, **2:** 339
Speer, Albert, **3:** 214, 362
Speier, Hans, **3:** 357; **6:** 412; **8:** 341
Spheres of influence, **8:** 263
Spiegel, Steven L., **8:** 215
Spielmann, Karl F., Jr., **8:** 347
Spilerman, Seymour, **6:** 358
Spindler, James W., **3:** 218
Spiro, Herbert J., **3:** 241; **5:** 125, 130
Spiro, Melford E., **2:** 25
Sprague, John D., **2:** 200, 204, 206, 207, 208
Sprout, Harold, **6:** 398; **8:** 89, 91, 201, 233, 340
Sprout, Margaret, **6:** 398; **8:** 89, 91, 201, 233, 340
Sputnik, **8:** 293–294, 325
  launching of, **6:** 84
Srinivas, M. N., **3:** 25
Srole, Leo, **2:** 23
SSRC Committee on Comparative Politics, **3:** 3, 91
St. Augustine, **1:** 11, 230, 231, 241, 245, 248, 252, 260, 263
St. Thomas Aquinas, **1:** 10, 241, 260, 263
Staats, Elmer B., **6:** 96
Stability-disruption-protest model, **2:** 260–262, 265–267, 270–272, 274, 280, 287–294, 297–298, 304, 307
Stabler, John R., **2:** 119
Staff, Ilse, **3:** 222
Staffieri, J. Robert, **2:** 119

Staley, Eugene, **8:** 31
Stalin, Joseph, **3:** 201, 206, 218, 219, 221, 224, 225, 238, 241, 245, 246, 247, 251, 262, 336, 338, 340, 342, 344, 362
Stalin Constitution, **3:** 199–200
Stalinism, **3:** 177, 240, 362
Stalker, G. M., **2:** 357
Stanković, S. A., **3:** 362
Stanley, David T., **5:** 183, 202, 203
Stanley, Julian C., **6:** 453; **7:** 146, 217, 231, 232, 237, 238, 243
Stanyer, J., **6:** 339, 344, 362
Stark, Rodney, **3:** 614
Starsinic, Donald E., **7:** 297
"State," **1:** 230, 248
  definition of, **3:** 502
  in multiethnic societies, **3:** 332
State autonomy, economic threats to, **8:** 390
State legislatures, American, **5:** 296
Statements
  descriptive, **1:** 316
  metaethical, **1:** 316
  normative, **1:** 316
  of regularity, **7:** 88
States General of the Netherlands, **5:** 292
Statesmanship, **5:** 40
Statistical decision theory, **2:** 348
  maximum likelihood, **2:** 348
  null hypothesis, **2:** 348
Statistical independence, **7:** 215
Statistical inference, **7:** 142–143, 148, 153, 154, 157–158
  causal inference, **7:** 144, 153
Statistical practices, **7:** 147–153, 168–169, 189, 201
  components of, **7:** 148
  criticism of, **7:** 152–153
  foundations of, **7:** 147–148
  traditions of, **7:** 148, 150–151, 153, 154–155
Statistical procedures, **7:** 157–167
Statistical traditions, **7:** 148, 150–151, 153, 154–155, 201
Statistical training, **7:** 157
Statistics
  branches of, **7:** 142–143, 148
  descriptive, **7:** 146, 148, 152, 158
  inferential, **7:** 143
  origins of, **7:** 141–142
  standards used in, **7:** 158
  use of in experimental research, **7:** 143

Status consistency, **7:** 272–273
Status inconsistency, **2:** 131; **7:** 272–273, 335; **8:** 149
Stauffer, Robert B., **5:** 268
Stedry, Richard, **2:** 328, 349
Steed, Robert P., **7:** 240
Steele, A. T., **6:** 413
Stein, Arthur, **8:** 238
Stein, Eric, **6:** 93; **8:** 345
Stein, Harold, **2:** 324; **6:** 390; **8:** 303, 326
Stein, Herbert, **6:** 76
Stein, Janice, **6:** 384, 390
Stein, Michael, **5:** 106
Stein, Morris I., **6:** 15
Steinberg, Blema, **6:** 384, 390
Steinbruner, John D., **6:** 382, 389, 390, 395, 400, 405, 421, 422; **8:** 324, 346
Steiner, Gilbert Y., **5:** 426; **6:** 114, 117, 143, 149, 152, 154, 158, 161, 192, 212, 215, 221
Steiner, Peter O., **6:** 77
Steinmetz Archives, **7:** 51
Stember, C. H., **2:** 134
Stepan, Alfred, **3:** 239, 248, 293, 294, 295, 298, 303, 308, 333, 354, 364, 364, 365, 367
Stephan, Frederick F., **7:** 268, 269, 307, 308
Stephens, G. Ross, **6:** 312, 356
Stephens, J. H., **5:** 421
Stephenson, Gilbert Thomas, **6:** 245, 257, 263, 276
Stephenson, Peter, **7:** 288
Stephenson, William, **7:** 248
Stern, Fritz, **3:** 363
Stern, Philip, **6:** 93
Stern, Robert L., **7:** 27
Stevenson, Charles L., **1:** 319, 324, 378
Stewart, J. D., **4:** 176, 213
Stewart, Philip, **3:** 336
Stiefbold, Rodney, **2:** 112, 115
Stimulus-response model, **8:** 123–128
Stinchcombe, Arthur, **3:** 618, 619; **8:** 76
Stoessinger, John, **8:** 315
Stoicism, **1:** 245
Stoics, **1:** 9–10; **5:** 18
Stokes, Donald E., **1:** 231; **2:** 9, 49, 103, 124, 125, 127, 129, 134, 137, 184, 332, 362; **3:** 443; **4:** 27, 64, 85, 90, 94, 98, 99, 100, 110, 113, 133, 149, 150, 152, 153, 154, 157, 158, 159, 160, 162, 234, 245, 247, 248; **6:** 215; **7:** 146, 218, 277, 282, 283, 286, 302, 303, 304
Stokes, Sybil L., **5:** 373

Stokes, William S., **5:** 133
Stolberg, Winton, **5:** 109
Stoljar, S. J., **5:** 30
Stoll, Clarice, **7:** 3
Stolz, Otto G., **5:** 150
Stone, Alan, **5:** 401
Stone, Julius, **5:** 327; **7:** 16
Stone, Lawrence, **3:** 485, 544
Stone, Philip, **7:** 53, 284
Stone, Walter J., **6:** 458
Storing, Herbert J., **4:** 215
Stouffer, Samuel A., **2:** 115, 116, 134; **7:** 281, 290, 295, 308, 316, 317, 318, 328, 330, 331
Stradling, Robert, **2:** 100, 101, 106, 112, 113, 115; **5:** 223
Strange, John H., **6:** 296
Strategic Air Command (SAC), **8:** 259, 278–279, 288
  selection of air bases for, **8:** 291
Strategic Arms Limitation Talks (SALT), **8:** 306
Strategic forces, **8:** 270, 289, 305, 307
Strategic studies, **8:** 286, 305–313, 317–321, 335–339
Strategic superiority, **8:** 306–307
Strauss, A. L., **7:** 107
Strauss, Eric, **5:** 413
Strauss, Leo, **1:** 273, 275
Strauss, Murray A., **7:** 289
Strayer, Joseph R., **3:** 87
Strickland, Stephen P., **6:** 85
"Strife events," **3:** 494
Strikebreakers, **6:** 279–280
Stritch, Thomas, **3:** 306
Strong equilibrium point, **7:** 394
Strothmann, Dietrich, **3:** 358
Strotz, Robert H., **3:** 449
Strunk, Mildred, **7:** 325
Struve, W. C., **3:** 363
Stuckey, John, **8:** 13, 144, 148
Stuhler, Barbara, **2:** 115
Stupak, Ronald J., **6:** 403
Sturm, Thomas A., **6:** 93
Styskal, Richard, **2:** 325
Suárez, Andrés, **3:** 366
Subcultural pluralism, **3:** 152–153
  and polyarchy, **3:** 153
Subject headings, library, **7:** 11–13
Subjective interest approach, **2:** 257, 269, 273–274, 279–280, 294–295, 299

Subjective probability, **2:** 341; **7:** 144
Submission of Recorded Presidential Conversations, **5:** 304
Subramaniam, V., **5:** 423, 424
Succession crises, **3:** 195, 340
Suchman, Edward, **6:** 15, 307; **7:** 240
Sudman, Seymour, **7:** 297, 298, 299
Suedfeld, Peter, **7:** 249
Suffrage, **3:** 134
Sugar, Peter E., **3:** 63
Suicide rate, as index of disequilibrium, **3:** 491
Sullivan, John D., **8:** 94, 99
Sullivan, John L., **6:** 223
"Sultanistic" regime, **3:** 179, 259–263
Summers, Gene F., **7:** 305
Sundquist, James L., **4:** 138, 139, 141, 147, 247; **5:** 149, 220, 234; **6:** 168, 176, 177, 221, 222
Sunk costs, **2:** 333
Sunshine, Jonathan, **3:** 6, 98
Supek, Rudi, **3:** 346, 361
Supergame strategy, **7:** 394
Suppes, Patrick, **3:** 438; **7:** 146, 182
Supplemental Security Income (SSI), **6:** 154–155
Suppression of Communism Act in South Africa, **6:** 257, 275
Supranational organizations, **8:** 74
Supreme Court, **5:** 177, 178, 180, 299
Supreme Soviet, **5:** 266
Surkin, Marvin, **1:** 114
Surveillance, **5:** 265
Survey instruments
    interview schedule, **7:** 286–287, 329
    questionnaire, **7:** 270, 298, 329
Survey panel, **7:** 224
Survey research, **2:** 36; **3:** 2; **7:** 230, 265–336
    purposes of, **7:** 306–327
Survey Research Center, **7:** 292, 296, 312, 324
Survey sample, **7:** 218–219, 224, 269
Surveys
    Continuous Work History Sample, **7:** 307
    cross-cultural, **7:** 288
    Current Population Survey, **7:** 320
    definition of, **7:** 266, 268, 329
    of demographic attributes, **7:** 268–274
    effects on theory, **7:** 327–336
    Equality of Educational Opportunity Survey, **7:** 321–323
    Financial Survey of Urban Housing (1934), **7:** 307

history of, **7:** 268–271, 306–327
    item wording in, **7:** 289–296
    National Health Survey, **7:** 307, 323
    1937 Enumerative Census of Unemployment, **7:** 307
    omnibus, **7:** 324
    panel design of, **7:** 275
    Project TALENT, **7:** 321–323
    samples, **7:** 218–219, 224, 269, 271, 308
    social survey movement, **7:** 268–274, 307
    Study of Consumer Purchases (1935-1936), **7:** 307
    Survey of Economic Opportunity, **7:** 319–320
    time budget, **7:** 284
    uses of, **7:** 269–272, 324–327
Sutherland, Donald, **7:** 309
Svalastoga, Kaare, **3:** 139
Swanson, Bert E., **2:** 164, 180, 197, 228; **6:** 16
Swartz, Marc J., **3:** 364, 365
Swayze, Harold, **3:** 358
Swearer, Howard R., **3:** 360
Sweeney, John W., **7:** 250
Sweezy, Paul M., **3:** 366; **5:** 59; **6:** 252; **8:** 17, 29, 77, 228
Swift, Betty, **2:** 129, 130
Switzerland, federalism of, **5:** 94, 99, 112, 117
Symbols, **1:** 251
System-function approach to political development analysis, **3:** 3
System persistence, **2:** 112–114
System support, **2:** 116
Systematic taxonomy, **7:** 431
Systemic hypotheses, **8:** 141–151
Systemic theory, **8:** 12, 16
Systems analysis, **6:** 306; **8:** 290–291, 303, 304, 323
Systems theory, **6:** 389–390; **8:** 43–65
    and assumptions, **8:** 43–44
    and the balance of power, **8:** 68
    and change, **8:** 50–51, 52, 55, 60
    criticism of, **8:** 68
    and expectations, **8:** 55
    and interactions, **8:** 43, 62–63
    and structure, **8:** 43, 50, 52, 55, 60, 63
    and unintended consequences, **8:** 44
Szalai, Alexander, **7:** 284, 285

Tacitus, **5:** 273, 274
Tactical forces, **8:** 270

Taeuber, Alma F., 6: 292
Taeuber, Karl E., 6: 292
Taft, Philip, 3: 516; 4: 180
Taft, William Howard, 2: 40; 5: 224
Tahim, G. S., 8: 191
Taiping rebellion, 3: 530–531
Tajfel, Henri, 2: 118
Talbot, Nell S., 4: 159
Talbot, Ross B., 4: 215
Talmon, J. L., 1; 390; 3: 230
Tanenhaus, Joseph, 1: 27, 35, 38, 39, 42, 48, 67, 72, 124; 2: 116; 5: 321, 420
Tang, Peter S. H., 3: 366
Tannenbaum, Edward R., 3: 358
Tannenbaum, Frank, 6: 263
Tannenbaum, Percy H., 2: 140
Tanter, Raymond, 3: 3, 40; 8: 130, 131, 133, 134, 135, 141
Tanzania, political opposition in, 3: 127
Tapp, June L., 2: 133
Tarlton, Charles D., 5: 142, 158
Tarrow, Sidney, 2: 9, 101, 136, 139; 3: 40, 97, 249; 7: 122
Task Force on Foreign Affairs, 6: 401
Task Force on Organization of Social Services, 6: 144
Tatum, Lawrence B., 8: 323
Tautologies, in measuring power, 7: 184–185
Taxation, 5: 282; 6: 44–47, 66–69
    federal taxes, 6: 66
    negative income tax, 6: 60, 151, 216–219
    reform, 6: 67, 68
    and revolutionary claims, 3: 527, 528
    social security taxes, 6: 67–68
    state and local taxes, 6: 66
Taylor, Alice, 6: 221
Taylor, Charles, 1: 168, 170, 220, 318; 3: 97, 358; 7: 64
Taylor, Eric, 5: 281
Taylor, George, 2: 102, 106, 107, 108, 113, 115, 138
Taylor, Lily Ross, 3: 116
Taylor, Maxwell, 8: 284
Taylor, Michael, 1: 351, 395; 2: 321, 334, 337, 342, 343, 347; 3: 440, 454; 4: 240; 7: 204, 375
Taylor, Paul, 1: 315, 316, 317, 330
Taylor, Philip B., Jr., 3: 358
Taylor, R. W., 7: 248
Taylor, Robert L., 2: 11
Taylor, Theodore B., 8: 333

Technical and administrative competence, 2: 324
Technobureaucracy, 3: 297
Technological and economic growth
    assessment, 7: 433–438
    neo-Malthusian conclusions on, 7: 412
    postindustrial perspective, 7: 413
Techno-organizational establishment, 5: 3–4
Teeters, Nancy H., 6: 76
Teleology, 7: 168
Teller, Edward, 8: 284, 301
Temperance movement, 3: 511
Temple, Sir William, 5: 95
Temporality, 7: 244–245
Tennessee Valley Authority, 3: 586, 587, 588, 589; 5: 397, 409
Territoriality, 8: 248, 315
Terror, political, 3: 188, 193, 195, 217–228
    in authoritarian regimes, 3: 223–224
    characteristics of, 3: 218
    concentration camps, 3: 219
    counterrevolutionary social categories, 3: 219
    differences in forms of, 3: 224
    executions, 3: 219
    functions of, 3: 226–227
    ideological basis, 3: 221, 222
    legalization of, 3: 220
    in takeover stage, 3: 223
Terrorism, 5: 264–265; 8: 224–225, 335
Test Ban Treaty, 8: 301
Teune, Henry, 1: 175; 4: 207; 6: 387; 7: 133, 288
Textor, Robert, 1: 312; 3: 62, 352; 7: 83; 8: 131, 141
Thalheimer, August, 3: 314, 366
Thayer, Charles, 6: 404
Theil, Henri, 3: 449, 450
Theocentric humanism, 1: 239, 241, 245, 246, 248–249
Theoretical adjustment, 1: 202
Theoretical concepts, 1: 298
Theory, 1: 133, 134, 140–145, 204, 210, 251; 7: 86–92
    analytic, 8: 12
    and associations, 8: 4–5, 6, 12
    and assumptions, 8: 11
    balance-of-power, 8: 33–43
    bureaucratic, 8: 16
    as collections of laws, 8: 3
    and commonsense clues, 8: 8
    "correspondence" rules, 1: 143

and data, **8:** 5–6, 8, 9, 14
deductive system of, **7:** 234
definition of, **8:** 4, 13–14
as distinct from law, **8:** 3
effect of surveys on, **7:** 327–336
empirically interpreted terms, **1:** 143
expectations of, **8:** 15
as explanation, **8:** 3, 4
falsification of, **1:** 145–148
formal, **7:** 351–399
"grounded," **7:** 107
and hypotheses, **8:** 5, 14
hypothetico-deductive system, **1:** 143
inductive, **8:** 6–10
and interpretive explanations, **1:** 186
from law to theory, **8:** 10
of the middle range, **8:** 65–66
minimal sense of, **7:** 90
multivariate, **7:** 129
nature of, **7:** 86
"orthodox" view, **1:** 141–145
power of, **7:** 133
and prediction, **8:** 4
primitive terms, **1:** 142
process of building, **7:** 91, 134
quality of, **8:** 12–13
and reality, **8:** 9
reductionist, **8:** 15–33, 66
scientific, **7:** 351, 353, 354
self-verifying, **8:** 25–26
semantic rules, **1:** 142
and simulation, **7:** 223
stating of, **8:** 13
and structure, **8:** 8
as system of hypotheses, **7:** 216
systemic, **8:** 12, 16
testing of, **1:** 145–153; **8:** 12, 14–15
theoretical terms, **1:** 143
uninterpreted postulate system, **1:** 142
uses of the term, **1:** 141
and variance, **8:** 7
Thernstrom, Stephan, **5:** 271, 272
Thibaut, John W., **1:** 195
Third World, **3:** 2, 284
military coups in, **3:** 321–322
Thomas, Hugh, **3:** 71, 366
Thomas, L. Eugene, **2:** 126
Thomas, Norman, **2:** 189, 192, 193; **5:** 207, 429
Thomassen, Jacques, **4:** 160
Thompson, Dennis F., **4:** 4, 5
Thompson, James, **2:** 319, 353, 356

Thompson, John E., **6:** 418
Thompson, Kenneth W., **1:** 236; **6:** 382; **8:** 199
Thompson, Leonard M., **3:** 73, 327
Thompson, Robert, **8:** 346
Thompson, Victor, **2:** 323; **5:** 428
Thomson, James C., Jr., **5:** 379
Thorndike, Edward L., **6:** 355, 361, 362, 363
Thornton, Thomas P., **3:** 335
Thorp, Bruce, **4:** 204
Thorson, Stuart, **1:** 131
Threat strategies, **3:** 457, 460
Thucydides, **1:** 236
Thurow, Lester C., **6:** 77, 99, 184, 283
Tiao, George C., **6:** 454, 467
Tigrid, Pavel, **3:** 337
Tillett, Paul, **5:** 183
Tilly, Charles, **3:** 9, 92; **7:** 54, 56
Tilman, R. O., **2:** 112, 115; **5:** 124
Timocracy, **5:** 40
Tinbergen, Jan, **3:** 370
Tingsten, Herbert, **3:** 40, 41; **4:** 112, 159; **7:** 302
Tiryakian, Edward A., **7:** 289
Titmuss, Richard M., **6:** 184, 185, 219, 220
Titus, David Anson, **3:** 365
Titus, H. Edwin, **2:** 49
Tobey, Ronald, **6:** 83
Tobin, James, **6:** 75, 149
Toharia, José Juan, **3:** 224
Tökés, Rudolf L., **3:** 228
Tolley, Howard, Jr., **2:** 100, 102, 106, 107, 116, 140
Tollison, Robert, **2:** 329; **8:** 368
Tomasevich, Jozo, **3:** 286
Tomkins, Calvin, **7:** 32
Tønnesson, Kare, **3:** 499
Tonnines, Ferdinand, **5:** 4
Topham, N., **6:** 321, 339, 342, 344, 362
Torgerson, Ulf, **4:** 268
Torgerson, W. S., **1:** 370; **7:** 306
Torney, Judith V., **2:** 94, 97, 98, 106, 111, 115, 119, 122, 129, 140; **7:** 61, 278, 302
Tort law, **5:** 339
Totalitarian elements in preindustrial society, **3:** 242
Totalitarian movements, **3:** 247
Totalitarian party, **3:** 198–216
bureaucratic character of, **3:** 202
class appeal of, **3:** 231
conflicts in, **3:** 207–208
functions of, **3:** 204, 208–211
mobilization of members in, **3:** 203–204

party leadership, **3:** 206–208
purges in, **3:** 202, 210
recruitment in, **3:** 210
and state, **3:** 211–213
youth organization in, **3:** 209
Totalitarian regimes, **3:** 187–264
alienation from, **3:** 194
attraction of, **3:** 194
characteristics of, **3:** 191–192
conceptual delimitations, **3:** 188–189
conditions for in modern societies, **3:** 247–251
and conflicts between church and state, **3:** 192–193
critiques of concept of, **3:** 241–247
definitions of, **3:** 187–196
distinction from other nondemocratic regimes, **3:** 189
and economy, **3:** 231–232
ideologists in, **3:** 235–236
and ideology, **3:** 196–198
internal dynamics of, **3:** 228–230
leadership in, **3:** 238–239
of the "Left" and the "Right," **3:** 230–240
membership, **3:** 200–201
military authority in, **3:** 189–190
Mussolini on, **3:** 177
policy diversion in, **3:** 213
political justice in, **3:** 222
political pluralism in, **3:** 190
social structure in, **3:** 232–233
stages of development, **3:** 244
subtypes of, **3:** 244
terror in, **3:** 217–228
transformations within, **3:** 191, 229–230
typology of, **3:** 191
in underdeveloped countries, **3:** 250
voting in, **3:** 210
without terror, **3:** 195, 218
Totalitarianism, future of, **3:** 356
Toulmin, Stephen, **1:** 216, 218; **8:** 4
Tourtellot, Arthur Bernon, **5:** 224
Towle, Charlotte, **6:** 121
Town meeting, New England, **5:** 269–270
Townsend, James R., **3:** 204, 209, 224, 366: **4:** 2
Trade unions, **3:** 322, 531, 532, 570–571, 575
Tradition, **1:** 4
Traditional society, **3:** 41–42, 45, 49, 50, 54–55
Traditional statification systems, **5:** 264
Trager, Frank N., **5:** 124; **8:** 347
Transformation curve, **8:** 156, 159, 161

Transforming social conflict, **2:** 246, 252, 278, 293–294, 301, 307
Transgovernmental relations, **8:** 398–399
Transitions, presidential, **5:** 194
Transitivity, **7:** 357
of individual preferences, **7:** 356
of majority rule, **7:** 369, 372
of social choice, **7:** 374
Transkei Constitution, **3:** 329
Transnational actors, **8:** 393
Transnational movements, **8:** 73
Travaglini, Thomas, **3:** 223
Treadgold, Donald W., **3:** 366
Treasury Department, **6:** 40, 42, 48
Treaties, **8:** 418–419, 420, 424
unequal, **8:** 419
Treaty of Paris of 1783, **5:** 108
Treaty of Versailles, **8:** 263
Treharne, R. F., **5:** 308
Treiman, Donald J., **2:** 131; **7:** 272
Trends
projection of, **7:** 406
in technology and economic growth, **7:** 406
Trial courts, **5:** 350–356, 357, 358
as fact finders, **5:** 353–356
Triepel, Heinrich, **5:** 113
Trilling, Richard J., **4:** 162
Trindade, Helgio, **3:** 233, 315
Triska, Jan F., **3:** 236, 335
Troika, **6:** 38
Trotsky, Leon, **3:** 177, 223, 357, 368, 519, 558, 560, 568, 569, 573; **8:** 23, 40
Trotter, R. G., **5:** 112
Trow, Martin, **3:** 618; **4:** 182
Trudeau, Pierre-Eliott, **5:** 135
Trueblood, Felicity, **6:** 309, 313, 334
Truman, David B., **2:** 246, 248, 249, 252, 262, 263, 264, 265, 266, 275, 285, 286, 301, 307, 308, 309, 310; **4:** 173, 174, 175, 185, 186, 187, 189, 190, 191, 193, 196, 197, 198, 208, 220, 264; **5:** 134, 259, 306, 308, 394, 414; **7:** 298, 312
on government institutions, **2:** 265
on objective interest approach, **2:** 263
on political process, **2:** 263
on potential groups, **2:** 266–267
on stability-disruption-protest model, **2:** 265–267
his stress on political structures, **2:** 247
typology of groups, **2:** 264
view of interest and politics, **2:** 263–264

Truman, Harry, **2:** 32; **6:** 404
Trythall, J. W. D., **5:** 267
Tsou, Tang, **5:** 384
Tucker, Robert C., **2:** 1, 23, 31, 40, 212, 213; **3:** 206, 229, 246, 340, 362, 365
Tucker, Robert W., **6:** 467; **8:** 203, 363
Tudor, Jeannette F., **2:** 119
Tufte, Edward, **7:** 204; **8:** 6
Tugwell, Rexford G., **5:** 232
Tukey, John W., **7:** 142, 146
Tullock, Gordon, **1:** 205, 220; **3:** 424, 428, 444, 445, 453, 454, 470; **5:** 408; **7:** 86, 397
Tully, Andrew, **6:** 391, 406
Tunkin, Grigorii I., **8:** 431
Tuohy, William S., **3:** 363
Turkevich, John, **6:** 100
Turkey, political institutions in, **3:** 62–64
Turner, Henry A., **3:** 316, 369
Turner, J., **4:** 162
Turner, James, **5:** 266, 400, 402
Turner, John B., **6:** 387
Turner, John E., **6:** 362
Turner, Julius, **4:** 242, 264
Turner, Ralph H., **6:** 402
Turner, Victor, **3:** 364
Tuthill, John W., **6:** 408
Tyranny, **5:** 41
Tversky, Amos, **1:** 371; **3:** 438; **7:** 159
Two-step flow of communications, **7:** 328, 329
Tyler, Stephan A., **2:** 8
Types and typology
  achievement motivation, **2:** 62
  active-negative, **2:** 56
  active-positive, **2:** 56
  activists, **2:** 45, 68, 76
  advertisers, **2:** 54, 61
  aristocrat, **2:** 44
  authoritarian, **2:** 44, 46, 47, 48, 50, 51, 56, 57, 58, 61
  democrat, **2:** 44
  diagnostic categories, **2:** 45
  dogmatism, **2:** 50, 51
  ego-defensive authoritarianism, **2:** 57, 59
  lawmakers, **2:** 54, 61
  life-cycle (genetic) antecedents, **2:** 46
  literature on, **2:** 44–56
  Machiavellian, **2:** 50, 51
  multi-case studies of, **2:** 44–60
  nuclear, **2:** 46
  passive-negative, **2:** 56
  passive-positive, **2:** 56
  political personality, **2:** 41, 53
    reluctants, **2:** 54, 61
    rigidly held beliefs, **2:** 50
    spectators, **2:** 54, 61
    syndromes, **2:** 44–45, 48
    timocrat, **2:** 44
    tyrant, **2:** 44
Tyrell, Albrecht, **3:** 368

Ueberhorst, Horst, **3:** 204
Uelmen, Gerald F., **6:** 342
Ugalde, Antonio, **3:** 363
Uhlig, Heinrich, **3:** 232
Ulam, Adam B., **3:** 359; **8:** 342
Ulman, Lloyd, **6:** 77
Ulmer, S. Sidney, **7:** 397
Ulrich, Junker, **5:** 206
Unamuno, Miguel de, **5:** 80, 81, 82, 86
Unanimity, **1:** 391
Uncertainty, **1:** 345–347; **2:** 325, 331, 332, 333, 334, 347
  distinguished from risk, **2:** 341, 344
  and objective probability, **2:** 344
Unconstitutionality, concept of, **5:** 68–69
Underdevelopment, **3:** 271
Unemployment, racial differentials in, **6:** 282
Unemployment insurance, **6:** 192
Unfreedom, **1:** 287, 288, 301, 305
Ungari, Paolo, **3:** 367
Ungs, Thomas D., **7:** 248
Unintended consequences of action, **1:** 182, 184, 208
Union of Utrecht of 1579, **5:** 95
Unionization, **3:** 296
United Nations, **6:** 315; **8:** 49, 206, 218, 230, 253, 420, 425, 428, 429
  Charter, **8:** 417, 429, 431
  Economic and Social Council, **6:** 312
  General Assembly, **8:** 416, 417, 424, 429
  Security Council, **8:** 417, 424
  statistical study of, **7:** 159–178
United Nations Educational, Scientific and Cultural Organization, **2:** 179
United States, federalism of, **5:** 37–40, 95, 118, 154
United States Code, **7:** 21
United States Code Congressional and Administrative News, **7:** 23
United States Commission on Civil Rights, **6:** 288
United States Commission on Organization of the Executive Branch of Government, **6:** 401

United States Congress, House, Committee on Foreign Affairs, Subcommittee on National Security Policy and Scientific Develpments, **6:** 409

United States Congress, House, Ways and Means Committee, **6:** 125

United States Congress, Joint Economic Committee, **6:** 130, 422

United States Congress, Joint Economic Committee, Subcommittee on Fiscal Policies, **6:** 221, 222, 223

United States Congress, Senate, Committee on Finance, **6:** 222

United States Congress, Senate, Committee on Government Operations, **5:** 404

United States Congress, Senate, Committee on Government Operations, Subcommittee on National Policy Machinery, **6:** 406

United States Congress, Senate, Committee on Government Operations, Subcommittee on National Security Staffing and Operations, **6:** 403, 422

United States Congress, Senate, Select Committee on Small Business, **5:** 403

United States Department of State, Division of Research for Europe, Office of Intelligence Research, **3:** 362

United States Geological Survey, **6:** 83

United States government, documents by and about, **7:** 18–23. *(See also listings for individual sources.)*
  archives, **7:** 27–34
  Congress, **7:** 18–23
  courts, **7:** 25–27
  federal executive, **7:** 23–25
  manuscript collections, **7:** 27–28, 34–38

United States Government Manual, **7:** 14, 24

United States Information Agency, **7:** 315

United States National Resources Commission, **7:** 270

United States–Soviet relations, **2:** 343

United States Statutes at Large, **7:** 18, 21

United States Strategic Bombing Survey, **7:** 313, 314

Universalism, **8:** 420

Uno, Toru, **3:** 43

Uphoff, Norman, **6:** 16, 460

Urban conditions, **6:** 319, 347

"Urban," definition of, **6:** 312

Urban government
  national role of, **6:** 311
  structure of, **6:** 306–307

Urban life, quality of, **6:** 305, 310, 314, 347–349, 350, 351, 355

Urban performance
  determinants of, **6:** 320, 330, 332–346
  developmental models, **6:** 328–330
  eclecticism, **6:** 328
  equilibrium theory, **6:** 324–325
  evaluation, sociology of, **6:** 349–358
  factor analysis, **6:** 327
  formal legal methods, **6:** 331–332
  incrementalism, **6:** 329
  and party ideology, **6:** 323, 345–346
  and politics, **6:** 336–346
  and region, **6:** 323, 328
  and religion, **6:** 323, 326–327
  resources, needs, and dispositions, **6:** 325–327
  shift to, **6:** 305–310
  and situational variables, **6:** 343
  systems models, **6:** 331

Urban policy
  determinants of, **6:** 316, 320, 324, 332–346
  diversity of, **6:** 316–332
  impact of, **6:** 307
  international comparisons, **6:** 333–335
  intranational range, **6:** 316, 336–346
  outcomes, range of, **6:** 346–358
  and the quality of life, **6:** 347–349, 350, 351, 355
  range of, **6:** 310–332

Urban policy studies, **6:** 305, 348
  achievements, **6:** 310
  goals of, **6:** 309
  nonperformance approaches, **6:** 308–309
  political implications of, **6:** 358–360

Urbanization, **3:** 40; **6:** 307, 308, 310

Urmson, J. O., **1:** 320

Urwick, Lyndall, **2:** 351; **5:** 397

Urwin, Dereck, **4:** 162, 245

Utilitarian power, **8:** 382

Utilitarian resources, **3:** 503

Utilitarianism, **1:** 360–361, 388; **3:** 444–451; **5:** 44

Utility function, **1:** 197, 203
  cardinal, **3:** 444–451, 457; **7:** 380, 389, 395
  ordinal, **3:** 439
  quadratic, **3:** 442, 449
  of von Neumann and Morgenstern, **3:** 446–448, 449

Utopia, **1:** 244

U-2 reconnaissance aircraft, **8:** 295

Uyehara, Cecil H., **6:** 93

Vaillancourt, Pauline Marie, **2:** 100, 119, 121, 122, 127, 129, 134, 136
Vaker, Nicholas, **3:** 363
Valcárcel, Daniel, **3:** 75
Valen, Henry, **2:** 172, 181, 204, 220, 226; **4:** 248; **7:** 45, 303
Valentine, Charles, **6:** 221
Validity, **2:** 75; **7:** 219, 222, 238, 251
  criterion, **7:** 247
  external, **7:** 222, 246, 247, 251, 252
  internal, **7:** 221, 229, 244
  threats to internal, **7:** 231–232, 237, 243, 250, 251
Vallauri, Carlo, **3:** 307, 367
Vallier, Ivan, **3:** 78
Value cognitivism vs. value noncognitivism, **1:** 319
Value judgments, **1:** 315, 317
  instrumental, **1:** 316
Values of science, **1:** 134
van den Bergh, George, **4:** 241
Van den Berghe, Pierre L., **3:** 67, 72, 327; **6:** 245, 258, 276
van den Bogaard, P. J., **3:** 449
Van der Mehden, Fred, **3:** 79
Van Doorn, Jacques, **3:** 367
Van Dyke, Vernon, **1:** 140; **6:** 467
Van Horn, Richard L., **7:** 227
Van Riper, Paul P., **5:** 183, 424
Van Til, Sally, **6:** 201
Van Wagenen, Richard W., **8:** 401
Vann Dicey, Albert, **5:** 4, 25, 31, 63
Variables in research, **8:** 88, 89, 90, 94
  analysis of, **8:** 93
  association between, **8:** 89
  covariation between, **8:** 89
  directional, **8:** 110, 111
  nondirectional, **8:** 110
Vatikiotis, P. J., **3:** 367, 369
Veblen, Thorstein, **8:** 23, 24, 31, 76
Venkataraman, K., **5:** 150
Verba, Sidney, **1:** 170, 306; **2:** 18, 25, 61, 95; **3:** 16, 17, 27, 32, 34, 35, 36, 78, 91, 97; **4:** 1, 3, 6, 11, 13, 16, 17, 22, 26, 32, 34, 35, 39, 40, 41, 42, 49, 50, 58, 60, 62, 64, 66, 70, 76, 77, 149, 150, 151, 152, 153, 154, 155, 158, 160, 162, 179, 199, 220, 221; **6:** 387, 394, 421; **7:** 95, 97, 99, 100, 103, 104, 110, 115, 133, 135, 215, 275
Vermeil, Edmond, **3:** 363
Vernier, Bernard, **3:** 367, 369
Vernon, Ray, **3:** 63; **8:** 227, 391

Versluis, J., **3:** 449
Verstehen, **1:** 180, 184, 294–297
Veysey, Laurence, **1:** 22; **5:** 289
Vickrey, William, **3:** 430, 452
Viereck, Peter, **3:** 363
Vierhaus, Rudolf, **3:** 206, 215, 362
Vietnam, **4:** 60
  political acculturation in, **3:** 21, 89
Vietnam War, **8:** 304–305, 321
Vile, M. J. C., **5:** 176, 178, 181
Villard, Henry S., **6:** 404
Viner, Jacob, **8:** 6
Vines, Kenneth N., **6:** 16
Vinogradoff, Sir Paul, **5:** 29
Vinyard, Dale, **5:** 228, 308
Violence, **3:** 483, 512–519
  "brute harm" conception of, **3:** 513
  collective, **3:** 495, 514–517
  domonstration, **3:** 515
  in fascism, **3:** 215
  Hitler on, **3:** 223
  labor, **3:** 516
  level of, **3:** 537
  political action and involvement in, **3:** 517–519
  repressive, **3:** 495
  in revolutions, **3:** 226
Vital, David, **6:** 383; **8:** 233
Vizierial government, **3:** 255
Vlastos, Gregory, **1:** 387
Vocational politics, **2:** 162
Voegelin, Eric, **1:** 231, 232–233, 245, 249, 256, 273, 275, 276; **3:** 178, 311
Vogel, Ezra, **3:** 224, 363, 366; **6:** 335
Vogelsang, Thilo, **3:** 303
Von der Muhll, George, **2:** 112
von Hippel, Frank, **6:** 91
Von Lave, Theodore H., **8:** 40
Von Leyden, W., **1:** 325
Von Mehren, Arthur, **5:** 331, 342
Von Neumann, John, **2:** 336, 346; **3:** 446, 447, 448, 449, 450, 451, 458; **7:** 382, 389, 399
Von Wright, Georg Henrik, **1:** 163, 164, 165, 166, 184–185, 216, 218, 219, 300, 302, 330; **7:** 143, 168, 170, 171, 191, 194, 195, 196, 201
Vose, Clement E., **4:** 188, 197, 199, 208; **7:** 14, 67, 322
Voss, Joachim, **3:** 369
Vote trading, **3:** 445; **7:** 397
Voting, **1:** 164–165, 169, 199; **4:** 9–10, 13, 15–16, 19–20, 66

community context and, **4:** 35
costs of, **3:** 466
in India, **4:** 22
initiative required for, **4:** 26
paradox of, **3:** 428
sincere, **3:** 463
sophisticated, **3:** 464
strategic, **3:** 461–464, 469
in totalitarian systems, **3:** 210
in Yugoslavia, **4:** 16
Voting behavior, **7:** 266, 276, 277, 297, 335, 388
defection, **4:** 134, 138–139, 144
issue voting, **4:** 120, 121, 124, 128, 132
nature of, **4:** 111–158
rational voting, **4:** 120, 121
in the United Kingdom, **7:** 282–283
voting choice, determinants of individual, **4:** 113–136
voting systems, macrocosmic change in, **4:** 136–148
Voting participation, urban and rural, **3:** 40–41
Voting predispositions, **7:** 154, 168, 170
Voting procedures, **7:** 376
binary, **7:** 388
sincere, **7:** 388
sophisticated, **7:** 388–389
straightforward, **7:** 388

Wade, L. L., **7:** 86
Wage-price guideposts, implementation of, **6:** 55–56, 58–59
Wagley, Charles, **3:** 26
Wagner, Richard E., **4:** 193; **5:** 143, 148, 149
Wagner, W. J., **5:** 145
Wagner Act, **2:** 302
Wahlke, John C., **1:** 231; **2:** 190, 191; **4:** 162, 264; **5:** 303; **6:** 16
Waismann, Friedrich, **1:** 309
Waite, P. B., **5:** 112
Waldo, Dwight, **1:** 80, 83; **5:** 373
Walker, Jack L., **2:** 110, 248; **4:** 4, 70, 103, 159; **5:** 224, 226; **6:** 349; **7:** 332; **8:** 371
Walker, Mabel L., **6:** 307
Walker, Malcolm T., **3:** 365
Walkland, S. A., **5:** 235, 297, 307
Wallace, Anthony F. C., **2:** 26; **3:** 507
Wallace, David F., **7:** 3
Wallace, Michael, **8:** 144, 145, 149, 150, 151
Wallas, Graham, **2:** 30
Wallerstein, Immanuel, **3:** 322, 370; **4:** 233

Walles, Malcolm, **5:** 306
Wallis, W. Allen, **7:** 54, 134
Walsh, Annemarie Hauck, **6:** 313, 335
Walters, Richard H., **2:** 42
Walther, Regis, **6:** 403
Waltz, Kenneth N., **2:** 63; **4:** 266; **5:** 222; **6:** 384, 392, 413, 414; **8:** 16, 47, 66, 91, 92, 193, 213, 214, 215, 220, 227, 231, 235, 238, 250, 315, 344, 363, 370, 375, 376
Walzer, Michael, **3:** 538
Wamsley, Gary L., **5:** 427
Wanamaker, Daniel K., **6:** 343
Want-satisfaction, **1:** 388
War
amount of in the system, **8:** 146, 150
and the balance of power, **8:** 36
and capitalism, **8:** 20
causes of, **8:** 15–16, 18–19, 66–67, 141–151, 176
correlates of, **8:** 146
and domestic insecurity of elites, **8:** 49
duration of, **8:** 171
effect of alliances on, **8:** 146
frequency of, **8:** 164, 169
historical approach to, **8:** 92
and imperialism, **8:** 17
legalistic approach to, **8:** 92
limited, **8:** 260, 279, 283–285, 317–321
magnitude of, **8:** 146
"mutually exclusive," **8:** 167
probability of, **8:** 168, 169
severity of, **8:** 146, 150, 151
study of, **8:** 95
systemic, **8:** 142
"War fighting," **8:** 318
War on Poverty, **6:** 130, 134–136, 146, 167–182
Community Action, **6:** 171, 175–182, 187
ends and means of, **6:** 173–175
National Emphasis Programs, **6:** 167, 177, 179, 181
Poverty Program, **6:** 195
and race, **6:** 170
"War termination," **8:** 318
Ward, Benjamin, **3:** 430
Ward, Norman, **5:** 202
Ward, Robert E., **2:** 124, 126; **3:** 91, 365
Ware, Alan, **3:** 358
Warnecke, Steven, **8:** 385
Warner, Amos, **6:** 164, 221
Warner, W. Lloyd, **5:** 183; **7:** 309
Warnock, Geoffrey, **1:** 397

Warr, Peter B., **7:** 236, 248
Warren, M. Q., **6:** 467
Warren, Sidney, **5:** 222, 224
Wartofsky, Marx W., **1:** 219
Warwick, D. P., **2:** 127, 128, 130, 131
Washburn, Sherwood L., **6:** 278
Washby, Stephen L., **6:** 467
Watanuki, Joji, **3:** 45
Waterbury, John, **3:** 365
Watson, Frank B., **6:** 221
Watson, Richard, **4:** 181
Watts, R. L., **5:** 112, 115, 116, 117, 123, 124, 125, 126, 127
Watzlawick, Paul, **8:** 78
Weaver, Warren, **5:** 410; **8:** 12
Webb, Eugene J., **7:** 222
Webb, James E., **6:** 89
Weber, Arnold R., **6:** 77
Weber, Eugen, **3:** 315
Weber, Hermann, **3:** 221
Weber, Max, **1:** 161, 219, 220, 234, 338; **2:** 157, 161, 204, 352, 353, 354; **3:** 200, 230, 253, 254, 259, 260, 306, 309, 339, 364, 367, 368, 525, 560, 596, 619; **5:** 303, 304, 388, 390; **6:** 333
Webster, Murray, Jr., **2:** 61
Webster, Richard A., **3:** 359
Webster, T. B. L., **5:** 272
Wechsler, Herbert, **5:** 134
Weede, Eric, **8:** 131, 139, 140
Weekly Compilation of Presidential Documents, **7:** 24
Wehler, Hans-Ulrich, **8:** 76
Weiker, Walter F., **3:** 185
Weil, Gordon L., **5:** 292, 295
Weiler, Hans N., **2:** 112
Weimar Republic, **5:** 98, 103, 113
Weinberg, Gerhard L., **3:** 238; **5:** 306
Weinberg, Ian, **3:** 370
Weiner, Myron, **3:** 30, 66, 68, 88, 91, 160; **4:** 1, 2, 233; **5:** 136; **7:** 105
Weiner, Stephen M., **3:** 218
Weingrod, Alex, **3:** 97
Weinkauff, Hermann, **3:** 222
Weinstein, A. A., **3:** 438
Weinstein, Franklin B., **6:** 385
Weinstein, Fred, **2:** 31
Weinstein, James, **5:** 405
Weinstein, Leo, **2:** 248, 253
Weinstein, W. L., **1:** 289
Weisband, Edward, **8:** 418
Weisberg, Herbert, **3:** 428; **4:** 161, 162

Weisbrod, Burton, **2:** 329, 331
Weiss, Carol H., **7:** 240
Weiss, Robert S., **6:** 467; **7:** 240
Weissberg, Robert, **2:** 94, 96, 115, 116
Weisz, Alfred E., **2:** 11
Welch, Claude E., Jr., **3:** 9; **5:** 125
Welch, Holmes, **3:** 322, 359
Welch, R. E., **6:** 356
Welch, William, **6:** 413, 440
Weldon, Thomas D., **1:** 284, 396
Welfare, characteristics of the "old," **6:** 157
    administrative complexity, **6:** 160–161
    ambivalence, **6:** 158–159
    bureaucratic accountability, **6:** 160
    continuity, **6:** 159–160
    federalism, **6:** 163–164
    intractability, **6:** 157–158
    professionalism, **6:** 162–163
    public-private relations, **6:** 164–167
    technicality, **6:** 160
Welfare policy
    bureaucratic accountability, **6:** 209
    and the civil rights movement, **6:** 169–170, 180
    clientele participation, **6:** 205–206
    community power, study of, **6:** 171–172
    federal expenditures, **6:** 190, 191, 194
    goals, **6:** 187, 201
    ideology, **6:** 210–212
    income redistribution, **6:** 195–199, 217
    income supports, **6:** 125, 148, 190–195, 199–203
    in-kind programs, **6:** 193
    judicial decisions affecting, **6:** 159–160
    manpower policy, **6:** 175
    mental-health strategy, **6:** 171
    and the "new welfare," **6:** 167–182
    in perspective, **6:** 156–157
    policy analysis, **6:** 172, 206, 209
    and political science, **6:** 113–115, 203
    politics of, **6:** 212–216
    and poverty, **6:** 182–203
    professionalism, **6:** 204, 209
    and race, **6:** 179, 184
    and religion, **6:** 165
    sectors of, **6:** 188–189, 198–199, 218, 220
    social planning approach, **6:** 205
    social services, **6:** 186–195, 218, 220
    stratification approach, **6:** 184–185
    universality-selectivity, **6:** 186–187, 193–194, 201–202
Welfare reform, **6:** 148–156

Welfare state, concept of, **6:** 111–112, 136
Welk, William G., **3:** 367
Welles, Benjamin, **5:** 267
Wellmer, Albrecht, **1:** 167, 217
Wells, Richard S., **2:** 205
Weltman, John J., **8:** 79
Werner, Andreas, **3:** 215
Wesson, Robert G., **5:** 266
West, J., **2:** 123
West, Ranyard, **2:** 31
Westerfield, H. Bradford, **6:** 415
Western positive state, **5:** 2
Westernization, **3:** 30
Westphal, Albert C. F., **6:** 401
Whaley, Barton, **6:** 17
Wharton, Vernon L., **6:** 260
Wheare, K. D., **5:** 98, 99, 102, 103, 104, 105, 106, 115, 116, 117, 127, 131, 258, 281
Wheatley, Paul, **5:** 12
Wheaton, Eliot Barculo, **3:** 368
Wheeler, Harvey, **5:** 66, 87
Wheeler, Richard S., **3:** 81
Wheelock, Keith, **3:** 369
Whichelow, Anthony, **5:** 297
Whig Revolution, **5:** 65–67
White, Alan, **1:** 293
White, Elliott S., **2:** 27
White, Leonard, **5:** 405, 413; **6:** 355
White, Lucia, **6:** 335
White, Mary K., **7:** 308
White, Morton, **2:** 255; **6:** 335
White, R. Clyde, **7:** 308
White, Ralph K., **2:** 118
White, Robert W., **2:** 9, 13, 34, 35, 51; **4:** 84; **7:** 278, 287
White, William S., **5:** 286
White House Office, **5:** 223
White House staff, **5:** 379
Whitehead, Alfred North, **8:** 7, 76
Whitelaw, W. Menzies, **5:** 112
Whitney, Richard E., **2:** 117, 120, 131, 140
Whitworth, William, **6:** 408, 419
Wholey, Joseph S., **6:** 307, 468
Who's Who in America, **7:** 7
Whyte, William Foote, **3:** 619; **7:** 119
Whyte, William H., Jr., **6:** 403
Wiarda, Howard J., **3:** 78, 235, 261, 311, 366
Wiarda, Ieda Siqueira, **3:** 78
Wiatr, Jerzy J., **3:** 344; **4:** 233
Wicker, Allan W., **2:** 137
Wicker, Tom, **6:** 395
Wiebe, Robert H., **5:** 289

Wiecking, Frederick A., **2:** 75
Wiener, Norbert, **8:** 63, 78
Wiesner, Jerome B., **6:** 93
Wiggins, James A., **7:** 238
Wight, Martin, **8:** 36, 78, 204
Wigmore, John Henry, **5:** 335, 342
Wildavsky, Aaron B., **2:** 164, 245, 322, 324; **3:** 569; **4:** 260; **5:** 110, 135, 173, 174, 183, 187, 208, 215, 222, 224, 227, 398, 406, 418, 419; **6:** 87, 90, 97, 206, 306, 329, 330, 350, 355, 357, 404, 440, 447, 462, 467
Wilensky, Gail, **6:** 359
Wilensky, Harold L., **3:** 618; **5:** 379, 391; **6:** 92, 143, 406
Wilensky, Norman, M., **2:** 188
Wilkenfeld, Jonathan, **6:** 386; **8:** 100, 101, 130, 134, 135, 136, 137
Wilkes, John, **6:** 319
Wilkinson, David O., **6:** 382
Wilkinson, Rupert, **2:** 46
"Will of all, the," **5:** 41
Willame, Jean-Claude, **3:** 354, 369
Willcox, William B., **2:** 21
Willems, E., **3:** 85
Willett, Thomas D., **8:** 368
Willey, R. J., **7:** 118
Williams, Bernard, **1:** 387
Williams, Edward J., **3:** 78
Williams, J. D., **7:** 398; **8:** 343
Williams, John E., **2:** 119, 133
Williams, Marcia, **5:** 224
Williams, Mary Frase, **3:** 180
Williams, Oliver P., **6:** 312; **7:** 67
Williams, Philip M., **5:** 189, 195, 198, 204, 237
Williams, Robert J., **7:** 286
Williams, Roger, **6:** 98
Williams, Walter, **6:** 464, 465, 467; **7:** 240
Williams, William Appleman, **6:** 416; **8:** 77
Williams v. *Mississippi,* **6:** 272
Williamson, Oliver E., **3:** 428
Willner, Ann Ruth, **3:** 362
Willoughby, W. F., **5:** 259
Willoughby, W. L., **2:** 351
Willoughby, Westel W., **1:** 36, 39
Willrich, Mason, **8:** 333, 347
Willson, F. M. G., **5:** 183, 198, 202
Wilson, A. Jeyaratnam, **3:** 79
Wilson, Bryan, **1:** 217; **3:** 81, 82
Wilson, B. R., **3:** 81
Wilson, David A., **3:** 255
Wilson, Harold, **5:** 222
Wilson, Howard E., **2:** 94

Wilson, James Q., **1:** 387; **2:** 163, 202, 289, 308; **4:** 184, 249, 250, 252, 256; **5:** 6, 69, 70, 71, 72, 73, 385, 387, 389, 412, 425, 429; **6:** 274, 305, 309, 340, 349; **7:** 267
Wilson, Robert, **3:** 448, 470; **7:** 396, 397
Wilson, Woodrow, **1:** 31, 33, 91; **2:** 1; **5:** 278, 279, 281, 386, 405
Winch, Peter, **1:** 167, 168, 169, 170, 178, 180–181, 184, 217, 295, 296
Windelband, W., **7:** 96
Windsor, Philip, **3:** 337
Winkler, Heinrich August, **3:** 316, 364
Winner, Langdon, **6:** 86
Winsborough, Hal W., **2:** 176
Winter, David G., **2:** 75
Winter, Ralph K., Jr., **5:** 407
Winters, Richard, **4:** 64; **6:** 223, 306, 467, 468
Wirt, Frederick A., **6:** 467
Wise, David, **6:** 406; **8:** 329
Wiseman, H. V., **3:** 357; **5:** 235
Wish, Myron, **7:** 175
Wissel, Peter A., **7:** 241
Witte, Edwin E., **6:** 126, 220
Wittfogel, Karl A., **3:** 55, 251
Wittgenstein, Ludwig, **1:** 216, 289
Wittner, Lawrence S., **4:** 194
Wnek, Denna, **7:** 249
Wohlstetter, Albert J., **6:** 95, 467; **8:** 288, 289, 292, 294, 344, 346
Wohlstetter, Roberta, **6:** 406
Wold, Herman, **6:** 452
Wolf, Eric, **3:** 263, 497, 498, 511, 528
Wolfe, Alan, **1:** 114
Wolfe, Arthur G., **4:** 158, 162
Wolfe, Bertram D., **3:** 370
Wolfe, Thomas W., **8:** 331
Wolfenstein, M., **2:** 40, 75, 104
Wolfers, Arnold, **8:** 203, 204, 250, 340, 345, 363
Wolff, Hans Julius, **5:** 322
Wolff, Richard D., **8:** 77
Wolff, Robert Paul, **1:** 274, 325, 326, 391; **3:** 422, 454
Wolfgang, Marvin E., **6:** 273
Wolfinger, Raymond E., **2:** 165, 248, 289, 310; **3:** 617; **6:** 323, 340, 341
Wolgemuth, Kathleen L., **6:** 247
Wolin, Sheldon, **1:** 8, 254, 255; **7:** 156, 157
Wolpe, Howard, **3:** 13, 68
Woman's suffrage, **3:** 511
Wood, Ellen Meiksins, **1:** 213
Wood, Oscar P., **2:** 5
Wood, Robert C., **6:** 81, 90, 91, 100, 312, 327

Woodroofe, Kathleen, **6:** 221
Woodward, C. Vann, **6:** 272
Woodward, Julian L., **2:** 189; **7:** 312, 325, 327
Woolf, S. J., **3:** 315, 316
Woolsey, Theodore, **1:** 39
Wootton, Graham, **4:** 187
Workmen's compensation programs, **6:** 192
Works Progress Administration, **7:** 308
"World government," **8:** 207–208, 217
World politics, **8:** 363–364, 394–401
World War I, **2:** 29
World view, animistic, **5:** 9–10, 78–79
Wormuth, Francis D., **5:** 2, 25, 34, 35, 36, 46, 48, 73, 75
Woshinsky, Oliver H., **2:** 75, 217, 233
Wriggins, W. Howard, **3:** 79
Wright, Benjamin F., **5:** 32
Wright, Charles R., **4:** 102, 198; **6:** 16; **7:** 286
Wright, J. Skelly, **6:** 222
Wright, Jack M., **7:** 306
Wright, Lawrence, **6:** 361
Wright, Quincy, **6:** 401; **8:** 142, 153, 154, 155, 169, 170, 171, 172, 173, 315, 316
Wright, Sewell, **6:** 467
Wrights, Carrol D., **7:** 268
Wrigley, E. A., **3:** 499
Wu, Eugene, **3:** 366
Wu, Yuan-li, **3:** 366
Wulf, Joseph, **3:** 358
Wynia, Bob L., **5:** 426, 427

Yamani, Sheik Ahmed Zaki, **7:** 189, 198
Yanarella, Ernest J., **6:** 88
Yancy, William, **6:** 149, 184
Yang, C. K., **3:** 363
Yannopoulos, George, **3:** 286
Yanouzas, John, **2:** 319, 320
Yarmolinsky, Adam, **5:** 375; **6:** 281, 406, 409; **8:** 323, 326
Yates, Jacques F., **2:** 48, 49
Yeh, K. C., **3:** 366
Yglesias, José, **3:** 363
Yinger, Milton, **2:** 75
Ylvisaker, Paul, **5:** 141, 142, 143, 148; **6:** 113, 114
Yntema, D. B., **1:** 370
Yom Kippur War of 1973, **8:** 334
York, Herbert, **8:** 345
Young, Elizabeth, **8:** 223
Young, James Sterling, **5:** 207, 288
Young, Oran R., **2:** 248, 289; **4:** 175, 193; **8:** 75, 366, 367

Young, Roland, **5:** 308
Young, William B., **3:** 181, 322
Youth organization in totalitarian parties, **3:** 209
Yugoslavia, federalism of, **5:** 100, 126
Yule, G. U., **7:** 141
Yurchenko, O., **5:** 122

Zagoria, Donald S., **1:** 187, 188, 190; **3:** 359
Zajonc, Robert B., **7:** 274
Zald, Mayer N., **2:** 320, 322, 323; **5:** 427
Zaleznik, Abraham, **2:** 67
Zaller, Robert, **5:** 307
Zaninovich, M. George, **3:** 346, 361; **7:** 248
Zapf, Wolfgang, **2:** 159; **3:** 222, 232
Zariski, Raphael, **2:** 233
Zartman, I. William, **3:** 256, 365; **6:** 396
Zavoina, William, **7:** 241, 242, 395
Zeckhauser, Richard, **2:** 329, 330, 348; **8:** 221
Zeisel, Hans, **5:** 363; **7:** 146, 168, 169, 170, 175
Zeitlin, Maurice, **3:** 97
Zeller, Belle, **2:** 182
Zeller, Claus, **3:** 369
Zellman, Gail L., **2:** 106, 115, 116, 119, 129, 134, 140

Zeman, Zbynek A., **3:** 337
Zentral-archiv für Emperische Sozial-forschung, **7:** 51
Zetterberg, Hans, **7:** 214
Zeuthen, Frederik, **3:** 458, 459, 470; **7:** 395
Ziebill, Otto, **6:** 362
Ziegler, Harmon, **2:** 194, 245; **4:** 174, 180, 197, 202, 205, 206, 207, 208; **5:** 157
Ziegler, Heinz O., **3:** 178
Zimmerman, William, **6:** 397, 398
Zinn, Charles J., **7:** 21
Zinnes, Dina A., **7:** 140, 248; **8:** 2, 112, 115, 116, 120, 125, 126, 127, 128, 130, 134, 136, 153, 174, 190, 191, 193, 316, 340
Zinnes, Joseph L., **8:** 126, 127
Zionism, **3:** 316
Zionts, Stanley, **3:** 460
Zipfel, Friedrich, **3:** 359
Zisk, Betty H., **2:** 189, 191, 193, 307; **6:** 342
Zitter, Meyer, **7:** 297
Zmarzlik, Hans-Günter, **3:** 363
Zolberg, Aristide, **2:** 293; **3:** 31, 32, 323, 324, 325, 369
Zonis, Marvin, **3:** 255
Zurick, Elia, **2:** 101, 106, 112, 113; **5:** 223